Collaborative Strategies for Teaching
Reading Comprehension

MAXIMIZING YOUR IMPACT

JUDI MOREILLON

AMERICAN LIBRARY ASSOCIATION
Chicago   2007

While extensive effort has gone into ensuring the reliability of information appearing in this book, the publisher makes no warranty, express or implied, on the accuracy or reliability of the information, and does not assume and hereby disclaims any liability to any person for any loss or damage caused by errors or omissions in this publication.

Excerpts from *See the Ocean,* by Estelle Condra, copyright © 1994 by Estelle Condra, reprinted with permission of Inclusive Books, LLC; all rights reserved.

Excerpt from *The Wise Woman and Her Secret,* by Eve Merriam, text copyright © 1999 by Eve Merriam, reprinted with permission of Simon & Schuster Books for Young Readers, an imprint of Simon & Schuster Children's Publishing Division.

Excerpt from *The Important Book,* by Margaret Wise Brown, copyright © 1949 by Margaret Wise Brown, reprinted with permission of HarperCollins.

Excerpt from *Wild Dogs: Past and Present,* by Kelly Milner Halls, copyright © 2005 by Kelly Milner Halls, reprinted with permission of Darby Creek Publishing.

Excerpts from *Song of the Water Boatman, and Other Pond Poems,* by Joyce Sidman, text copyright © 2005 by Joyce Sidman, reprinted with permission of Houghton Mifflin Company; all rights reserved.

The paper used in this publication meets the minimum requirements of American National Standard for Information Sciences—Permanence of Paper for Printed Library Materials, ANSI Z39.48-1992. ∞

Library of Congress Cataloging-in-Publication Data

Moreillon, Judi.
  Collaborative strategies for teaching reading comprehension : maximizing your impact / Judi Moreillon.
    p.   cm.
  Includes bibliographical references and index.
  ISBN-13: 978-0-8389-0929-4 (alk. paper)
  ISBN-10: 0-8389-0929-9 (alk. paper)
  1. Reading comprehension—Study and teaching. 2. Lesson planning. I. Title.
LB1050.45.M667 2007
372.47—dc22   2006036132

ISBN-10: 0-8389-0929-9
ISBN-13: 978-0-8389-0929-4

Printed in the United States of America

11 10 09 08 07   5 4 3 2 1

*With gratitude to the expert
and generous colleagues
who have propelled my own
development as an educator*

Contents

Acknowledgments

There is nothing short of a legion of students of all ages, classroom teacher and teacher-librarian colleagues, administrators, researchers, and scholars who have stimulated my thinking, furthered my knowledge, and shaped my beliefs about teaching and learning. Each of you has enriched my life and has deepened my commitment to the vital role of literacies and libraries in our lives, and I thank you.

I am grateful for the support and trust of my editor, Patrick Hogan, and my library "connector," Connie Champlin. You are my superheroes!

My longtime friend and classroom teacher colleague, Denise Webb, gave me hours of her professional advice and critical feedback on the presentation of the lesson plans in this book as well as the Web support for these lessons. I am in your debt.

Thank you to my public librarian collaborator, Mary Margaret Mercado, and to Judy, Karen, and Tina at the Tucson-Pima Public Library Kirk–Bear Canyon branch for providing me with summer access to piles of children's literature from their collection and through interlibrary loan.

Finally, this book would not have been possible without my husband, Nick Vitale, and his fearless counsel, infinite patience, and enduring love.

Thank you all for teaching me.

Introduction

The goal of *Collaborative Strategies for Teaching Reading Comprehension: Maximizing Your Impact* is to help educators develop coteaching strategies to ensure student achievement. It is founded on the belief that two heads—or more—are better than one. Working together, teacher-librarians, classroom teachers, administrators, and families can create dynamic learning communities in which what is best for student learning is at the heart of every decision. In these communities everyone is invested in everyone else's success. Through coteaching and sharing responsibility for all students in the school, educators can strengthen their academic programs.

I wrote this book to support the collaborative work of elementary school teacher-librarians who want to develop their understanding of teaching reading comprehension strategies. I wrote it for educators who want to increase their expertise in using currently recognized best practices in instruction. The teacher-librarians with whom I hope to share this work understand that, in order to make an impact on student achievement, they must teach what really matters in their schools. The most effective way to do that is to teach standards-based lessons every day in collaboration with classroom teacher colleagues. Through effective classroom-library collaboration, teacher-librarians can help make others successful. They can support their colleagues in accomplishing their goals. These teacher-librarians are educators who intend to position themselves as essential partners in the literacy programs in their schools.

Preservice teacher-librarians are another readership for this book. As students of school librarianship prepare for their careers, I hope they embrace the mission of the school library as a hub of learning. The collaborative strategies offered in this book can help them make their instructional partner role their top priority. If this book can help preservice teacher-librarians learn the vocabulary and practices that guide the work of their classroom teacher colleagues, then they will enter their positions ready to create partnerships that will improve student learning.

Something magical happened among the villagers. As each person opened their heart to give, the next person gave even more. And as this happened, the soup grew richer and smelled more delicious.

—From *Stone Soup,* retold and illustrated by Jon J. Muth

I hope classroom teachers, instructional and literacy coaches, curriculum specialists, and principals find this book useful in their work. The collaborative strategies presented can be applied for the benefit of students in many coteaching situations. The book can support lesson study, professional reading study groups, and site-level or district-level staff development efforts. Teacher-librarians can share this book with their administrators and colleagues as a seed that can contribute to growing a culture of collaboration in their schools.

• • • • •

This book is about teaching reading comprehension strategies. The chapters describe the strategies and provide resources for teaching them. Sample lesson plans at three levels of reading development provide educators with opportunities to put the ideas and information in this book into action in their libraries and classrooms. The Web supplements for these lessons provide extensive support for teaching the sample lessons, including customized graphic organizers and rubrics. Completed teacher resources are provided to facilitate modeling the strategies. When appropriate, sample writing pieces or student work are available for reference. The Web supplements free up collaborators to focus on coteaching and monitoring student learning. Once educators have read the strategy chapters, the Web support makes these sample lessons ready to use on Monday morning. Find these supplements at http://www.ala.org/editions/extras/Moreillon09294/.

The sample lessons are built on five foundational best practices in school librarianship and instruction: evidence-based practice, "backward planning," aligning and integrating information literacy standards with the classroom curriculum, using research-based instructional strategies, and modeling with think-aloud strategies. Over the course of my career and in collaboration with classroom and special education teachers, art, music, and technology specialists, I have coplanned or cotaught all of the lessons or variations of them in K–5 school libraries, classrooms, and computer labs. I have seen that these lessons have improved the reading comprehension abilities of students with various cultural, linguistic, and socioeconomic backgrounds.

• • • • •

The collaborative teaching strategies recommended in this book are most compatible with open, flexibly scheduled school library programs. When the library schedule can accommodate consecutive days of coteaching or extended study periods, teacher-librarians find their teaching has a greater impact on student learning. The ideas in this book are for schools that strive to treat all educators as equals, endeavor to structure collaborative planning time into the school day, and are open to the potential of job-embedded professional development.

If this does not describe your teaching environment, this book can support you in initiating conversations about how the school library could be used to maximize student learning. There are many single-session lessons included in this book that can be taught or used as models for coplanned lessons at your school site. Find a collaborator with whom to teach these lessons, and then gather student data to show the positive impact on student achievement that results from coteaching these lessons. Lower the student-to-teacher ratio at the point of instruction and document student progress. Make a case for moving the library program into a central role in the academic program in your school.

• • • • •

If you are not yet serving in a school with a strong collaborative culture and a collaborative teaching model, please read chapters 1 and 2 before you tackle the strategy chapters (3–9). Talk about the ideas and information presented there with colleagues and administrators. Then, before coteaching the sample lessons, read the strategy background chapters. With your collaborator, assess the students' prior knowledge of the target strategy and determine a developmental reading level. Read the lesson plans and the children's literature. Print out all of the Web supplements to support the lesson and determine whether or not they need to be adapted for your students. Decide which collaborator will take which role or roles during instruction. Monitor and adjust the lesson as you coteach, and assess student work and evaluate the lesson together.

Give yourself the gift of learning on the job with supportive colleagues and continue learning far beyond this book. Codesign, coimplement, and coassess collaborative lessons that include collaborative teaching strategies in all areas of the curriculum. Read and learn more about the best practices embedded in the sample lessons and continue to use them in your teaching. Share the student learning that results from your collaborative work with a wide audience. Keep on teaching and learning together.

· · · · ·

From my experience as a teacher educator, I learned that beginning classroom teachers need help locating appropriate resources. They need a great deal of support to learn curriculum design. They need to know how to integrate performance objectives from more than one content area into each of their lessons. They benefit from explicit modeling and from specific feedback about their teaching. With more and more novices entering the profession, there is a real need to provide support for new teachers so they can be successful—so they remain in the profession and continue to develop as educators.

With members of an undergraduate teacher education program, I am in the process of conducting a longitudinal study titled "Two Heads Are Better Than One: The Factors Influencing the Understanding and Practice of Classroom-Library Collaboration." I have published a preliminary report on the pilot study (Moreillon 2005). At the time of this writing, most of the study participants are beginning their first year of full-time classroom teaching. This is what I've learned so far. When these preservice teachers stepped into the building where they conducted their student teaching experience, little of what we had done in the university classroom made a significant difference. If their cooperating teacher had a value for classroom-library collaboration and worked with the teacher-librarian, so did the student teacher. If the teacher-librarian was someone who reached out to support the work of new teachers in the building, then the student teacher worked with the library program. If there was a paraprofessional or an incompetent teacher-librarian serving in the library, or if a rigid library schedule did not provide opportunities for classroom teachers to have their curriculum needs met, then the student teacher did not collaborate with the library staff. If the library staff was unwelcoming, the student teachers and the children in their care simply did not use the library at all.

The bottom line is this: each teacher-librarian is the representative of the profession for the administrators, classroom teachers, student teachers, students, and families in that school community. Our profession is only as strong as each individual who serves in the role of teacher-librarian.

Something magical can happen when educators contribute their expertise and willingness to learn to cocreate more responsive and more effective instructional programs. The complexity of 21st-century literacy and learning requires collaborative educators to ensure that all students, regardless of their backgrounds, develop tools for success. Through collaborative teaching, teacher-librarians are in an ideal position to become teacher leaders in their schools. As declared in a widely distributed Dewitt Wallace–Reader's Digest Library Power Project poster (circa 1994), "Teaching is too difficult to do alone; collaborate with your teacher-librarian."

Collaborative Teaching in the Age of Accountability 1

At the dawn of the 21st century, school districts and states struggle with accountability for student achievement in the form of data on standardized tests. It is no wonder that the classroom teachers and principal depicted in *Testing Miss Malarkey* feel anxious on the morning of "the test." Today's educators must cope with incredible pressure about students' test scores. Among the variables and factors that determine if a student, a classroom teacher, a school, a school district, or a state meets academic goals is the quality of instruction. How can the teacher-librarian be an essential contributor on the teaching team that impacts student achievement through best practices in instruction?

In the age of accountability spawned by the No Child Left Behind Act of 2001, teacher-librarians cannot afford to be considered on the periphery in education, nor can they be considered "support" staff by any education stakeholder. It certainly has not helped that, when this legislation defined the criteria for "highly qualified" educators, teacher-librarians were not listed among those in "core academic subjects" who need to have particular course work and credentials. As a result, educators' qualifications for serving as teacher-librarians continue to vary widely from state to state, and paraprofessionals occupy the position in far too many schools. At the time of this writing, the National Center for Educational Statistics still classifies teacher-librarians as "support-services-instructional," a classification outside the "instructional" category that classroom teachers occupy. While these

That morning there were more teachers than kids waiting for the nurse.

—From *Testing Miss Malarkey*, by Judy Finchler, illustrated by Kevin O'Malley situations are being corrected, teacher-librarians must "step up" to set high standards for themselves. They must have the skills and knowledge to position themselves in a central role in the academic program in their schools so they can make measurable contributions to students' learning.

A few old-timers know that the first set of national K–12 school library standards that defined the service functions of school librarians, *School Libraries for Today and Tomorrow,* was published by the American Library Association in 1945. Others know that standards established in 1969 emphasized the instructional role of school librarians in helping classroom teachers meet students' learning needs. But for most professionals serving in school libraries today, it wasn't until *Information Power: Guidelines for School Library Media Programs* (AASL and AECT 1988) and its 1998 successor that school librarians clearly understood the four roles of the teacher-librarian: teacher, information specialist, instructional partner, and program administrator. Viewed in this way, 75 percent of the teacher-librarian's job is directly concerned with teaching students.

A study conducted by KRC Research before the launch of the AASL @ your library campaign showed that study participants—parents, students, classroom teachers, and administrators—acknowledged that school libraries and librarians are important and have value, especially for elementary school children. Most of the participants, however, believed that school librarians primarily provide *support* functions that revolve around teaching students to find information or resources efficiently. Although classroom teachers and administrators were likely to see teacher-librarians and libraries as critical components of education, parents and students did not tend to see school librarians as educated professionals active in instruction.

A goal of AASL's campaign was to address the gaps between these perceptions and the critical teaching functions of librarians and library programs in students' education. To that end, these key messages were developed:

- School library media programs are critical to the learning experience.

- School library media specialists are crucial to the teaching and learning process.
- School library media centers are places of opportunity.

Read this study and learn more about the campaign at http://www.ala.org/ala/pio/campaign/schoollibrary/schoollibrary.htm.

With a focus on student achievement, the research studies that document the impact of teacher-librarians and school library programs on students' standardized achievement test scores should be of interest to every educational stakeholder. Figure 1-1 is a summary of selected reading and library program findings of research studies conducted in fifteen states between 1993 and 2004; for complete reports on these studies, visit the Library Research Service website at http://lrs.org.

Clearly, teacher-librarians and school library programs are significant in helping students achieve, and reading is definitely one core content area in which teacher-librarians must have the instructional skills and resources to maximize their impact on student learning. Although decoding skills are best taught in the classroom where classroom teachers can closely monitor the progress of individual children, the teacher-librarian is perfectly positioned to be a coteacher of reading comprehension strategies. With access to a variety of resources in various formats at a wide range of reading levels, what is the best way for teacher-librarians to realize their potential with regard to teaching reading comprehension?

Although research has consistently shown that ready access to a wide variety of reading materials increases the chances that students will become readers and choose to read (Krashen 2004), serving as recreational reading motivators and nurturers is not enough. All educators, including teacher-librarians, must support student achievement in reading through systematic instruction. Forming partnerships with classroom teachers to help teach students to employ their decoding skills in order to make meaning from text is natural for teacher-librarians and school library programs. These classroom-library

FIGURE 1-1
Selected Reading and Library Program Findings
from the School Library Impact Studies

STATE	YEAR	READING FINDINGS	LIBRARY PROGRAM FINDINGS
Alaska	1999		Test score increases correlate to frequency of library/information literacy instruction from teacher-librarians
Colorado	1993, 2000	Size of school library staff and collection explains 21% of variation in 7th-grade reading scores (1993)	21% higher reading scores in elementary schools with the most collaborative teacher-librarians (2000)
Florida	2002		Positive relationship between library program staffing and test scores at all levels
Illinois	2005		11th-grade ACT scores highest in schools with classroom teacher and teacher-librarian collaboration
Indiana	2004		Higher-performing teacher-librarians and programs in schools with collaborative teachers
Iowa	2002	Students with highest reading scores use more than 2½ times as many library books as lowest-scoring students	
Massachusetts	2002		Higher test scores at all levels in schools with library programs
Michigan	2003	Reading scores rise in relation to certified teacher-librarian staffing	
Minnesota	2003	66.8% of schools with above-average reading test scores had full-time teacher-librarians	
Missouri	2003		10.6% impact on student achievement from school library services
New Mexico	2002		Achievement scores rise with school library program development
North Carolina	2003	Significant impact on reading test scores by school library programs at all levels	
Oregon	2001	Incremental improvements in school library programs yield incremental improvement in reading scores	Collaborating high school teacher-librarians twice as likely to impact reading scores
Pennsylvania	2000	Positive and significant relationship between library staffing and reading test scores	
Texas	2001	10% more students in schools with teacher-librarians met minimum reading standards	

Adapted from Scholastic Research and Results (2006).

interactions begin at the level of providing the necessary resources and develop to full collaboration in which teacher-librarians and classroom teachers are equal partners who codesign, coimplement, and coassess lessons, including "how-to" reading comprehension strategy lessons. *Taxonomies of the School Library Media Program* (Loertscher 1988) specifies these levels of programmatic involvement.

Resources do provide a foundation for classroom-library collaboration. Children's literature should not be housed only in the school library; classroom libraries are a critical part of providing students with a rich literacy environment. For Serafini (2006, 37), at least 100 books per child is the benchmark for a well-stocked classroom library. He recommends 2,500–3,000 resources at all reading levels and in all genres for an ideal classroom collection. But few school districts support classroom teachers in developing class libraries of this size, and the cost of providing these critical resources falls entirely on the classroom teacher.

Even though conscientious classroom teachers visit garage sales and other sources of used books, write grants, and spend their own money to collect the resources their students need to be successful, schools with well-managed and fully integrated school library collections are vital in students' literacy development. In schools with open-access libraries and curriculum-based library collections that also meet learners' independent reading needs, students can have access to an ever-wider range of materials on more diverse topics at all reading levels than they could ever have in a classroom library. Clearly, there is a need for both classroom and school library access points for learners. In an open, flexibly scheduled library with sufficient support staff, students can browse, search, read, and check out books and other resources at the point of need. It is essential that school library programs be responsive to spontaneous teachable moments as well as to planned classroom-library collaboration.

The practices put forward in this book move the teacher-librarian up the taxonomy to the highest instructional design level, where they serve as full partners with classroom teachers in coteaching

lessons supported by the resources of the school library. In the age of accountability, this level of involvement in the school's academic program is a necessity. Throughout the school day, teacher-librarians serve in various capacities, depending on students' and classroom teachers' needs, but the goal should always be to spend the most time and energy at the top of the taxonomy, as full-fledged collaborating members of their school's instructional teams.

Strategies for Collaborative Teaching

What is collaboration? Friend and Cook explain interpersonal collaboration as "a style for direct interaction between at least two coequal parties voluntarily engaged in shared decision making as they work toward a common goal" (1996, 6). Collaboration describes *how* people work together rather than *what* they do. It is a dynamic, interactive process among equal partners who strive together to reach excellence. In the 21st century, educators' overarching common goal is increasing achievement for all learners.

Collaboration can happen in the planning, implementation, and assessment stages of teaching. It begins with planning the partnership itself. In formal collaborations, collaborators must schedule time to meet. Ideally, they preview the lesson ideas to each other in advance of the meeting so that planning can be more focused. Each person can then bring possible goals and objectives to the meeting, along with ideas for curriculum integration, instructional strategies, student grouping arrangements, and potential resources. In the planning process, educators establish shared goals and specific learning outcomes for students as well as assessment tools to evaluate student achievement. They discuss students' background knowledge, prior learning experiences, and skill development and determine what resources will best meet learners' needs. Educators decide on one or more coteaching approaches, assign responsibilities for particular aspects of the lesson, and schedule teaching time based on the needs of students and the requirements of the learning tasks. They may set up another meeting before teaching the lesson and schedule a follow-up time to coassess student work and to evaluate the lesson itself.

Using a collaborative planning form can help guide the initial planning meeting. (Web Supplements 1A, 1B, and 1C are sample planning forms; these planning documents do not replace formal lesson plans.) The goals and objectives are the most important sections on classroom-library collaborative planning forms. While negotiating the best way for the teacher-librarian to coteach curriculum standards and to integrate information literacy skills, the "backward planning" framework (Wiggins and McTighe 1998) charges educators with knowing where they are going before they begin determining instructional strategies and resources. This planning model is centered on student outcomes. Many teacher-librarian resources provide sample collaborative planning forms. The software program *Impact! Documenting the LMC Program for Accountability* (Miller 1998) combines both advanced planning and lesson plan support. It also helps teacher-librarians create reports that graphi-

cally and statistically document their contributions to the school's academic goals.

During lesson implementation, collaborators can assume different coteaching roles. In *Interactions: Collaboration Skills for School Professionals*, Friend and Cook describe various coteaching approaches (1996, 47–50). Figure 1-2 shows possible coteaching configurations. Depending on the lesson, the students' prior knowledge and skill development, the expertise of the educators, and their level of trust, collaborators can assume one or more of these roles during a lesson or unit of instruction.

Of these five approaches, team teaching requires the most collaboration and is the approach needed to teach the sample lessons offered in this book most effectively. Team teaching requires careful planning, respect for each educator's style, and ultimately a shared belief in the value that this level of risk taking can offer students and educators themselves. Teacher-librarians, working within a supportive learning community, must develop interpersonal skills as well as teaching expertise that can allow team teaching to flourish.

FIGURE 1-2

Coteaching Approaches

One Teaching, One Supporting	One educator is responsible for teaching the lesson while the other observes the lesson, monitors particular students, and provides assistance as needed.
Station or Center Teaching	After determining curriculum content for multiple learning stations, each educator takes responsibility for facilitating one or more learning centers. In some centers, students may work independently of adult support.
Parallel Teaching	After collaborative planning, each educator works with half the class to teach the same or similar content. Groups may switch or reconvene as a whole class to share, debrief, and reflect.
Alternative Teaching	One educator preteaches or reteaches concepts to a small group while the other educator teaches a different lesson to the larger group. (Preteaching vocabulary or other lesson components can be especially valuable for English language learners or special needs students.)
Team Teaching	Educators teach together by assuming different roles during instruction, such as reader or recorder or questioner and responder, modeling partner work, role playing or debating, and more.

Adapted from Friend and Cook (1996).

Collaboration can also occur during assessment. After coplanning and coimplementing lessons and units of instruction, it is logical that evaluating student learning is part of a shared responsibility for instruction. Checklists, rating scales, and rubrics, developed with colleagues and in some cases with students in advance of instruction or early in the lesson, establish the criteria for postlesson assessment. Students should use these tools to guide, revise, and self-assess their work. Educators can use the same criteria to inform their teaching and modeling, guide student practice, and assess students' learning process and final products.

Educators may decide to divide assessment on the basis of components of the lesson for which each one took primary responsibility. For example, teacher-librarians may take the lead in teaching notemaking skills and may then take responsibility for assessing students' notes with a rubric. Joint assessment can happen before designing a lesson when educators administer pretests to determine the students' level of skill development or prior knowledge of a particular concept. Even if they did not coteach a lesson, educators might ask one another to provide another set of eyes to evaluate the effectiveness of instruction based on students' learning products. In *Assessing Learning: Librarians and Teachers as Partners,* Harada and Yoshina (2005) provide a comprehensive guide to best practices in assessment.

Coassessing the lesson or unit of instruction is too often overlooked. After coplanning, coteaching, and coassessing students' work, collaborating educators must make time to debrief in order to determine which aspects of the lesson went well and which could use revision. If educators are team teaching, then some of this evaluation occurs as they share responsibility for monitoring and adjusting the teaching and learning while the lesson is in progress. Taking the time to reflect on the lesson after it has been taught is important for professional growth. Reflection helps educators more clearly articulate the relationships between their goals and objectives for student learning and student outcomes. Reflective practitioners focus on students'

learning as well as on improving their own practice. In "TAG Team: Collaborate to Teach, Assess and Grow," Schomberg (2003) offers a glimpse into her learning team's collaborative teaching journey, a journey through the initial planning stages, coteaching and modeling learning tasks, coassessing student work, and sharing responsibility for revising the team's solar system unit for future use.

Collaboration and School Reform

Why is collaboration necessary in our schools? What could happen if classroom teachers and teacher-librarians combined their expertise and talents to share responsibility for teaching students? Barth (2006, 11) observes that collegial relationships in schools are both "highly prized" and "highly elusive" preconditions for school reform, and in a collegial school he would expect to see

- Educators talking about practice.
- Educators sharing craft knowledge.
- Educators observing one another while they are engaged in practice.
- Educators rooting for one another's success.

Classroom-library collaboration meets all four of these criteria. When educators coplan, coimplement, and coassess lessons and units of instruction, they cannot help but talk about practice, share craft knowledge, observe one another teaching, and root for one another's success. Through collaborative teaching, educators develop a common language, a common set of practices, and channels for communication that can increase student learning and help the entire school community better serve the academic and social needs of students and families.

In *What Works in Schools: Translating Research into Action,* Marzano (2003) shares thirty-five years of research related to improving student achievement. He delineates school-level, teacher-level, and student-level factors that affect student achievement. At the school level, a guaranteed and viable curriculum, challenging goals and feedback, parent and community involvement, a safe and orderly environment, and collegiality and professionalism all had positive impacts on student outcomes. At the teacher level, instructional strategies, classroom management, and classroom curriculum design improved student achievement. At the student level, the home atmosphere, learned intelligence and background knowledge, and motivation all affected students' learning. Many of these factors, including collegiality, instructional strategies, and curriculum design, are directly addressed in this book, but there is one additional factor that research has shown to affect student learning: class size.

Researchers have been conducting studies about reducing class size for many years. In a meta-analysis of these studies, Glass and Smith (1979) concluded that a class size of less than fifteen is optimum and that the benefits of small class size are greatest for elementary-age students. Surely the school, student, and educator characteristics make a difference, but lowering the student-to-teacher ratio through coteaching makes sense, particularly for children who enter formal schooling with fewer school-like literacy experiences.

Two research studies support the notion that reducing class size or lowering the student-to-teacher ratio has a significant impact on student achievement, particularly for minority students. Tennessee legislators initiated an experimental study called Student-Teacher Achievement Ratio (STAR). Conducted between 1985 and 1988, kindergarten through third-grade students were randomly assigned to three different class configurations: small (13–17 students), regular (22–26 students), and regular-sized classes with both a certified classroom teacher and a teacher's aide. Students in small classes outperformed students assigned to the other two configurations and continued to do so through middle school and into their high school education. In addition, minority students' test scores improved the most. In the late 1990s, Wisconsin's Student Achievement Guarantee in Education (SAGE) program placed K–3 children from high-poverty schools in classes of fifteen students for all or part of the day. Similar to the STAR study, test scores for SAGE minority students made the greatest gains (Reichardt 2001).

Across the United States, states lack the will and commitment to authorize the level of funding necessary to continuously support smaller class size. Although hiring a full-time credentialed and professional teacher-librarian to serve as a collaborator does not lower class size (and school statistics should not be manipulated to suggest otherwise), classroom-library collaboration can lower the student-to-teacher ratio at the point of instruction. The results of the SAGE program in which students may have been assigned to smaller classes only for core subjects such as reading, writing, and math suggest that classroom-library collaboration could have a similar impact.

Students come to us with varying background knowledge, learning styles, linguistic and cultural heritages, values, and beliefs about learning and schooling. The resulting diversity among students requires that schools continuously adapt and step up to meet individual learner's needs. Today's school reform movements are based in large part on the challenge of making sure all students have every opportunity to reach their potential. Collaborative teaching between classroom teachers and teacher-librarians using the strategies suggested in this book benefits students because it puts the focus on learning outcomes. But that's not all it does. Coteaching positively impacts adult learning as well. Figure 1-3 outlines the benefits of collaborative teaching to both students and educators.

In school restructuring, the most powerful impediment to reform is teacher isolation (Lieberman 1995, 10). Just as learning is social for students, it is also social for adults. Innovations in teaching cannot spread throughout a learning community if educators remain isolated, separate in their classrooms. As figure 1-3 clearly shows, educators who teach collaboratively not only improve student learning but also create learning opportunities for themselves and for each other.

FIGURE 1-3
Benefits of Classroom-Library Collaboration Based on Coteaching

FOR STUDENTS	FOR EDUCATORS
More individualized attention	More opportunities to work one-on-one with students
Better-designed lessons	Clarification of goals and objectives through joint planning; coassessment of lesson effectiveness
Increased opportunity for differentiated instruction	Improved facilitation of differentiated instruction
Access to information at the point of need	Literature and information literacy skills integrated in a meaningful way into the classroom curriculum
Access to multiple resources, including technology	Shared responsibility for gathering engaging, effective resources
More engagement because of fewer distractions	Fewer classroom management issues
More material or deeper investigations into concepts and topics	More teaching time (because of fewer management issues and scheduling to achieve student learning objectives)
Expanded opportunities for creativity	Expanded opportunities for creativity
Acquiring skills for lifelong learning	Personal and professional growth opportunities through coteaching and coassessment of student learning
Integrated learning	Integrated teaching

Professional Development at the Point of Practice

Team teaching with another professional gives educators job-embedded professional development, which is currently considered a best practice in education. The profusion of classroom teacher support roles such as literacy and instructional coaches shows that more and more school districts understand the value and effectiveness of faculty development at the point of practice. Rather than being a formal one-day or separate event, effective professional development should be more informal, a regular part of educators' everyday professional work. Ongoing, continuous improvement in teaching practices is necessary if educators are to ensure that diverse learners have the maximum opportunity for achievement.

"The single most effective way in which principals can function as staff development leaders is providing a school context that fosters job-embedded professional development" (DuFour 2001, 14–15). School principals are central figures in building a culture of collaboration within the school learning community. They must provide educators with time to coplan during contract hours. They can support coteaching by endorsing collaborative teaching for performance evaluations and by spotlighting effective collaborative teaching in faculty meetings and newsletters to families. They must also model collaborative practices by inviting another principal to cofacilitate a faculty meeting or to observe them doing the work of the principalship. As instructional leaders, principals are pivotal in establishing value for collaborative teaching.

What do principals expect of teacher-librarians? Haycock reported that principals value both formal and informal staff development facilitated by teacher-librarians. An informal example is as simple as offering "short sessions for individuals and interested small groups on new resources, whether print or electronic, and how they might be incorporated into instruction" (2004, 6). Using resources as an entrée, teacher-librarians have natural opportunities to begin curriculum conversations. These conversations provide doors through which teacher-librarians can invite and initiate classroom-library collaboration for instruction. The model for collaborative teaching offered in this book is founded on parity and shared risk taking. The resulting coteaching fosters job-embedded professional development for both classroom teachers and teacher-librarians that will impact the literacy learning in their schools.

With increasing retirements and a high turnover in teaching positions, principals must be vigilant about inducting new teachers into collaborative learning communities. Teacher preparation programs tend to focus on classroom teachers' individual interactions with students rather than on collaborative activities among educators (Hartzell 2002). As a result, if classroom teachers learn to collaborate, they do so after they arrive on the job. Teacher-librarians must be ready to develop interpersonal skills and best practices for successful classroom-library collaboration alongside both new and veteran teachers.

If educators hope to prepare young people for living and working in the 21st century, and they target information literacy and 21st-century skills objectives in their lessons, then they should be mindful of the ways they do or do not model these behaviors for students. What is the covert curriculum in our schools? What attitudes and behaviors are educators modeling as they teach the covert standards-based curriculum? *Information Power: Building Partnerships for Learning* (AASL and AECT 1998) and organizations such as the Partnership for 21st Century Skills (www.21stcenturyskills.org) charge educators with teaching learning and thinking skills such as critical thinking, problem solving, collaboration, communication, and information and media literacy. How can educators practice as well as demonstrate these skills for students? Collaborative teaching is one way. When educators collaborate for instruction, they not only teach these skills, they model them as well, and in the process both students and educators learn.

Summary

The organic nature of the classroom-library collaboration model offers on-site, job-embedded professional development integrated into the daily practice of educators. Through shared responsibility, collaborators create opportunities for reciprocal mentoring and ongoing shared reflection. Collaboration for instruction lowers student-to-teacher ratios. More students have opportunities for individualized attention, and groups of students can be better supported as they learn essential skills and content in different ways. Two or more educators can monitor, adjust, and assess the students' work as well as evaluate the lessons themselves. The opportunity to learn alongside a colleague as an equal improves teaching practices for novice as well as veteran educators.

Among those who actively support the use of the term *teacher-librarian*, there are those who believe it is essential that the name clearly state the teacher-librarian's role and priorities. If teacher-librarians have earned teaching credentials, their title should reflect that, because their effectiveness as coteachers may hinge on being considered a peer by classroom teacher colleagues and equals with classroom teachers by administrators. Just as classroom teachers have duties beyond teaching, teacher-librarians have library administration duties. But none of these responsibilities can compete with the imperative to impact student achievement through effective instruction. Until teacher-librarians serve as full members of instructional teams, their true value as educators cannot be measured.

2 Maximizing Your Impact

Reading was just plain torture. When Sue Ellyn read her page, or Tommy Bob read his page, they read so easily that Trisha would watch the top of their heads to see if something was happening to their heads that wasn't happening to hers.

—From *Thank You, Mr. Falker*, by Patricia Polacco

Although there are ongoing debates among educators about best practices in reading instruction, there is universal agreement on the goal of giving our nation's youth the tools they need to become lifelong readers. Educators at every grade level must serve as partners with parents and take responsibility for inviting young people into the "literacy club" (Smith 1998). They must ensure that students have limitless opportunities to develop the skills necessary to be effective readers. Educators must design lessons that stimulate readers' curiosity and help them make connections and find relevance between school-based and community-based literacy. Only by doing so can educators help students become strategic readers who understand that their proficiency in reading for information and for pleasure will impact all their life choices.

What is reading? Simply put, reading is making meaning from print and from visual information. But reading is not simple. Reading is an active process that requires a great deal of practice and skill. It is a complex task which, as Polacco's autobiographical character Trisha noted, seems to go on inside people's heads like so much magic in a magician's top hat. In order to be readers, learners must take their ability to pronounce words and to "read" pictures and then make the words and images *mean* something. Reading comprehension strategies are tools that proficient readers use to solve the comprehension problems they encounter in texts.

Zimmermann and Hutchins (2003) identify seven reading comprehension strategies:

1. Activating or building background knowledge
2. Using sensory images
3. Questioning
4. Making predictions and inferences
5. Determining main ideas
6. Using fix-up options
7. Synthesizing

Each of the following chapters defines one of these reading comprehension strategies, discusses considerations for teaching it, offers children's literature resources, and presents three sample "how-to" strategy lessons that help teach students *how to* use the strategies to make meaning. Although the lessons can be taught by individual educators, the sample lessons are designed to maximize educators' opportunities for coteaching and lowering the student-to-teacher ratio during instruction.

Foundations and Best Practices for Teaching Reading Comprehension Strategies

The how-to lessons presented in this book provide models that can guide educators as they help students acquire reading strategies. The strategies define what is taught, but how the lessons were designed and how they are taught are equally important. These lessons are based on five foundational best practices in school librarianship and instruction: evidence-based practice, backward planning, aligning and integrating information literacy standards with the classroom curriculum, using research-based instructional strategies, and modeling with think-aloud strategies.

Teacher-librarians can confidently build collaborative practices on the firm foundation of the findings of the impact studies (see figure 1-1), but they must continually demonstrate to students, classroom colleagues, school administrators, parents, and the public that what they do in their daily

practice results in improved student achievement. Teacher-librarians must understand that everyone is "from Missouri" and needs to be shown that school library programs make a difference. Todd notes that this evidence-based practice is "critical to the future sustainability of the profession, and represents one of the most significant challenges facing school librarianship" (2001, 1). Teacher-librarians can use the sample lessons offered in this book to take action at their school sites and advance local academic goals that connect with what matters in most elementary schools—achievement in reading. By coteaching reading comprehension strategies alongside classroom teachers, teacher-librarians can gather evidence that their instruction makes a difference in student learning.

According to Wiggins and McTighe (1998), effective instructional design begins with determining student learning outcomes. Commonly called backward planning, this conceptual framework requires that educators first select learning objectives (based on curriculum standards). Next, they determine and describe the learning tasks and the criteria on which student work will be assessed as well as a tool with which to assess it. All learning tasks are then designed to help students meet these criteria. This is all accomplished before the teaching methods and resource materials are selected and long before the lesson begins. The how-to lessons in this book were designed with this framework, except that one aspect of the teaching method, collaborative teaching, was assumed.

With its focus on outcomes, the backward design framework is ideal for evidence-based classroom-library collaborations. Collaborative planning must always begin with learning objectives as well as criteria and tools for assessing student outcomes. When students are capable of setting their own learning goals, however, educators may modify this framework by inviting learners to establish their own assessment criteria in advance or early in the learning engagement. This level of ownership in outcomes can address motivation issues and support students in becoming self-directed learners. It should also be noted that sometimes rubrics or other assessment tools need to be adjusted during instruction. If this situation arises, educators will appreciate the benefit of putting two or more minds to that task.

Information literacy standards, as delineated in *Information Power: Building Partnerships for Learning* (*IP2*), are also integrated into each of these reading comprehension strategy lessons. Unfortunately, the information literacy keywords are not readily found in the core subject curriculum standards. For example, a reading standard that requires students to locate specific information by using organizational features of expository texts is congruent with Information Literacy Standard 1, which involves accessing information efficiently and effectively. Or a social studies standard that requires students to summarize information relates directly to Information Literacy Standard 3, which suggests that an information-literate student uses information accurately. The guidelines and standards as outlined in *IP2* are undergoing revision, so it is especially important that teacher-librarians be proficient at identifying the terms used in the content area standards that relate to information literacy.

Notemaking is one information literacy skill that is used across the strategy lessons. Figure 2-1 is a chart that states the goal of notemaking and some commonly used types of notes. (This chart is also available as Web Supplement 2A.)

In this book, the term *notemaking* is used rather than the term *note taking*. Notemaking implies that learners record information in their own words; note taking implies that learners have copied verbatim from texts. When students copy verbatim, they are rarely prioritizing or analyzing information. Educators can model recording a direct quote, passing that information through their prior knowledge and experience, and then making a note or two in their own words to show what they understand or have learned from the quoted sentence or passage. Demonstrating this process in all content areas and with many different kinds of text is an important part of teaching notemaking.

Notemaking also requires that students carefully record information in order to be able to cite their sources. Teacher-librarians can contribute various kinds of support for students to keep track of their resources in the form of paper or electronic graphic organizers; students and educators may also have access to computer software that helps students record their sources and link them to their notes. Matching up bibliographic forms and notemaking graphic organizers is one way to ensure that students know the source of their information, can return to it for clarification if need be, and can cite it in their final products; see the advanced lesson plan in chapter 9 for examples of these graphic organizers. Educators can also facilitate a discussion of plagiarism and provide guidelines for avoiding plagiarism, the most important of which are to make notes in one's own words, to quote copied material, and to record sources. Clearly, these are information literacy skills that can be integrated in many content-area, standards-based lessons at the elementary school level.

In *Classroom Instruction That Works: Research-Based Strategies for Increasing Student Achievement*, Marzano, Pickering, and Pollock (2001) offer a summary of a meta-analysis of studies conducted by researchers at Mid-continent Research for Education and Learning. These studies analyzed the effectiveness of specific components of instruction. The authors identified nine instructional strategies that have a strong effect on student achievement; six of these are used as support for the how-to lessons in this book. Figure 2-2 identifies the strategies selected for the lessons and the related percentile gains for student achievement on standardized tests.

FIGURE 2-1
Notemaking Chart

Notemaking = Information in your own words
Types of notes
    Single words and phrases
    Lists
    Abbreviations
    Drawings
    References to a page number

FIGURE 2-2

Instructional Strategies That Affect Student
Achievement on Standardized Tests

CATEGORY	PERCENTILE GAIN
Identifying similarities and differences	45
Summarizing and note taking	34
Nonlinguistic representations	27
Cooperative learning	27
Setting objectives and providing feedback	23
Questions, cues, and advance organizers	22

Selected from Marzano, Pickering, and Pollock (2001).

These gain figures in figure 2-2 are based on an average student being exposed to a particular strategy compared with a student who was not instructed in the strategy. The authors used a statistical conversion table to transform study effect sizes into student percentile gains. For example, if a student learns to employ the similarities and differences strategy, then her score on achievement tests may increase by as much as 45 percentage points. These test score gains suggest that students learn reading comprehension strategies more effectively by using research-based instructional strategies in the learning process.

These instructional strategies were integrated into the sample lesson plans on the basis of their appropriateness in supporting the learning objectives. Four forms of identifying similarities and differences are used in the lessons: comparing using Venn diagrams, classifying using category matrices and webs, creating metaphors (or similes), and creating analogies. Summarizing is used in the main ideas strategy lessons as well as in reflective paragraphs in lessons in other chapters. Notemaking is used throughout the lessons. Drawing pictures, creating graphs, and kinesthetic activities are three types of nonlinguistic representation students use to show their learning in the sample lessons. Educators role-play cooperative strategies, and students engage in cooperative learning in many lessons. Setting objectives and providing feedback are essential components of every sample lesson offered in this book. In lessons targeted for several different strategies, cues,

questions, and advance organizers help students activate their prior knowledge and prepare them for the learning tasks.

Finally, using think-aloud strategies during modeling is a common thread throughout the how-to lessons offered in this book. This research-based best practice in reading instruction makes the invisible cognitive processes of reading "visible" to students. Research has shown that people learn better when they are more aware of their own thinking processes. Providing models for less developed readers, proficient readers share how they solve comprehension problems by using think-alouds while reading a text. For example, while reading *Thank You, Mr. Falker,* a reader may stop and say, "I can't understand why Trisha is reacting this way. She seems so hurt and angry. Has anyone ever made me feel this way? Maybe if I replay the scene in my mind, if I visualize it, I will understand her actions." The reader is showing how using her background knowledge and visualizing the action can help her understand the character's behavior. Not only is this approach to literacy instruction helpful to elementary-age learners, it is being applied more broadly across the K–12 spectrum (see Wilhelm 2001).

To become expert in these best practices in education, teacher-librarians should go to the sources mentioned to read and understand these strategies in depth. The goal of integrating these best practices into the how-to strategy lessons is to help educators, and teacher-librarians in particular, gain experience using these practices. This also gives collaborators a common vocabulary and set of practices that can be applied across contexts—in the classroom and in the library. A glossary of terms is provided at the end of the book.

The Metaphor of the Elephant and the Seven Reading Comprehension Strategies

In his retelling of an ancient East Indian fable, "The Blind Men and the Elephant," author-illustrator Ed Young gives young and mature readers alike the perfect metaphor for the seven reading comprehension strategies presented in this book. In this tale, each blind mouse goes out to investigate the "strange Something" by their pond. Each one describes a part of the "Something" while considering its shape and relating it to a familiar object. The elephant's tail is thought to be a rope, its ear a fan, and so on. All but the final mouse comprehend only isolated parts of the elephant and therefore come to partial and erroneous conclusions based on those single aspects alone. It is only when the seventh blind mouse considers all the parts that the mice are able to make sense of the whole; they are able to fully comprehend the elephant.

Unlike the blind mice who consider only shape, readers can relate parts of an elephant to the seven reading comprehension strategies based on the function they serve. Constructing metaphors is one of the research-based instructional strategies that increases student achievement (Marzano, Pickering, and Pollock 2001). Although the tail is found at the end of the elephant, background knowledge comes first, because without it readers have no place to begin. Sensory imagery symbolized by the ear follows because using sensory imagery is more than using visual information or visualizing. It requires readers to engage all their senses to make meaning. Sensory connections are also an aspect of our background knowledge. Asking questions, represented by the elephant's probing tusks, and making predictions and inferences, the head, require higher-order thinking skills that stretch the reader to go beyond a text's denotation on the page or screen to explore connotations. The legs, which support all the weight, represent the main ideas. Readers must analyze texts to determine the main ideas and to compose summaries. The fix-up strategy, suggested by the multitasking trunk, allows readers to recover lost comprehension. It uses a set of options that can be taught one by one, but altogether they show the complexity of monitoring and recovering meaning. And finally, synthesis, the whole elephant, requires that the reader use all the strategies to bring together ideas and

evidence from multiple texts and combine them with their own interpretations to transform information into knowledge. Strategic readers are readers who apply these strategies seamlessly in their reading process.

The metaphors serve as handy shorthand for students and educators to communicate about the meaning of the comprehension strategies. The Web-based support for this book includes bookmarks that can be used to remind students of these metaphors. On one side, the parts of the elephant and the comparable reading comprehension strategies are listed. The reverse side of the bookmark lists fix-up options at three levels of sophistication: beginning with eight options for merging readers (Web Supplement 2B), twelve for advancing readers (2C), and all sixteen for advanced readers (2D). Students can refer to the bookmarks as they read and practice the strategies.

Like the blind mice, educators and students could be deceived by perceiving each reading comprehension strategy as able to stand alone, isolated from the others. In truth, all of these strategies use aspects of the others. When applying background knowledge, readers recall sensory images. Predictions are often based on our background knowledge, what readers know from life experiences or from reading other texts. Identifying main ideas and synthesizing are common aspects of our thinking processes in all of these comprehension strategies. Many of the fix-up options are based on the strategies themselves: try to visualize, ask a new question, make a prediction, and so on. Active readers utilize multiple comprehension strategies as they engage with texts. Teachers and students must remember that the ultimate goal is to utilize combinations of strategies when they are appropriate to different types of text, purposes for reading, and comprehension challenges. (The order of the chapters in this book reflects a logical sequence for building students' comprehension strategy repertoires rather than following the order of the elephant parts as presented in Young's book.)

Sample Lessons and Lesson Format

This book offers sample lesson plans at three levels of reading development: emerging, advancing, and advanced. Emerging readers have a working knowledge of decoding; they are primed to develop their independent reading abilities. Advancing readers, while still mastering the finer points of decoding, are regularly reading texts independently. Advanced readers have mastered decoding and are reading more sophisticated texts independently. These levels of literacy development are not related to specific grade levels. A lesson that may be appropriate for kindergarten students in one classroom may be equally effective for second-grade students in another. It is up to educators, who have assessed the students' level of proficiency before initiating instruction, to determine which lesson level or levels is appropriate. Observation, self-reporting questionnaires, interviews, and formal pretests are some diagnostic tools educators can use to determine students' proficiency levels or readiness for new learning.

All readers can benefit from specific instruction in reading comprehension strategies. As readers continue to practice the strategies with the support of educator modeling, they should begin to take increasing responsibility for guiding the strategy lessons. When they effectively apply these comprehension strategies in their independent reading, the strategies become skills and there is no longer a need for explicit instruction. Educator Janet Allen describes a skill as "a strategy that's gone underground."

Figure 2-3 shows the lesson format for the how-to strategy lessons offered in this book. The planning section extends from the reading comprehension strategy through the standards; the lesson implementation or process follows. All of the lessons assume that educators have determined in advance that students will benefit from learning the target reading comprehension strategy. Learning and practicing the strategy are the overarching objectives for the lesson. The lesson format lists the level of reading development, followed by the research-based instructional strategies selected to support this lesson. The lesson length is an average. One "session" is about forty-five minutes of instructional time. Depending on the learners' characteristics, educators may need to revise the lesson length. It is assumed that lessons are taught in whatever location is best for the students, educators, and content, be it the library, computer lab, or classroom. The purpose for

FIGURE 2-3
Sample "How-To" Strategy Lesson Format:
Planning and Implementation

PLANNING	IMPLEMENTATION
Reading Comprehension Strategy	Process
Reading Development Level	Motivation
Instructional Strategies	Student-Friendly Objectives
Lesson Length	Presentation
Purpose	Student Participation Procedures
Objectives	*or*
Resources, Materials, and Equipment	Student Practice Procedures
Children's Literature	Guided Practice
Websites	Closure
Graphic Organizers	Reflection
Materials	Extensions
Equipment	
Collaboration	
Assessment	
Standards	
Reading and Writing	
Listening and Speaking	
Other Content Areas	
Information Literacy	
Educational Technology	

the lesson is directly related to the students' need and readiness for the instruction.

The objectives for each lesson use terms taken from performance objectives found in the Arizona state standards. Other state standards are likely to use similar terms. If necessary for local documentation, educators can conduct electronic searches of standards' documents to locate the keywords found in the objectives. To manage lesson length, picture books are used as anchor texts for these lessons. In this book, the term *text* refers to a work in its totality, words and illustrations. The term *print* refers to the words only, and the term *illustration* refers to artwork and a variety of other graphic features.

In the list of children's literature at the end of each chapter, the starred titles indicate the books used in the lessons. At the time of this writing, all of the children's literature chosen for the lessons was available for purchase, and some of the titles were available in Spanish. Educators are not limited to using these books, but the characteristics of titles should be considered if substitute texts are selected. Only websites with relative permanence are included in this book. I will maintain Internet pathfinders to ensure that websites are functional. A complete set of graphic organizers and rubrics is available as part of the Web support for this book. Required materials are listed, as is equipment. When the terms *post, project,* and *class-sized graphic organizer* appear in the lesson plans, educators can use overhead transparencies, data projectors, or interactive whiteboards to share documents with students. The resources and materials were carefully selected to support the instructional objectives of each lesson.

In the collaboration section of each lesson plan, collaborative strategies for teaching the lessons are described. These strategies can and should be adapted to fit the needs of students, educators, and the particular learning environment. In making adjustments, educators should remember that the lessons were designed to lower the student-to-teacher ratio during the presentation or guided practice components of the lessons. The sources for assessment of student outcomes are given in the "assessment" section. It is critical that educa-

tors share the assessment criteria with students in advance of the guided practice and that they model using the rubrics and other assessment tools. If the completeness of a graphic organizer is the assessment, educators need to be especially careful to establish the criteria through modeling.

The curriculum standards are listed as keywords. Like the terms used in the lesson objectives, educators can search standards documents for these keywords. The lessons are interdisciplinary in order to maximize students' ability to transfer their learning and to make connections across content areas. Designing instruction in this way also helps educators cover the curriculum more efficiently. With children's literature serving as anchor texts, lesson extensions often address educational technology standards. If the resources are available, educators and students can use electronic webbing and other thinking tools when appropriate. Depending on the needs and proficiency levels of students, all written work can be keyboarded or presented electronically, and all artwork can be created using applicable software. The curriculum standards suggested are not exclusive; educators may certainly add to them when appropriate.

The implementation or process section of the lesson plans is guided by the essential elements of instruction, also known as the Madeline Hunter model. The lessons begin by offering motivation for participating in the learning engagement. Student-friendly objectives are listed next and should be posted for students and educators to refer to during the lesson. The presentation components of the lesson are what the educators do to model and prepare students to practice the reading comprehension strategy. If the presentation includes opportunities for student participation, a list of student participation procedures is provided; these too can be posted for students' and educators' reference. If the lesson moves from presentation to guided practice, there is a list of student practice procedures that should be posted. The guided practice specifies what educators pay attention to as they monitor students' work. The lesson closure includes student sharing or a review of the strategy and an assessment. The reflection is offered in the form of questions that can be posted and responded to orally or in writing. Possible extensions to the lesson conclude the format. Because all lesson plans are guides rather than prescriptions, educators are advised to modify and adapt lesson procedures to fit the needs of students, the curriculum, and their own teaching styles.

Considerations for English Language Learners

As schools welcome more and more English language learners (ELLs), teacher-librarians and classroom teachers must consider these students' needs as they carefully plan and implement instruction. Across the United States, school districts, state departments of education, and colleges of education are recognizing the necessity of providing practicing and preservice educators with tools that help students acquire and learn English. The sheltered instruction approach is one model that has gained widespread use (Echevarria, Vogt, and Short 2004). In elementary schools where classroom teachers are responsible for instruction in all areas of the curriculum, language arts objectives are often integrated into every lesson. If ELLs are members of the classroom community, then ELL language arts standards must be integrated into each lesson as well. As educators learn to articulate and plan language objectives clearly, they are advised to collaborate with colleagues who are trained in sheltered instruction or other English language teaching and learning approaches.

All of the reading comprehension strategies highlighted in this book are specified in the sheltered English instruction approach. Basing lessons on published standards, clearly stating content and language objectives orally and in writing, and posting participation and practice procedures offer procedural support for ELLs. Teaching strategies that use think-alouds and modeling explicitly are cornerstones of the sheltered approach. For ELLs who must simultaneously learn language and content, graphic organizers offer important instructional scaffolds that help them organize information. Educators can modify the provided graphic organizers to meet the needs of ELLs by embedding concept definitions or elaborations that further explain the content. These strategies and methods are important for all learners, but they are imperative for ELLs.

Summary

There is no better way to promote the teaching role of the teacher-librarian and the importance of the school library program than to document how classroom-library collaboration impacts student outcomes. Coteaching the how-to lessons in this book is one place to begin. Collecting pre- and postlesson data, gathering and assessing student products, and sharing these results with administrators, other classroom teacher colleagues, and parents help educate the stakeholders in the learning community about the value of classroom-library collaboration.

Coteaching reading comprehension strategies with classroom teachers gives teacher-librarians a tangible and effective way to contribute to student achievement in reading, one of the core subjects that matters in every school. Working together, teacher-librarians and classroom teachers can gather meaningful evidence that demonstrates that student learning has increased as a direct result of their collaborative efforts. They can use backward planning to design effective lessons that focus on student outcomes. Through collaborative teaching, teacher-librarians can teach the information literacy skills that are found in the performance objectives in many content areas. By using research-based instructional strategies, collaborators employ recognized best practices and adapt and develop them to meet the needs of the students in their charge. Educators offer students cognitive scaffolds for developing reading skills by using think-alouds as they coteach and model reading comprehension strategies.

The seven reading comprehension strategies described in this book and addressed in the sample lesson plans are skills that are used by strategic readers. Through purposefully designed lessons using think-alouds and modeling, teacher-librarians and classroom teachers make these internal processes evident to students. Readers can practice and develop these strategies until they can use them automatically when they engage with texts—until they become reading skills. The goal of teaching reading comprehension strategies is to give readers the tools they need to be effective readers and independent learners. Unlike Trisha in *Thank You, Mr. Falker*, they will no longer watch each other's heads in search of reading magic. Instead, students will understand the reading process from the inside out.

Children's Literature Cited

Seven Blind Mice, by Ed Young

Thank You, Mr. Falker, by Patricia Polacco

Reading Comprehension Strategy One
Activating or Building Background Knowledge

When I was young in the mountains, I never wanted to go to the ocean, and I never wanted to go to the desert. I never wanted to go anywhere else in the world, for I was in the mountains. And that was always enough.

—From *When I Was Young in the Mountains,*
by Cynthia Rylant, illustrated by Diane Goode

Before we open a book, link to a website, or sit down in a movie theater or in front of the TV, our adult minds begin to activate what we already know, think, or believe about the topic of the literacy event we are about to enter. We developed this skill over the course of many years of meeting and greeting new experiences. Our brains seek out patterns; our thinking involves making connections. Understanding the importance of background knowledge to comprehension is critical because we connect new information with prior knowledge before we integrate and organize the new information. Like the elephant's tail, background knowledge is always behind us backing up our comprehension. It is the sum of the prior experiences we bring to each new encounter with text.

Rosenblatt (1978) developed a theory of reading as a transaction among the reader, the text, and the intention of the author. She posited that each reader brings his own feelings, personality, and experiences to the text and that each reader is different each time he revisits a particular text. Background knowledge is what the reader brings to the reading event. Each reader's interpretation and each reading of the text are potentially unique. This theory helps explain our individual responses to literature, art, and music and can be applied more broadly to our generalized responses in all areas of learning.

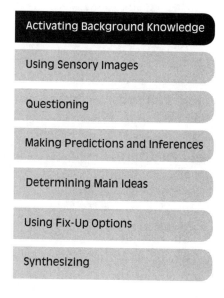

Activating Background Knowledge

Using Sensory Images

Questioning

Making Predictions and Inferences

Determining Main Ideas

Using Fix-Up Options

Synthesizing

As we go through life meeting and revisiting ideas and information, we organize our understandings into schemas. According to McGee and Richgels, a schema is a "mental structure in which we store all the information we know about people, places, objects, or activities" (1996, 5). If we have no schema for a particular topic, we begin that encounter with an immediate loss of comprehension, as the following incident clearly shows.

What's a Grand Canyon?

After months of preparation and anticipation, the children waited enthusiastically for the writing prompt for their annual state-mandated writing assessment. The classroom teacher opened the booklet and read aloud to her students: "Write a story about the day you took a pack mule trip into the Grand Canyon."

In this Tucson, Arizona, elementary school 350 miles from the Grand Canyon and 60 miles from the Mexican border, twenty-eight wiggling eight-year-old arms flew into the air. "Teacher, teacher," they called out in unison. "What's a Grand Canyon?"

The third-grade students attending this elementary school had never seen a photograph of the Grand Canyon, much less visited it. Only one student said she had ridden a mule, but when the teacher translated that word to "burro," at least half the class reported having had that experience. In short, these children had no schemas to support their writing on this topic.

These students did not have contextual background because they had never visited the Grand Canyon, and they did not have decontextualized book knowledge because they had not yet read or viewed a film about the place or the experience of riding a mule down its steep slopes.

Keene and Zimmermann (1997) liken schemas to "homes in the mind." This metaphor helps educators think in terms of the necessity of familiarity and comfort with a topic if the reader is to be successful at making meaning. By assessing students' schemas and activating or building background knowledge, they offer students critical support for comprehension.

Educators cannot assume that students have prior experiences with any school-based domains. Introducing lessons and units of study with brainstorms and questions about what prior ideas and information children possess on particular topics is an essential component of lesson design. In order to find a firm starting point for student learning, educators often utilize K-W-L charts, or some variation of this tool, to help the class or individual students assess their background knowledge. If students have the necessary schemas, they have support for leaping into the learning experience. If they do not yet have a schema, then it is up to the educator to help them build background knowledge. Extending the K-W-L chart allows for the possibility that educators will need to help students build their background knowledge before identifying what they already know and want to learn:

- *Build* background.
- What do we already *know*?
- What do we *wonder* about?
- What did we *learn*?
- What are our new *questions*?

This B-K-W-L-Q chart, based on the work of Janet Allen (2004), also acknowledges that inquiring is a dynamic process that can generate as many questions as it answers.

We can also think of background knowledge as learned understandings about specific domains. Background knowledge becomes part of what some researchers call "crystallized intelligence." This type of intelligence is associated with facts, generalizations, and principles. "The strong correlation between crystallized intelligence and academic achievement helps to explain the strong relationship between background knowledge (or 'prior knowledge' in some studies) and achievement" (Marzano 2003, 134).

If we attempt to read or write in a domain for which we have no prior knowledge, we struggle with comprehension. Readers need the support of schemas as they encounter new ideas and information.

By explicitly modeling and practicing prior knowledge assessment, educators can help students develop their own procedures for assessing their background knowledge before they begin explorations into new learning territories. They can help children determine what they already know or if they need to build their background knowledge before they begin. If students determine that they need more prior knowledge, educators should give them time to build it before encountering a new concept. They can also provide students with background knowledge as a means of demonstrating the critical importance of these understandings to reading comprehension. When explicitly taught, this strategy provides children with both the rationale and the experience of utilizing background knowledge to support effective reading.

How to Teach the Strategy

The process of sharing your own stories and learning about students' experiences is a natural part of building relationships in the classroom and library. We store memories and much of our learning in story format because the brain functions narratively. Children often share their knowledge and experiences in story form (Christie, Enz, and Vukelich 2003, 57). In the process of activating background knowledge, educators and students engage in storytelling that builds connections. While this strategy aids comprehension, it also offers the additional benefit of developing community; getting to know classroom teacher colleagues as well as students more fully is an enriching side benefit of collaboratively teaching the background knowledge comprehension strategy.

When teaching background knowledge strategy lessons, educators focus on modeling the many ways that making connections before, during, and after reading supports meaning-making. Educators should let students know what ideas come into their minds before beginning to read a book or other resource. Sharing background knowledge during the reading requires that educators stop and reflect; this helps students understand that reading is a complex, nonlinear process that goes beyond the literal denotations of the words on the page. After reading, sharing connections helps readers access the messages and themes suggested by the text. Talking about how these connections support comprehension is an important part of learning to activate and use background knowledge. Educators should be specific in sharing how their background knowledge helped them comprehend the text and encourage students to be specific as well. Figure 3-1 shows a sample of how to model making connections before, during, and after reading a story.

Connection Types

Keene and Zimmermann (1997) suggest that readers make three types of connection: text-to-self, text-to-text, and text-to-world. Readers can use each of these frames to identify the source of their prior knowledge connections. These frames also provide ways to think and talk about books and help readers build schemas. Questions related to each of these types of connection provide educators with tools to engage students in active reading. After educators practice metacognition by thinking aloud and sharing their connections orally, they can use these questions to engage students in making their own connections and thinking about how connections help them comprehend texts.

As with all the strategies, young readers should ultimately internalize these questions and utilize them as a means of exploring the ways they are connecting to what they read, hear, and view. We know that connections help us remember what we read. Connections also give value to literacy events in which we engage. Building connections not only supports comprehension, it also enriches our literate lives by giving deeper significance to literacy experiences.

FIGURE 3-1

Making Text-to-Self, Text-to-Text, and
Text-to-World Connections

Text: *When I Was Young in the Mountains,* by Cynthia Rylant, illustrated by Diane Goode

BEFORE READING	
Making Connections	*How Connections Support Comprehension*
From reading the book title and looking at the cover, I know this book is going to be about living in the mountains. I have visited the mountains, but I've never lived there. I remember that it's quieter in the mountains than in the city where I live. (Text-to-self) The characters' clothes make me think this story happened some time in the past. We don't wear clothes like this now. (Text-to-world)	Knowing that this story is set in the mountains and probably takes place some time ago, I suspect this story will be quiet and slow. I think I will learn some things about living in the mountains long ago because I don't know that much about it now. This helps me listen for what is different about the characters' lives from my own life. These connections help me get ready to enter the story.
DURING READING	
Making Connections	*How Connections Support Comprehension*
I have had the same experience as the narrator, but not from eating okra. (Okra was my grandmother's favorite vegetable —yuck!) One time I ate too much chocolate candy, and I had to pay the price. I swam in a muddy creek once. I couldn't see the mucky bottom. It felt a little creepy because I didn't know what other creatures were swimming with me! (Text-to-self)	These connections help me think about how the character feels and what she experiences. I realize now that, even though we live in different locations, we have some of the same feelings and experiences. This helps me get into the story, share the character's life, and connect it with my own.
AFTER READING	
Making Connections	*How Connections Support Comprehension*
This story reminds me of a movie called *Heidi.* In the film, a girl went to the mountains to live with her grandfather. At first she was unhappy there, but then she came to love her grandfather and her new mountain home. Heidi even got homesick for the mountains and grandfather when she had to return to the city. (Text-to-text) Like the narrator, I'm happy about where I live. Part of that feeling comes from the place, but it also comes from the people who live with me and the things we do together. (Text-to-self)	This connection reminds me that the setting in a story can make a difference. Different things happen in different places. Both of these stories help me make a connection to something I believe: people are an important part of what we think of as "home." This connection helps me understand the message of the story. I think the author wanted to tell readers it's important to have loving people in your life. I agree with this idea.

Text-to-Self Connections

Text-to-self connections require that educators know the children in their care and be familiar with students' home lives and local communities. Classroom teachers often bring a deeper knowledge of individual students to the classroom-library collaboration. Teacher-librarians often bring a broader knowledge of the literature available in the school library, through interlibrary loan, and by way of Web resources. Through collaboration, classroom teachers and teacher-librarians can connect children's background knowledge with a rich array of children's literature and resources, thereby providing readers with exceptional opportunities for making connections based on the familiar experiences of the students themselves.

When modeling text-to-self connections, educators can use think-aloud questioning to share their thinking processes. Posing and answering questions can be an effective vehicle for making comprehension through background knowledge accessible to students. These sample questions center on three areas of text-to-self connection: feelings, experiences, and ideas:

- Have you ever felt like the character(s) in this story? Describe what happened and how you felt.

- Have you had a similar experience? Compare your experience to that of the character(s).

- Have you heard or read this information before? What does this information mean to you?

- How does connecting a story or information to your own life experiences help you better understand it?

Text-to-Text Connections

When educators make effective connections between children's home and school lives, and as children build their school-based background knowledge, learners can be guided to make connections between texts. In a broad sense, a text can be any communication from which a person makes meaning. This includes all forms of paper-based documents as well as oral communication, visual images, and electronic resources. This view of a text offers learners a wide range of possible sources for making connections. When children begin to notice commonalities between texts situated both inside and outside of school, they may begin to find more relevance in their school-based learning experiences.

The following sample questions center on making text-to-text connections. They can be used to guide educators' and students' thinking as they model and practice this strategy:

- Have you ever read another book or seen a movie in which the characters have feelings or experiences similar to the ones in this story? Describe how they are the same.

- Have you ever read another book or seen a movie in which a story element (setting, plot, conflict, theme, or style) is similar to the one in this story? Describe how they are the same.

- Have you read another book or seen a movie in which the writer used language or text structure similar to that in this story? Describe how these texts are similar.

- How does making connections to familiar texts help you comprehend the new text?

Text-to-World Connections

With text-to-world connections, readers stretch their thinking beyond the particulars of what they read, hear, and view to connect story themes with larger life issues. These topics often include social and political problems related to historical or current events.

For instance, before reading *Fly Away Home*, written by Eve Bunting and illustrated by Ronald Himler, educators can share a current newspaper article about homelessness. During the reading, educators and students can compare the situations and issues in the story to those in the article or to other experiences or information related to this social problem. During or after the reading, some students may make connections to homeless people they have seen or to news broadcasts or other newspaper articles on this topic.

When students make intertextual connections such as these, they are beginning to explore using literacy as a tool for forming opinions about social and political issues. Readers can grow to understand that authors and illustrators create for purposes that may include messages or perspectives on world events. The author's intention, part of Rosenblatt's reading transaction, should be one ingredient of the meaning made by the reader.

These are some questions that can be used to guide educators' or students' thinking as they practice making text-to-world connections:

- What do you think the author's message or purpose was in writing this story or presenting this information?
- Did the author suggest a message that connects with bigger ideas about the way things are in the world? What do you already know about these issues?
- What do you think was the author's opinion or perspective on the big ideas in this text? Do you agree? Why or why not?
- How does making connections to larger issues help you comprehend this text?

Making Literature Connections

Books of all genres that relate to students' life experiences provide fertile soil for background knowledge strategy lessons. Students can quickly learn to make connections to books whose story elements, topics, authors, or illustrators are familiar to them. School-based events are a place to begin because they represent shared experiences. Characters, settings, and plots may be particularly strong in readers' connections to these texts. Branching out from school stories to students' home and community experiences is a natural progression, one that requires educators to know their students well.

With practice, students begin to make their own text connections spontaneously, and the educators learn even more about their students' schemas.

Connections to the immediate or regional community also provide effective support for building prior knowledge. Historical events and monuments, national parks and forests, museums, and landmarks can make particularly powerful connections, especially if students can take actual or virtual field trips to these locations before, during, or after reading about them. Initial practice at assessing background knowledge is successful when readers find relevance and familiarity in their texts. Students can then build on these successes as they advance as readers, and they more easily recognize when their loss of comprehension is related to a lack of background knowledge.

Informational books on topics in children's areas of interest and expertise provide effective support for background knowledge strategy lessons. Working in partnerships, classroom teachers and teacher-librarians can model this strategy effectively with texts that relate to their own areas of interest and expertise. Students who have a passion for dogs, dump trucks, or deep-sea diving will quickly see the process of activating background knowledge as one in which they are already engaged when they select a new book on their favorite subject. For supporting this connection during independent reading, it is important to guide the student to the "right" book, a longtime charge of classroom teachers and teacher-librarians alike. Informational books are a rich resource for practicing this strategy.

Text sets developed by classroom teachers and teacher-librarians are another powerful support for students who are learning to build background knowledge and make connections (Short, Harste, with Burke 1996). Text sets of five to fifteen or more books can be organized around topics, genres, story elements, structural patterns, story variants, and author-illustrator studies. Figure 3-2 shows a variety of possible concepts around which educators can build text sets.

Supported by text sets, author-illustrator studies can invite making connections that result from

FIGURE 3-2
Conceptual Frameworks for Organizing Text Sets

CONCEPT	EXAMPLES
Topics	Content-area topics such as weather (science), Civil War (history), measurement (mathematics)
Genres	Biographies, poetry, science fiction, mysteries
Story Elements	Similar settings, characters, plots and conflicts, themes, cultural features, illustration media or styles
Story Structures	Cumulative and patterned language stories, fables, myths
Story Variants	Fairy-tale and folktale variants, such as Cinderella stories
Author and Illustrator Studies	Multiple works by the same author or illustrator

building a repertoire of prior knowledge with the characters, settings, plots, themes, and styles found in literature created for children. Just like adult readers, young readers often choose books on the basis of their previous experiences with the author's or illustrator's work. When engaging in whole-class author-illustrator studies, educators model making connections among story elements and share how these connections increase their enjoyment as well as their understanding of the texts. Author-illustrator studies also help readers develop reading preferences, an important foundation for lifelong reading.

Figure 3-3 shows a category matrix, intended to be reproduced on large butcher paper that can be completed while engaging with a story-variant text set. Using one of the variants, the teacher-librarian and classroom teacher can model completing each category on the basis of information found in the print as well as in the illustrations. Students can continue the study by reading the other variants in small groups and taking responsibility for contributing an entry in each category. (Color coding the categories facilitates cross-text comparisons. For example, all students' contributions in the setting category could be recorded on green paper.) The completed matrix provides a rich resource to support readers as they compare the various story elements in these books.

Using text sets selected by educators, students can be guided to make connections—with the ulti-mate goal of creating their own text sets based on self-selected topics, text types, and themes. Web Supplement 3A is an annotated text set built on a theme of cultural interactions. It includes both picture books and novels from a wide variety of genres including biography, historical and realistic fiction, informational books, and poetry. Developed through classroom-library collaboration, text sets of all types provide rich resources for background knowledge strategy lessons.

Summary

Assessing and building background knowledge provide critical support for reading comprehension. This strategy can be taught by making text-to-self, text-to-text, and text-to-world connections before, during, and after reading. Teacher-librarians and classroom teachers working in partnership can effectively model their thinking and demonstrate their individual prior knowledge, identify the need for additional background information, and share unique responses to texts. They can use questioning to provide students with windows into their own connections and help students understand how background knowledge is necessary information that makes texts more comprehensible.

Both fiction and informational children's literature that relates to students' prior knowledge and understandings can support these how-to lessons.

FIGURE 3-3
Cinderella Variant Category Matrix

TITLE, AUTHOR, ILLUSTRATOR	SETTING	CHARACTERS	PLOT	CULTURAL FEATURES	ILLUSTRATIONS	THEME
Cendrillon: A Caribbean Cinderella (San Souci/Pinkney)						
Cinderella (Perrault/Jeffers/ Ehrlich)						
The Egyptian Cinderella (Climo/Heller)						
Estrellita de oro: Little Gold Star (Hayes/Perez and Perez)						
Mufaro's Beautiful Daughters: An African Tale (Steptoe)						
Sootface: An Ojibwa Cinderella Story (San Souci/San Souci)						
Yeh-Shen: A Cinderella Story from China (Louie/Young)						

Texts that offer vocabulary, concepts, and experiences outside of students' current schemas can help make the case for assessing when background knowledge must be built before comprehension can occur. By lowering the student-to-teacher ratio and reinforcing these strategies in classroom and library settings, educators can help students learn to utilize background knowledge to make sense of the myriad of texts they encounter for school-based assignments as well as for independent reading and inquiry.

Children's Literature Cited

Starred titles are used in the lesson plans.

*Amber on the Mountain, by Tony Johnston, illustrated by Robert Duncan

Cendrillon: A Caribbean Cinderella, by Robert D. San Souci, illustrated by Brian Pinkney

Cinderella, by Charles Perrault, retold by Amy Ehrlich, illustrated by Susan Jeffers

The Egyptian Cinderella, by Shirley Climo, illustrated by Ruth Heller

Estrellita de oro: Little Gold Star, by Joe Hayes, illustrated by Gloria Osuna Perez and Lucia Angela Perez

Fly Away Home, by Eve Bunting, illustrated by Ronald Himler

*Froggy Goes to School, by Jonathan London, illustrated by Frank Remkiewicz

*Look Out Kindergarten, Here I Come! by Nancy Carlson

Mufaro's Beautiful Daughters: An African Tale, by John Steptoe

*My Name Is Yoon, by Helen Recorvits, illustrated by Gabi Swiatkowska

*Sing Down the Rain, by Judi Moreillon, illustrated by Michael Chiago

Sootface: An Ojibwa Cinderella Story, by Robert D. San Souci, illustrated by Daniel San Souci

When I Was Young in the Mountains, by Cynthia Rylant, illustrated by Diane Goode

Yeh-Shen: A Cinderella Story from China, by Ai-Ling Louie, illustrated by Ed Young

Lesson Plans

In the following how-to lessons, classroom teachers and teacher-librarians use think-aloud strategies to demonstrate how and why they are accessing and assessing their background knowledge and how they are using it to comprehend new texts before, during, and after the reading. The lessons are constructed for students at three levels of development. Readers at all levels can benefit from how-to lessons until these reading strategies are integrated into their repertoires as reading skills. The organization of instruction in the lessons maximizes the benefit of two equal-partner collaborators by lowering the student-teacher ratio.

Each lesson utilizes a different type of connection to demonstrate this strategy: text-to-self, text-to-text, and text-to-world. Although it is recommended that strategy lessons focus on one connection framework at a time, readers should not be limited in making a particular type of connection; these examples simply share one dominant connection framework. Whether the text is assigned or read by the student independent of school, the ultimate goal of these lessons is for readers at all levels of development to learn to notice when they need to connect or to build background knowledge before, during, or after reading.

Using Background Knowledge

Reading Development Level	Emerging
Instructional Strategies	Cues and Questions, Classifying, and Comparing
Lesson Length	1 session
Purpose	The purpose of this lesson is to use background knowledge to make connections between excited and nervous feelings and experiences that children have before and on the first day of school.
Objectives	After reading *Look Out Kindergarten, Here I Come!* or *Froggy Goes to School*, students will be able to

1. Classify ideas about the main character's feelings and experiences on a category matrix.
2. Identify and record text-to-self comparisons on a Venn diagram.
3. Use prior knowledge to make text-to-self connections as they respond to literature orally, through art, or in writing.

Resources, Materials, and Equipment	*Look Out Kindergarten, Here I Come!* by Nancy Carlson
	Froggy Goes to School, by Jonathan London, illustrated by Frank Remkiewicz
	Graphic Organizers: Category Web (Web Supplement 3B), Venn Diagram (Web Supplement 3C), Text-to-Self Connections Rubric (Web Supplement 3D)
	Overhead, data projector, or interactive whiteboard
Collaboration	The teacher-librarian works with half the class; the classroom teacher works with the other half. Each group hears a read-aloud and records their understandings of the main character's feelings and experiences on a class-sized category web (Web Supplement 3B). After each educator models using a class-sized Venn diagram (Web Supplement 3C), students compare their own experiences to that of the book character on individual Venn diagrams.
Assessment	Students' Venn diagrams show their ability to identify similarities and differences. Students' contributions to the class-sized category web and their oral, artistic, or written responses can be assessed using a rubric. In all cases, the educators are looking for the students' proficiency at making text-to-self connections.
Standards	*Reading keywords:* describe characters; compare or relate literary text to their own experience; respond
	Listening and speaking keywords: use effective vocabulary and logical organization to relate or summarize ideas
	Fine arts keyword: illustrate
	Information literacy keywords: select information appropriate to the problem or question at hand; organize information for practical application
Process	*Motivation*

Cues and Questions: Before reading, ask students to think back to the night before school started this year. What did you think about the first day of school? Were you scared to meet your new classmates and classroom teacher? Were you excited to see your friends from last year? What were your expectations for the new school year?

Student-Friendly Objectives

1. Classify ideas on a category matrix.
2. Record text-to-self comparisons on a Venn diagram.
3. Tell, write, or draw a response.

Presentation

Read the title and the author's and illustrator's names on the book jacket. Ask students what they think the book may be about. Examine the expressions on the characters' faces. Is this how students felt on their first day of school? Students think-pair-share.

Cue: As we read, notice how the main character feels and what happens to him on the first day of school.

Read: Look Out Kindergarten, Here I Come! or *Froggy Goes to School* from beginning to end.

Reread the story. During the reading, think aloud about how the main character is feeling. What are the clues in the text? What do the illustrations tell us about how he is feeling? Review the types of notes (figure 2-1 or Web Supplement 2A). Model by recording at least one feeling and one experience on the class-sized category web.

Show the Text-to-Self Connections Rubric (Web Supplement 3D) and talk about student participation on the category web. Students share their ideas. Educators record students' ideas in notemaking format on the category web.

Student Participation Procedures

1. Raise a hand to pause the reading.
2. Name the category (feelings or experiences).
3. Tell your idea.

Guided Practice

The goal is for each student in the half-class group to contribute at least one idea to the category web. Record students' names in parentheses beside their ideas.

Presentation

Using think-alouds, model completing a class-sized Venn diagram while comparing the educator's own feelings and experiences to those of the main character. (Remember: It is important to record parallel ideas on both sides of a Venn diagram. For instance, record a feeling on one side and a feeling on the other.) Record both feelings and experiences. Refer to the rubric.

The students share orally with a partner before recording ideas on a Venn diagram.

Student Practice Procedures

1. Think-pair-share feelings and experiences.
2. Write "same" ideas in the middle of the Venn diagram.
3. Write "different" ideas on either side.

Guided Practice

Monitor partners for sharing both feelings and experiences and correct use of individual Venn diagrams.

Presentation

Bring the two groups together. Each educator models making text-to-self connections in response to the book. Ideally, one educator tells and writes his response, and one tells and draws his response. (Example: Henry was excited about going to kindergarten. I was excited and scared too.) Review the rubric.

Students write and illustrate a sentence or two.

Student Practice Procedures

1. Talk with partner.

2. Write a sentence.

3. Illustrate the sentence.

Guided Practice

Monitor students' discussions and writing. Educators can take dictation from students who share their sentences orally.

Closure

Students can share their sentences and illustrations in half-class groups with the educators facilitating. Students self-assess using the rubric (Web Supplement 3D). The educators utilize the same rubric for assessment.

Reflection

How did text-to-self connections help readers comprehend the feelings and experiences of these characters? When we connect our own experiences to those of the characters, do we feel part of the story? How does that change our experience of the story?

Extension   Students can dramatize their responses with small skits. They can work in like or dissimilar feelings or experiences groups.

READING COMPREHENSION STRATEGY
Using Background Knowledge

Reading Development Level	Advancing
Instructional Strategies	Cues and Questions, Classifying, and Comparing
Lesson Length	3 sessions
Purpose	The purpose of this lesson is to use and to build background knowledge to make text-to-text connections between two books about characters that are learning to read and write.
Objectives	After reading *Amber on the Mountain* and *My Name Is Yoon*, students will be able to

1. Categorize their ideas about characters' literacy experiences using the five Ws and How.

2. Compare these two book characters' literacy experiences.

3. Make text-to-text connections as they respond to literature in writing and through drawing.

Resources, Materials, and Equipment	*Amber on the Mountain*, by Tony Johnston, illustrated by Robert Duncan
	My Name Is Yoon, by Helen Recorvits, illustrated by Gabi Swiatkowska (two copies)
	Graphic Organizers: Five Ws and How Category Matrix (Web Supplement 3E), Text-to-Text Connections Rubric (Web Supplement 3F)
	Overhead, data projector, or interactive whiteboard
Collaboration	While sharing one book, the educators model completing a category matrix, then divide the class in half. Each group compares the second text to the first after completing a category matrix about the new text.
Assessment	The students' contributions to the half-class category matrix show their ability to identify and categorize details of the story. They think-pair-share the connections between the texts. Students respond to one or both books by writing a paragraph. Their text-to-text connections are assessed using a rubric. In all cases, educators look for the students' proficiency at making text-to-text connections.
Standards	*Reading keywords:* describe characters (e.g., traits, roles, similarities) within a literary selection; compare and contrast; comprehension; respond; story elements
	Listening and speaking keywords: use effective vocabulary; follow multistep directions; prepare and deliver information by generating topics and organizing ideas
	Fine arts keyword: illustrate
	Information literacy keywords: select information appropriate to the problem or question at hand; organize information for practical application
Process	*Motivation*
Day 1	*Questions:* Activate prior knowledge. Students think-pair-share as the educators ask questions. Think back to how you first learned to read and to write. Who were the people who helped you? What tools did you use? Were you at home or in school? How old were you? What made you want to learn to read or write? How did you do it?

Cues: Read the title and the author's and illustrator's names on the book jacket of *Amber on the Mountain*. Ask students to think-pair-share what they think the book may be about. Tell students: As we read, notice how the main character feels and what happens to her as she learns to read and write. Review the five Ws and How and the categories for thinking about the story elements, then ask students to listen for these ideas during the reading.

Student-Friendly Objectives

1. Listen for the five Ws and How.

2. Categorize ideas.

Presentation

Read *Amber on the Mountain*. One educator rereads the book while the other records information on the class-sized category matrix.

During the second reading, both educators use think-alouds to model how they identify information in the story that corresponds to the categories (questions) on the matrix. Review the types of notes (figure 2-1 or Web Supplement 2A). Solicit student input regarding the appropriate category for each note on the class-sized matrix.

Closure

After the reading, review the information recorded on the category matrix. Project the Text-to-Text Connections Rubric (Web Supplement 3F) and discuss criteria for assessment.

Day 2 ### Student-Friendly Objective

1. Categorize ideas using the five Ws and How.

Presentation

Divide the class in half. Both educators read and reread *My Name Is Yoon*. Remind students to listen for the five Ws and How. If appropriate, use think-alouds to model the process of gathering and recording information on a Five Ws and How Category Matrix (Web Supplement 3E).

The students offer ideas during the second reading while the educator records notes on the class-sized category matrix.

Student Participation Procedures

1. Raise hand to pause the reading.

2. Identify the category and then share the idea.

Guided Practice

The goal is for each student in the half-class group to contribute at least one idea to the category matrix. Record students' names with their ideas.

Closure

To review, ask students to think-pair-share connections between the characters' feelings and experiences in both books. Ask for volunteers to share a few ideas.

Day 3 ### Student-Friendly Objectives

1. Compare two book characters' experiences.

2. Write a paragraph with text-to-text connections.

3. Illustrate the paragraph.

Presentation

Bring the two groups together. Put the new category matrices based on *My Name Is Yoon* side by side with the original *Amber on the Mountain* matrix. Remind students that they will be writing a paragraph comparing these two characters' feelings and experiences.

The educators take turns reading by category from the matrices. Involve students in making text-to-text connections. Use one color marker to circle similarities and another color to circle differences between the characters' experiences.

Educators provide an oral example of a possible paragraph. (If necessary, provide a written model by facilitating a shared writing.)

Brainstorm possible illustrations for this paragraph. Review the rubric (Web Supplement 3F).

Students use the matrices as prewriting. They compose paragraphs, participate in writing conferences, and illustrate their paragraphs.

Student Practice Procedures

1. Read through the matrices and the rubric.

2. Write a three- to five-sentence paragraph with one, two, three, or more text-to-text connections.

3. Conference with an adult or classmate.

4. Illustrate the paragraph.

Guided Practice

Educators conference with individual students. They monitor students' ability to write about text-to-text connections.

Closure

Form an inside-outside circle. Students take turns reading their paragraphs to a partner and sharing their illustrations. Rotate and repeat.

Students use the rubric to self-assess their text-to-text connections.

Reflection

How did text-to-text connections help readers comprehend the feelings of the main characters in these two stories? Are there other books or movies we have read or seen that share how the characters learned to read and write?

Extensions   Create a thematic text set that focuses on literacy learning. Ask the students to choose books from the text set and complete their own category matrices. Ask students to respond to these texts using a variety of sign systems, including writing, art, drama, music, and mathematics. (A possible mathematical representation for *Amber on the Mountain* could be represented in print or illustration: Friendship + Books = Learning to Read and Write.) Involve students in literature circles or engage students in discussions about how making text-to-text connections helps readers comprehend characters' experiences.

READING COMPREHENSION STRATEGY
Building Background Knowledge

Reading Development Level	Advanced
Instructional Strategies	Cues and Questions, Classifying, Notemaking and Summarizing, and Comparing
Lesson Length	3 or 4 sessions
Purpose	The purpose of this lesson is to provide background knowledge to prepare students to read about an unfamiliar cultural tradition and to make text-to-world connections between the worldviews suggested by these traditional practices and those of present-day U.S. mainstream culture.
Objectives	After they have researched and performed a choral reading of *Sing Down the Rain,* students will be able to

1. Identify the need for background knowledge.

2. Make notes from websites and print resources.

3. Use the background knowledge they gathered to understand new text.

4. Develop fluency through the practice and performance of a choral reading.

5. Identify which information helped them better comprehend the narrative poem.

6. Analyze and compare the cultural practices and ecological view of traditional Tohono O'odham culture with present-day U.S. mainstream culture.

Resources, Materials, and Equipment	*Sing Down the Rain,* by Judi Moreillon, illustrated by Michael Chiago
	Choral Reading Transcript: http://storytrail.com/pages/choral.pdf (Make a class set of reader's theater scripts for the choral reading.)
	Tohono O'odham Pathfinder: http://storytrail.com/pages/TTPathfinder.html
	Graphic Organizers: Teacher Resource: Category Web (Web Supplement 3G), Category Web (Web Supplement 3H), Teacher Resource: Notemaking Graphic Organizer (Web Supplement 3I), Notemaking Graphic Organizer (Web Supplement 3J), Teacher Resource: Bibliography Graphic Organizer (Web Supplement 3K), Bibliography Graphic Organizer (Web Supplement 3L), Notemaking and Bibliography Graphic Organizer Rubric (Web Supplement 3M), Teacher Resource: Venn Diagram (Web Supplement 3N), Venn Diagram (Web Supplement 3O)
	Overhead, data projector, or interactive whiteboard
Collaboration	Educators work with the entire class. Both educators support students as they conduct research and practice and perform a choral reading reader's theater script. At the end of the study, the educators facilitate a text-to-world discussion centered on culture and ecology.
Assessment	Students' notemaking and bibliography graphic organizers can be assessed using the notemaking and bibliography rubric. The complete category web shows what the students learned through their research and performance of the choral reading. The Venn diagram shows their ability to compare two cultures.

Standards

Reading keywords: use graphic organizers to clarify the meaning of text; use context to determine the meaning of words; use reference sources to determine the meaning of words; develop vocabulary in context; describe the historical and cultural aspects found in cross-cultural works of literature; fluency

Science keywords: ecology; describe the interaction between human populations and the environment

Social studies keywords: describe the different perspectives of Native American tribes; human cultures; locate information using a variety of resources; research skills

Information literacy keywords: recognize the need for information; develop and use successful strategies for locating information; organize for practical application; integrate information into one's own knowledge

Educational technology keywords: technology research skills

Process

Motivation

Day 1

Cues and Questions: Define ecology as the relationships among plants, animals, people, and the environment. What are students' connections to the concept of ecology? (Examples: recycling, planting trees, rescuing injured animals.) Describe the different kinds of relationships people have with the earth and with other organisms. Briefly discuss what students already know, if anything, about traditional Native American cultural views on the relationships among people, land, plants, and animals.

Teach or review the types of notes (figure 2-1 or Web Supplement 2A). Prompt students as the class fills in a class-sized category web about the Tohono O'odham. Speculate as to why students know little or nothing about these people, who are indigenous to the U.S. Southwest and northern Mexico. Let students know that, before they read and perform a narrative poem about a Tohono O'odham annual tradition, they will conduct research to build their background knowledge in order to increase their comprehension of traditional Tohono O'odham culture and the poem.

Student-Friendly Objective

1. Identify the need for background knowledge.

Presentation

Review the initial concept web. Ask: Do we have enough background knowledge about the Tohono O'odham to understand a narrative poem that describes their annual rainmaking ceremony? Conduct a bookwalk through *Sing Down the Rain*. Ask students what they notice in the illustrations. Generate and record students' questions. Where might we find the answers?

The educators project and share the Tohono O'odham pathfinder. Using the narrator's beginning stanzas, model thinking aloud about vocabulary and concepts to research. (Web Supplement 3I is a teacher resource.) Identify and circle or highlight the unknown words and concepts in the beginning stanzas.

Closure

Review the process; read and circle unknown words or concepts. Ask students: Where can we find information to help us understand these items?

Days 2 and 3   *Student-Friendly Objectives*

1. Make notes from websites and print resources.

2. Use new background knowledge to understand new text.

Presentation

Demonstrate searching, notemaking, recording reference numbers on the notemaking graphic organizer, and recording information on the bibliography graphic organizer. (Supplement 3K is a completed sample bibliography graphic organizer. Web Supplements 3J and 3L are student graphic organizers.) In addition to websites linked to the Tohono O'odham pathfinder, students can also use the book itself, the book's cultural advisor's notes, or other print resources.

Project the Notemaking and Bibliography Graphic Organizer Rubric (Web Supplement 3M). Discuss criteria. Use the rubric to assess the educators' examples.

Divide the students into "voice" groups based on the parts in the poem: narrator, clouds, saguaros, flowers, women, grandparents, medicine man, and headman. (Note: Voices are listed in order of their participation and in decreasing complexity.) The students collaborate on their notemaking.

Student Practice Procedures

1. Work in voice groups.

2. Identify and circle unknown vocabulary and concepts.

3. Use Tohono O'odham pathfinder to locate information and make notes.

4. Record resources used on bibliography form.

Guided Practice

Educators monitor students' ability to identify the need for background information. They support students in researching, notemaking, and bibliography recording skills.

Closure

Students meet in voice groups to discuss their notes. Let students know they will be practicing and performing the choral reading the next day.

Day 4   *Motivation*

Educators can bring in a text they do not understand and attempt to read it convincingly to students. Discuss this question: Does comprehension help us read more effectively and expressively?

Student-Friendly Objectives

1. Practice and perform the choral reading.

2. Identify which information supports comprehension of narrative poem.

3. Analyze and compare the cultural practices and ecological view of traditional Tohono O'odham with present-day U.S. mainstream culture.

Presentation

The educators chorally read the first three stanzas of the poem with a focus on listening to one another and on fluency (pacing, expression, and flow).

Student Practice Procedures

1. Listen to others while reading.
2. Find a pace that works for everyone in the group.
3. Read with expression.
4. Make it flow.

Performance

Perform the choral reading.

Presentation

After performing the choral reading, the educators model completing the third column of Notemaking Graphic Organizer (Web Supplement 3J). Both identify how background knowledge helped them comprehend a particular part of the poem or the entire poem. Project the rubric and review the criteria.

Project the Category Web (Web Supplement 3H). As a class, record an example in each category. (Use ideas from the teacher resource, Web Supplement 3G.) Students work with their voice groups to complete the notemaking sheet, to self-assess, and to fill out the category web.

Student Practice Procedures

1. Work with voice group.
2. Complete the third column of the notemaking sheet.
3. Use the rubric to self-assess notemaking and bibliography graphic organizers.
4. Complete an individual category web.
5. Contribute to a small group Venn diagram.

Guided Practice

Educators monitor students' completion of the graphic organizers.

Presentation

Project the Teacher Resource: Category Web (Web Supplement 3G). Compare students' ideas to those on this example.

Closure

Educators project the Tohono O'odham Ecology Web found on the Tohono O'odham pathfinder and invite students to discuss it.

Using the class-sized Venn diagram (Web Supplement 3O), educators model identifying similarities and differences between traditional Tohono O'odham culture and modern-day practices. (Supplement 3N is a completed Venn diagram.)

Students discuss similarities and differences in their voice groups and complete a group Venn diagram (Supplement 3O).

Lead a whole-class discussion and add to the class-sized Venn diagram. How does the ecological view of traditional Tohono O'odham compare with present-day U.S. mainstream culture? What questions do we have?

Reflection

How do we recognize the need for background information? When we need it, where can we get background information? How does background information help us comprehend text? Why is it important to compare new information with prior knowledge?

Extension   Students can generate questions based on the discussion of culture and ecological worldviews. They can conduct further study on the ecological view(s) of another people, which can culminate in a learning project: nonlinguistic representation, poem, dramatization, print or electronic report, or other format.

Reading Comprehension Stategy Two
Using Sensory Images

4

The ocean is an old, old man born at the beginning of time.
He breathes a loud, salty breath, and his beard blows white
on the sandy beach. Fish swim in his long wavy hair.

—From *See the Ocean,* by Estelle Condra,
illustrated by Linda Crockett-Blassingame

We first learn about the world through our senses. A newborn's skin responds to temperature, her eyes to light, her ears to the sound of her mother's voice, and her nose to her mother's scent. Her hungry mouth opens for nourishment and expresses a preference for the taste of her own mother's milk. Over time, babies gradually learn to distinguish one sense from the other and use their senses to explore and "make sense" of their surroundings.

Sensory experiences are a significant aspect of our background knowledge. Sensory imagery is an important part of our schemas. When we think about our sensory experiences, we are creating representations of those experiences in our memories (Marzano 2004, 35). In fact, our most powerful memories are attached to sensory experiences. A smell or a taste can trigger a long-cherished recollection—bread baking in the oven in grandma's kitchen, the damp earth that signals rebirth in nature each spring. The metaphor of the elephant's ears reminds us that we can tap into all of our senses, not just our sense of sight, as we read. When we bring our sensory knowledge to the reading of a text, we are the directors of the movie that plays inside our heads. The movies we create as we read are richer if they include a variety of sensory details.

Does the bombardment of visual information in 21st-century Western society diminish students' ability to imagine?

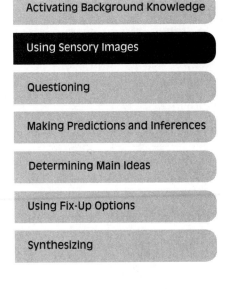

Activating Background Knowledge

Using Sensory Images

Questioning

Making Predictions and Inferences

Determining Main Ideas

Using Fix-Up Options

Synthesizing

Sousa (2005) notes that technology provides many images for students, which makes visualization more difficult for them. Like underused muscles, students' ability to use their imaginations is being reduced by the lack of opportunity. It is particularly important for educators to teach students to visualize by the time they are ready to read or listen to chapter books without illustrations. Readers transitioning to nonillustrated texts must be ready to apply their own imaginations and what they have learned through their experiences with visual media and other sensory input in order to create mental pictures and sensory images for characters, settings, and plots as well as information presented in texts.

Classroom teachers and teacher-librarians can emphasize sensory experiences in read-aloud lessons in both the classroom and the library. Reinforcing these experiences supports students' understanding of the significance of their senses in literacy, in learning, in memory and recall, and in life. Learning engagements that focus students' attention on each sense singly help readers develop their ability to identify and use each sense to improve comprehension. Young children associate senses with the sense organ that receives the input, such as eyes for sight. Later, they learn to classify their sensory experiences into the categories of sight, hearing, touch, taste, and smell. As students become more sophisticated in utilizing their senses, sensory imagery can be combined to show how the senses work together to enhance our understanding and enjoyment of text.

As educators collaborate to plan, implement, and assess sensory-focused lessons, it is essential that they take into account students' individual differences. Some children may not have typical eyesight or hearing. As a result, they may have developed keen sensory ability in another category. Some children may not have the mobility to engage in a variety of kinesthetic experiences; instead of touch, another sense may more fully capture sensory input for them. The classroom teacher's assessment of individual student needs is a critical component of the knowledge she brings to the collaboration. Lessons must be modified or adapted and must be

presented in such a way that all learners are given opportunities for sensory development in order to achieve comprehension.

Gardner's (1993) theory of multiple intelligences reminds us that people learn best in different ways. Some learners have diverse and strongly developed proficiencies for learning that emphasize one or more of their senses. Students with visual-spatial, musical, and body-kinesthetic intelligences may utilize their senses of sight, hearing, or touch spontaneously as they make meaning with text. Educators can capitalize on these preferences and invite these children to share their gifts with classmates. Classroom teachers and teacher-librarians themselves may be talented in utilizing one or more of their senses. Art, music, and physical education teachers can contribute their expertise and talents to collaborative teaching and learning focused on developing sensory knowledge. Other adults with these strengths can also provide outstanding support for teaching through the senses.

One of the research-based instructional strategies recommended by Marzano, Pickering, and Pollock (2001) is nonlinguistic representation. Generating mental pictures, drawing pictures and pictographs, and engaging in kinesthetic activities are brain-compatible strategies. As support for linguistic representations, they help learners connect both hemispheres of the brain. In *Worksheets Don't Grow Dendrites: 20 Instructional Strategies That Engage the Brain,* Tate (2003) provides strategies that rely on sensory input. Included in these strategies are drawing and artwork, the use of manipulatives and models, and activities that incorporate movement, music, drama, and visuals, as well as visualization and guided imagery. All of these strategies rely on the effective use of the senses in making meaning.

How to Teach the Strategy

As children learn to connect sensory experience with language, each sense can pose unique challenges. It is not easy, for example, to describe a smell without referring to taste. In fact, we often describe our sensory experiences in relation to other senses (Ackerman 1990). Writers use literary devices, such as similes and metaphors, to help shape our sensory experience of text, to help us make connections between our senses and language; understanding and creating metaphors is one of the research-based instructional strategies highlighted in this book. Many picture book authors offer readers powerful similes that connect sensory experiences to a particular time period, landscape, culture, or emotion that may be unfamiliar to a young reader. Figure 4-1 offers some similes that show how picture book authors use sensory comparisons to help readers make meaning.

Students who can make connections between their sensory experiences and language can then use their senses to comprehend text. In *Picture This: Teaching Reading through Visualization*, Rose (1989) offers a series of learning experiences to help students develop the ability to visualize. Her lessons involve guided visualizations, some of which are based on excerpts from children's literature. Rose provides listeners with a focus for their imaginations and a specific task to perform at the end of the visualization. In addition to developing the ability to make mental pictures while listening and reading, these lessons also encourage students to incorporate more vivid sensory details in their own writing.

The simple technique of adding aural components to read-alouds is one way to engage children's senses: a train whistle dramatizes *Train Song* (Siebert/Wimmer), a jingle bell enhances *The Polar Express* (Van Allsburg). Educators who understand the role of listener participation in read-alouds can add rhymes and songs to enrich the written text. For example, the perennial *Carrot Seed* (Krauss/Johnson) can be extended by adding a song (search the Web for "Carrot Seed Song"). Finger plays and kinesthetic movement activities involve touch. Augmenting stories by inviting children to manipulate props such as flannel boards and puppets appeals to the sense of touch as well as sight. Educators can find support for engaging students in this way in resources such as *Storytelling with Puppets* (Champlin 1998).

Many informational books, especially those published in the past decade, engage readers with vivid language as well as high-interest visuals. Science concept titles by Vicki Cobb, Laurence Pringle, Sandra Markle, Seymour Simon, and others can be used to help students visualize information. Susan Campbell Bartoletti, Russell Freedman, Jim Murphy, and Diane Stanley use rich descriptions and dramatic action in their biographies and books on social studies topics. Teacher-librarians can support the curriculum and the use of sensory imagery in particular through the selection and integration of such high-quality informational resources.

Inviting students into sensory experiences prompted by literacy engagements helps them deepen their comprehension as well as appreciate and learn the writer's craft of using language to involve the senses in the reading process. Educators must share their own experience of using their senses before, during, and after reading. The think-aloud strategy in figure 4-2 describes how a classroom

FIGURE 4-1
Similes That Compare Different Senses

Hearing with Sight

"Our barelegged mammas dance down the steps and join us in the fresh, clean rain . . . while the music from Miz Glick's phonograph shimmies and sparkles and streaks like night lightning." From *Come On, Rain!* by Karen Hesse, illustrated by Jon J. Muth

Taste with Touch

"Juicy, golden peaches, honey-sweet, like a gentle caress on the palm of my hand." From *Gathering the Sun: An Alphabet in Spanish and in English*, by Alma Flor Ada, illustrated by Simón Silva

Smell with Touch

"It [the perfume] was dark, velvety, seductive, . . . like the first soft touch of a pillow at the start of a deep, deep sleep." From *The Perfume of Memory*, by Michelle Nikly, illustrated by Jean Claverie

FIGURE 4-2
Sensory Imagery Literacy Engagement

Text: *See the Ocean,* by Estelle Condra, illustrated by Linda Crockett-Blassingame

Before Reading: Connecting to Prior Sensory Knowledge

Play ocean music softly. Read the title of the book. Ask the students to close their eyes and take a minute to imagine the sights, sounds, tastes, textures, and smells of the ocean. When they open their eyes, brainstorm as many ocean sensory images as possible. The educators can begin the brainstorm and can continue to contribute as the brainstorm builds. Input should be recorded with different colors, one for each sense: sight, hearing, taste, touch, and smell.

During Reading: Activating Sensory Images

One educator reads; one closes her eyes. The students also close their eyes during the readings of the three passages. Listeners imagine the ocean during the readings.

> "The ocean is an old, old man born at the beginning of time. He breathes a loud, salty breath, and his beard blows white on the sandy beach. Fish swim in his long wavy hair. On his head he wears a crown of pearls. On his feet he wears shoes of shells."

The listening educator shares her images and connections with the students. Example:

> I now live in the desert and grew up in the Midwest, far from the ocean. When the author wrote about how the ocean is an old man, a metaphor, she made it easier for me to imagine the ocean in my mind's eye. Although I have visited the ocean, I have more background knowledge of the images she shares of the old man and of the senses suggested by the words in this passage than I do of the ocean itself.
>
> I could imagine an old man's long white beard and how the waves that touch the shore are white. I have smelled salty breath. I'm thinking of my husband's breath after he's eaten popcorn or pickles. I could see the fish in my mind's eye, swimming up and down along the waves, waves like the old man's hair. It was fun to imagine the ocean as an old man with a crown of pearls on his head and shoes made from shells on his feet.

> "Sometimes the wind blows his hair about in big wild waves. Then he gets angry, and he roars and hisses and spits. When the sun shines, he laughs and gurgles and prattles in the rock pools. He smiles a wide silver and green smile on the beach. On his shoulders he carries ships and boats."

The listening educator shares her images and connections with the students. Example:

> The idea of the ocean changing conditions like people change their moods made sense to me. This helps me understand that the ocean is always changing. The words *gurgles* and *prattles* are onomatopoeia, words that make sounds. These words helped me hear the water in the rock pools.

> "But at night he's more beautiful than ever. At night he wears a dark, silvery gray cloak with moons and stars sprinkled upon it. Every night before he goes to sleep, he pulls a soft, misty blanket over himself."

The listening educator shares her images and connections with the students. Example:

> The final image was very beautiful. I am familiar with the moon and stars in the sky, and I could easily imagine the old man wearing them like a wizard's moon-and-stars cloak. The blanket of mist image wasn't as strong for me. I haven't seen mist very often in my life.

After Reading: Reflection

The listening educator shares her images and connections with the students. Example:

> I think the author, who uses the voice of the young girl in the story to describe the ocean in this way, gave me connections to sensory images that helped me experience the ocean more powerfully. I could picture the ocean in my mind because I could relate it to things with which I am familiar, such as an old man, salty breath, and a wizard's cloak. Picturing the ocean in my mind made this passage even more memorable to me. My visualization included sounds and smells as well as visual images. The author's figurative language made the ocean come alive for me. In these passages, the author's words created a truly beautiful movie in my mind.

teacher and teacher-librarian can collaborate to demonstrate the effective use of sensory images to achieve comprehension.

Making Literature Connections

To help students fully develop each sense, educators can design lessons that focus on individual senses. In *Sense-Abilities: Fun Ways to Explore the Senses,* O'Brien-Palmer (1998) offers a series of natural science learning experiences focused on each sense. Each section of the book begins with a piggyback song about one sense as well as a bibliography of fifteen or so sense-focused children's books. Diane Ackerman and Peter Sis have collaborated on *Animal Sense,* a book of animal poems composed around each sense. Books like these provide educators with an enjoyable way to bring together sensory experiences, science concepts, and literature.

Working in collaboration, teacher-librarians and classroom teachers can collect resources, such as those reviewed below, for lessons focused on each sense. Figure 4-3 shows a collection of Jack Prelutsky's poems from *The New Kid on the Block.* Each of these poems appeals to an individual sense. The poet's lively language helps listeners and readers imagine the characters, settings, and events presented in these poems. Students can be asked to identify the sensory focus and to create single-sense or multisensory poems of their own.

Sight

Our eyes tend to monopolize our senses. Readers can use their visual memory to create mental images. Guided visualizations like "Rock to Rock" in *Keepers of the Earth: Native American Stories and Environmental Activities for Children* (Caduto and Bruchac/Fadden and Wood), which invites students to visualize the rock cycle, are essential activities for teaching this strategy. Although texts with descriptive language and sensory imagery for which students have background knowledge are the easiest to visualize, educators can guide students as they practice this strategy with almost any text. Inviting students to close their eyes and imagine the text as it is read aloud, and then asking them to share the pictures in their heads, is the basic technique used to teach visualization.

Along with this practice, it is important to help students comprehend the impact of visuals on meaning-making. Classroom teachers and teacher-librarians should take full advantage of the richness and sophistication of illustration in children's picture books by focusing on the visual information and aesthetic experiences these titles provide. Conducting illustrator studies or studies based on

FIGURE 4-3
Sensory Poetry Classification Matrix

SIGHT	HEARING	TASTE	SMELL	TOUCH
"My Dog, He Is an Ugly Dog"	"Louder Than a Clap of Thunder!"	"Jellyfish Stew"	"Drumpp the Grump"	"I've Got an Itch"
"The Zoosher"	"I've Got an Incredible Headache"	"Yubbazubbies"	"Be Glad Your Nose Is on Your Face"	"Super-Goopy Glue"
"Baloney Belly Billy"	"Floradora Doe"	"Gussie's Greasy Spoon"		"Suzanna Socked Me Sunday"
"Forty Performing Bananas"	"Happy Birthday, Dear Dragon"	"When Tillie Ate the Chili"		
		"I'd Never Eat a Beet"		
		"I'd Never Dine on Dinosaurs"		

the media used in a selection of texts can focus students' attention on the visual feast offered by these books. Although it seems almost criminal to read aloud these highly illustrated books without sharing the artwork, educators can use this technique to prompt story listeners to compare the scenes they imagine in their minds with the illustrators' interpretations of the authors' words.

Variants of folktales illustrated with a variety of media can also be used to compare artists' interpretations of stories. Comparing movie versions of picture books to the original book illustrations also offers opportunities for examining the impact of visuals on comprehension. These learning engagements give readers input for making comparisons based on their sense of sight.

Wordless books provide one especially strong vehicle for visual literacy studies. A search of the library catalog using the keyword "wordless" or a subject search of "stories without words" will yield a selection of titles, some of them quite sophisticated. One such book is *A Circle of Friends* (Carmi). In this story, a young boy's act of kindness toward a homeless man comes full circle. As the story unfolds, author-illustrator Giora Carmi uses color to spotlight the new or critical story element on each page. Readers can use the visual information in this and other wordless books to create print to accompany the artwork and thereby demonstrate that pictures do indeed tell a story.

Hearing

Many children's books appeal to a listener's sense of hearing. The most important thing about these titles is that they must be read aloud, they must be heard, in order to be appreciated. This makes them perfect selections for the think-aloud strategies used in teaching reading comprehension strategies.

Poetry, which is written to be spoken, is a key genre for exploring how sound shapes our understanding. Rhythm and rhyme are two literary devices that poets use to engage listeners' hearts and minds. From a very early age, children respond to regular rhythms in language. Perhaps this har-

kens back to our first experiences of hearing the rhythmic lub-dub of our mothers' heartbeats. The popularity of Shel Silverstein's and Jack Prelutsky's work is a testimony to young people's preference for rhyming poems. Educators who share poetry or prose with rhyming lines can invite students to supply the rhyming words at the ends of lines to show how the poet-author's word choice supports prediction. A search of the subject heading "stories in rhyme" will yield hundreds of possibilities, including time-honored titles by Dr. Seuss and Bill Martin Jr.

Attention to poets' and authors' use of another literary device, onomatopoeia, demonstrates how words like *chirp, growl, tinkle,* and *rumble* invite readers to use sound to make meaning. Picture books like *Achoo! Bang! Crash! A Noisy Alphabet* (MacDonald) illustrate the impact of sound-making language on meaning. Texts with onomatopoeia make smashing read-alouds because these words embed drama in the print. *Snip Snap! What's That?* (Bergman/Maland) and *Clickety Clack* (Spence/Spengler) are examples that include repetition that encourages listeners to participate in the sounds of language that enhance meaning. Another example, *The Treasure of Ghostwood Gully: A Southwest Mystery* (Vaughan/Terry), is reviewed on the Southwest Children's Literature website. This book was used by Nadine Valukas as an invitation to students to play with sound in their own sentences and to illustrate with a focus on sound (http://storytrail.com/SWCL/pages/tgg2.htm). *Using Picture Books to Teach Literary Devices* (Hall 2002) is one professional resource for identifying picture books that support teaching onomatopoeia as well as other literary devices.

The relationship between poetry and music is undeniable. "Music speaks to us so powerfully that many musicians and theorists think it may be an actual language, one that developed about the same time as speech" (Ackerman 1990, 209). For many of us, our first songs were nursery rhymes set to music. *Hush Songs: African American Lullabies* (Thomas/Joysmith) is a collection of nursery rhymes and songs that brings the home and community culture into the literacy learning classroom. Similar resources in languages other than English, such as *Pío Peep! Traditional Spanish Nursery Rhymes* (Ada and Campoy/Escrivá), reflect the cultural and linguistic heritages of many students.

Combining song and poetry, *Take Me Out of the Bathtub, and Other Silly Dilly Songs* and *I'm Still Here in the Bathroom: Brand New Silly Dilly Songs* (Katz/Catrow) are collections of humorous poetry that piggyback on well-known tunes to support readers' performance of the poems. Traditional songs have been published with the work of various illustrators and have even spawned variants such as *She'll Be Comin' 'round the Mountain* (Sturges/Wolff), in which "she" is a bookmobile-driving librarian. Another example is *Over in the Garden* (Ward/Spengler), which adapts the original song's setting and the selection of mother and offspring characters from a meadow environment to the garden. Being able to sing along as they read supports young readers' comprehension; these texts are particularly effective for children learning a second language (Jackman 1997).

Touch

There are books that must be touched! The raised spider's web on the pages of Eric Carle's *Very Busy Spider* helps readers comprehend the single-minded focus of an arachnid whose friends attempt to divert her from her spinning task. After students make and play with *oobleck*, they understand the threat posed by this sticky stuff falling like rain from the sky in *Bartholomew and the Oobleck* (Seuss). A book like *The Goat in the Rug* (Blood and Link/Parker) demands that an educator supply young readers with opportunities to feel the textures of raw wool, yarn, and finished rugs.

Movement is another way for educators to appeal to the sense of touch. In addition to puppets and finger plays, hand clapping to rhymes and gesturing during reading increase readers' engagement with text. For instance, before reading a fictional or informational text about a butterfly, lead the students in a kinesthetic experience to learn the

parts of a butterfly's body by involving them with a piggyback version of "Head, Shoulders, Knees, and Toes":

> *The Butterfly*
> Head and thorax
> Abdomen, abdomen
> Head and thorax
> Abdomen, abdomen
> Eyes and wings
> And antennae and proboscis
> Head and thorax
> Abdomen, abdomen

If educators wonder about the potential of physical response to engage children, they need only spend a few minutes on the playground during recess watching children joyfully and effortlessly perform hand and jump-rope rhymes. The advancing lesson offered at the end of this chapter uses a kinesthetic experience to increase comprehension and recall.

Taste and Smell

Some books just beg to be tasted. For decades, educators have been serving *Green Eggs and Ham* and *Scrambled Eggs Super!* (Seuss), and these learning experiences have lingered long in students' literacy memories. More recently published, *Bee-bim Bop!* (Park/Lee) and *How to Make an Apple Pie and See the World* (Priceman) are two books that include recipes so readers can make and taste the delights described within the text before, during, or after the reading. Showing a turnip with the top still on and tasting it before reading *The Turnip: An Old Russian Folktale* (Morgan) or one of its variants can deepen readers' comprehension. The website www.cookingupreading.com offers children's literature and recipe connections. Most people, children included, can be motivated through their stomachs!

Educators can also make connections between taste and culture. Books such as *Everybody Cooks Rice* and *Everybody Brings Noodles* (Dooley/Thornton) can be used as springboards to similarities and differences in cuisine that help students understand a variety of cultures. For example, children can taste and smell rice or noodles spiced with Indian curry or Japanese soy sauce before reading picture books, folktales, or informational texts about those cultures. Best of all, families can be invited to prepare and share dishes that teach students about the diverse tastes, customs, and cultures of their classmates.

We smell with every breath we take, and many of our earliest and most vivid memories are associated with this sense. The beautiful children's book *The Perfume of Memory* (Nikly/Claverie) begins, "Everyone knows that a wonderful scent is a breath away from a memory." In this long-ago and faraway land, children were given the opportunity to study perfumery, for it was the dream of everyone in that place to become the Royal Perfume Maker. When an accident occurred, however, the people forgot the perfume formulas and lost their memories entirely. Through classroom teacher and teacher-librarian collaboration, educators can collect and share books that engage students with their sense of smell.

Using smell to achieve comprehension is arguably the most difficult skill to teach. Readers can bake bread with the Little Red Hen or bake cookies before reading *The Doorbell Rang* (Hutchins) to combine smell and taste. They can seek support in the natural environment for smells. This requires educators to be spontaneous and prepared for the teachable moment. Educators can open the classroom or library windows when it's drizzling to smell the wetness while reading about rain and spring. For practice imagining smells, read books such as *Dog Breath: The Horrible Trouble with Hally Tosis* (Pilkey) or *Walter the Farting Dog* (Kotzwinkle and Murray/Colman), if you dare.

• • • • •

As students become more proficient and sophisticated at using sensory imagery, combining two or more senses in a lesson can be a next step. Our eyes contain 70 percent of the body's sensory receptors, so we take in more information visually than through any of the other senses (Wolfe 2001, 152). Still, visual imagery is not enough for reaching deep comprehension. The visualization process can be significantly enriched by involving all five senses in mental re-creations of texts. For instance, visual imagery alone provides an incomplete picture of a Civil War soldier's experience in battle. When a reader can also imagine the taste of fear in the soldier's mouth, hear the anguished cries of fallen comrades and horses, feel the trembling of his fingers on a Springfield musket, and smell acrid gunpowder, she has achieved a "lived-through" experience. She no longer stands outside the text but has entered into it and participated in the action along with the characters.

Summary

Sensory images are part of the background knowledge that readers bring to a text. Helping students utilize all their senses as they read texts supports their comprehension. Sensory images also have the potential to increase readers' enjoyment and memory of their literary experiences. Educators can add sensory input to literary engagements to dramatize the powerful influene of our senses on meaning-making. Through modeling, educators share their unique sensory responses to the language and images presented in texts. Teacher-librarians and classroom teachers working in partnership can effectively model how to utilize one's own senses to comprehend text more fully and to gain increased pleasure from reading. Sensory images also help students store reading events in their memories.

Exposing students to rich language and vivid imagery is a key to utilizing this strategy across the curriculum in all content areas. Many books shelved in the fiction section of the library contain factual information. An increasing number of informational books include dramatic illustrations and graphics, poetry, and poetic prose. These books are more accurately described as multigenre texts. They provide effective support for developing students' ability to read with their senses fully engaged. The literature and lesson plans in this chapter support educators as they maximize the sensory impact of these types of text.

Through collaboration, educators can effectively design, implement, and assess lessons that demonstrate the use of sensory imagery to make meaning. By lowering the student-to-teacher ratio at the point of instruction, they can better monitor the cooperative learning strategies explored in the how-to lessons outlined in this chapter. As a team, they can more easily monitor and adjust teaching this sometimes difficult-to-assess strategy. When students learn to utilize background knowledge to create sensory images as they read, their literary lives and their background knowledge can be enriched significantly.

Children's Literature Cited

Starred titles are used in the lesson plans.

Sight and Multisensory

Animal Sense, by Diane Ackerman and Peter Sis

A Circle of Friends, by Giora Carmi

Come On, Rain! by Karen Hesse, illustrated by Jon J. Muth

Gathering the Sun: An Alphabet in Spanish and in English, by Alma Flor Ada, illustrated by Simón Silva

* Hello Ocean, by Pam Muñoz Ryan, illustrated by Mark Astrella

* The Important Book, by Margaret Wise Brown, illustrated by Leonard Weisgard

Keepers of the Earth: Native American Stories and Environmental Activities for Children, by Michael J. Caduto and Joseph Bruchac, illustrated by John Kahionhes Fadden and Carol Wood

The New Kid on the Block, by Jack Prelutsky

* Owl Moon, by Jane Yolen, illustrated by John Schoenherr

See the Ocean, by Estelle Condra, illustrated by Linda Crockett-Blassingame

* Until I Saw the Sea: A Collection of Seashore Poems, by Alison Shaw

* Water Dance, by Thomas Locker

Hearing

Achoo! Bang! Crash! A Noisy Alphabet, by Ross MacDonald

The Carrot Seed, by Ruth Krauss, illustrated by Crockett Johnson

Clickety Clack, by Rob and Amy Spence, illustrated by Margaret Spengler

Hush Songs: African American Lullabies, by Joyce Carol Thomas, illustrated by Brenda Joysmith

I'm Still Here in the Bathroom: Brand New Silly Dilly Songs, by Alan Katz, illustrated by David Catrow

Over in the Garden, by Jennifer Ward, illustrated by Kenneth Spengler

Pío Peep! Traditional Spanish Nursery Rhymes, by Alma Flor Ada and F. Isabel Campoy, eds., English adaptations by Alice Schertle, illustrated by Viví Escrivá

The Polar Express, by Chris Van Allsburg

She'll Be Comin' 'round the Mountain, by Philemon Sturges, illustrated by Ashley Wolff

Snip Snap! What's That? by Mara Bergman, illustrated by Nick Maland

Take Me Out of the Bathtub, and Other Silly Dilly Songs, by Alan Katz, illustrated by David Catrow

Train Song, by Diane Siebert, illustrated by Michael Wimmer

The Treasure of Ghostwood Gully: A Southwest Mystery, by Marcia Vaughan, illustrated by Will Terry

Touch

Bartholomew and the Oobleck, by Dr. Seuss

The Goat in the Rug, as told to Charles L. Blood and Martin Link by Geraldine, illustrated by Nancy Winslow Parker

The Very Busy Spider, by Eric Carle

Taste and Smell

Bee-bim Bop! by Linda Sue Park, illustrated by Ho Baek Lee

Dog Breath: The Horrible Trouble with Hally Tosis, by Dav Pilkey

The Doorbell Rang, by Pat Hutchins

Everybody Brings Noodles, by Norah Dooley, illustrated by Peter J. Thornton

Everybody Cooks Rice, by Norah Dooley, illustrated by Peter J. Thornton

Green Eggs and Ham, by Dr. Seuss

How to Make an Apple Pie and See the World, by Marjorie Priceman

The Perfume of Memory, by Michelle Nikly, illustrated by Jean Claverie

Scrambled Eggs Super! by Dr. Seuss

The Turnip: An Old Russian Folktale, by Pierr Morgan

Walter the Farting Dog, by William Kotzwinkle and Glenn Murray, illustrated by Audrey Colman

Lesson Plans

In these how-to lessons, classroom teachers and teacher-librarians use think-aloud strategies to demonstrate how and why they are using their senses to comprehend new texts before, during, and after reading. All three lessons use poetry or poetic prose to heighten a reader's sensory experience of text. Each lesson includes a writing component. When educators cofacilitate students' guided practice, they can more easily manage writing conferences. Lowering the student-to-teacher ratio and providing students with individual feedback can significantly improve students' writing.

READING COMPREHENSION STRATEGY
Using Sensory Images

Reading Development Level — Emerging

Instructional Strategy — Classifying

Lesson Length — 2 sessions

Purpose — The purpose of this lesson is to describe the impact of the senses on students' imagined experience and comprehension of a day at the ocean.

Objectives — After reading *Hello Ocean* and hearing poems from *Until I Saw the Sea: A Collection of Seashore Poems,* students will be able to

1. Classify sensory images by the sense organ and sense used for that experience.
2. Utilize background knowledge and the category matrix to compose a group poem and compose and illustrate an individual list poem about a day at the ocean.

Resources, Materials, and Equipment — *Hello Ocean,* by Pam Muñoz Ryan, illustrated by Mark Astrella

Until I Saw the Sea: A Collection of Seashore Poems, by Alison Shaw

Text set on the topic of oceans and beaches for browsing

Graphic Organizers: Category Matrix (Web Supplement 4B), Sensory List Poem Graphic Organizer (Web Supplement 4C), Sensory List Poem and Illustration Rubric (Web Supplement 4D)

Materials for Sensory Centers (Web Supplement 4A) and drawing materials

Overhead, data projector, or interactive whiteboard

Collaboration — Educators share the responsibility for organizing and facilitating the sensory input experiential centers. When presenting the book, one educator reads while the other records notes on the category matrix. Both educators facilitate shared writing of group poems and monitor and conference with students on their individual poem writing and self-assessment.

Assessment — Students' poetry demonstrates their understanding of sensory images and the use of these images to comprehend and compose text. Students are invited to illustrate their poems as well. Students and educators can assess the poems and illustrations with the poem rubric.

Standards — *Reading keywords:* story elements (setting); comprehend; respond

Writing keywords: expressive writing; expressive or descriptive phrases and short sentences

Listening and speaking keywords: effectively listen and speak; use effective vocabulary

Fine arts keyword: illustrate

Science: five senses and their related body parts; compare common objects using multiple senses

Information literacy keywords: select information appropriate to the problem or question at hand; organize information for practical application

Technology (extension): keyboard; illustrate; publish

Process

Day 1

Motivation

Name the five sense organs: eyes, ears, fingers/skin, nose, and tongue/mouth. (This is the order used in *Hello Ocean.*) Divide the students into five groups. Rotate students through five sensory centers. (Web Supplement 4A is a list of sensory center materials.) Let them know they will be using their senses to explore things related to the ocean. Ask the students to describe what they see, hear, feel, smell, and taste to their group members as they cycle through each center.

Student-Friendly Objectives

1. Use all five senses.
2. Classify sensory images.

Presentation

Bring the group together to hear *Hello Ocean.* Play ocean music softly during the reading. One educator and the students close their eyes and visualize during the reading. The other educator reads the book in sections by sense without showing the illustrations. The listening educator shares her visualization of the beach scenes with a focus on sensory details.

One educator rereads each section, focusing on each sense while asking students to identify notes for the class-sized Category Matrix: see/eyes, hear/ears, touch/skin, smell/nose, and taste/tongue (Web Supplement 4B). Ask students to think-pair-share their visualizations with a partner. Then ask for student volunteers to share with the class. The other educator records the students' ideas on the group matrix, using a different color marker for each sense. Collaborate to include sensory adjectives.

Student Participation Procedures

1. Think-pair-share.
2. Raise hand to share with the class.
3. Tell which sense and color of marker should be used to record information on the matrix.

Closure

One educator rereads the entire book to the class and shares the illustrations. Play ocean music while rereading.

Note: Make a second copy of the group category matrix for Day 2.

Day 2

Motivation

Play ocean music and read selections from *Until I Saw the Sea: A Collection of Seashore Poems.* Ask the students to use all their senses as they listen. Share the illustration after reading each poem. Let the student poets know they will be using the matrix to compose a group poem and an individual poem. They will illustrate their individual poems. Review the class-sized Category Matrix (Web Supplement 4B). Are there sensory details and adjectives that can be added?

Student-Friendly Objectives

1. Share ideas for a group poem.
2. Write an individual poem and an illustration about a day at the ocean.
3. Use the rubric to self-assess the poem and the illustration.

Presentation

Divide the class in half. Using the group category matrix as a word wall, each half of the class works with one educator to compose a group poem. Use the Sensory List Poem Graphic Organizer (Web Supplement 4C).

Bring the whole class together to share the two group poems. Project the Sensory List Poem and Illustration Rubric (Web Supplement 4D) and assess the group poems. Brainstorm ideas for illustrations that match the group poems.

Student Practice Procedures

1. Compose an ocean or beach poem using the poem graphic organizer.

2. Conference with a teacher.

3. Illustrate the poem.

4. Self-assess the illustration using the rubric.

5. Read books from the ocean text set.

Guided Practice

Educators monitor the poets' work. They ask the students how they are incorporating sensory imagery in their poems and remind them to use the rubric to guide their writing. When the student completes her poem, she conferences with an educator in order to self-assess with support, and then she independently illustrates her poem and self-assesses the illustration. The educators utilize the same rubric for assessment.

Closure

Bring the class together. Ask for volunteers to share their poems. Ask students to close their eyes as each volunteer reads his/her poem, with or without teacher support. Ask students to identify the strongest sense in each poem by whispering their answers to a neighbor. If the student has completed an illustration, she can share it after classmates have had the opportunity to visualize.

Reflection

Which senses did we use in this lesson? How did sensory images help us visualize the ocean? How did the sensory images help us understand spending a day at the ocean?

Extensions Students' poems and illustrations can be compiled into a class poetry anthology, or provide them with an electronic template of the Sensory List Poem Graphic Organizer (Web Supplement 4C) so they can keyboard their poems. Students can also utilize a computer drawing program to create their illustrations for a book or to create an electronic book or Web pages. Students can also create list poems and publish poetry collections about any topic they are studying in any content area.

READING COMPREHENSION STRATEGY
Using Sensory Images

Reading Development Level	Advancing
Instructional Strategies	Cues, Cooperative Learning, and Nonlinguistic Representation
Lesson Length	1 session
Purpose	The purpose of this lesson is to use sensory imagery and body-kinesthetic movement to learn, remember, and draw the water cycle.
Objectives	After reading *Water Dance,* students will be able to
	1. Recall the sequence of the water cycle as depicted in the book.
	2. Draw a diagram (nonlinguistic representation) of the water cycle.
Resources, Materials, and Equipment	*Water Dance,* by Thomas Locker
	Graphic Organizers: Student Sample: Completed Water Cycle (Web Supplement 4F), Water Cycle Checklist and Rubric (Web Supplement 4G)
	Materials: 11" by 14" sheet of white construction paper folded lightly into quadrants (or marked lightly with a pencil) for each student, one blue crayon for each student, other crayon colors, environmental CD with rain and thunder sounds
Collaboration	While one educator reads the book, the other makes hand movements to "illustrate" the water cycle. Together, the educators model recalling the sequence of the text. Both educators monitor students as they work in pairs to recall the water cycle and create individual nonlinguistic representations of the cycle.
Assessment	The students' nonlinguistic representations can be self-assessed and teacher-assessed using a checklist and rubric.
Standards	*Reading keywords:* restate facts; sequence; comprehend; respond
	Listening and speaking keywords: effectively listen and speak; use effective vocabulary
	Fine arts keyword: illustrate
	Science: water cycle; rain; water; weather; organize data; diagram
	Information literacy keywords: select information appropriate to the problem or question at hand; organize information for practical application
Process	*Motivation*
	Cues: Tell the students they will be learning about the water cycle. Let students know they will be using their senses to visualize. Review the senses. To help them think about the way they experience rain through their senses, play an environmental CD that includes rain and thunder sounds. Ask students to close their eyes and use all their senses to imagine a rainstorm. After the piece, each educator shares an example of one sensory image she visualized during this engagement. Ask students to think-pair-share one image with a partner. Ask for volunteers to share with the entire class.
	Student-Friendly Objectives
	1. Tell the water cycle in sequence.
	2. Draw a nonlinguistic representation of the water cycle.

Presentation

One educator reads *Water Dance* while the other produces the hand movements for the students to follow. (Web Supplement 4E is hand movements for *Water Dance*.) Repeat the hand movements in cumulative fashion after each new page.

At the end of the reading, ask students to visualize the text or their own personal experiences with rain and water as they repeat the cycle, along with the educators, using the hand movements only, without speaking or without viewing the illustrations.

The educators use the think-aloud process to model recalling the water cycle. They repeat the cycle verbally and with hand movements, supporting each other's ability to recall. The educators tell which sense they used most as they visualized the water cycle.

Replicate the students' individual papers by making a large rectangle with lightly marked quadrants on the board. Beginning in the high noon position and proceeding clockwise, the educators model illustrating the water cycle on the board. (Web Supplement 4F is a student sample.) Use blue marker/chalk until the end of the cycle; use more colors when adding a sun and a rainbow. Think aloud while planning the illustration. Repeat the hand movements to support recalling the water cycle sequence and invite students to do so as well.

Project a transparency of the checklist and rubric. As a whole class, assess the educators' nonlinguistic representation of the water cycle. Note: Final question on the checklist: Which of your senses helped you most in recalling the water cycle?

Depending on the proficiency of the students, the educators may erase their nonlinguistic representation to give students the opportunity to use only the hand movements and their memories. Students work with a partner as support for recalling the water cycle. Distribute one piece of construction paper and one blue crayon to each student.

Student Practice Procedures

1. Help your partner remember the cycle.
2. Illustrate the water cycle using a blue crayon.
3. Check your work with the checklist.
4. Raise your hand to request other crayons for the sun and rainbow.
5. Self-assess with the rubric.

Guided Practice

Educators monitor students' recall of the cycle as well as their execution of the illustrations. They make sure students are planning their illustrations. To keep students focused on sensory images, educators can also question students about which senses they are using as they draw. Educators monitor students' work in progress and suggest revisions if necessary before providing crayons for the sun and rainbow.

Closure

Display the water cycle illustrations around the room or in the hallway. Ask students to turn to face a partner. As a class, chorally recall the water cycle using hand movements. Ask students to tell their partners which of their senses they used most as they retold the cycle.

Reflection

Which senses did we use to remember the water cycle? How did the hand movements, the illustrations in the book, and the images in our minds help us remember the water cycle? How can we use visualization to help us comprehend text?

Extension   Students can add a title and label their nonlinguistic representations to convert them into scientific diagrams.

READING COMPREHENSION STRATEGY
Using Sensory Images

Reading Development Level	Advanced
Instructional Strategies	Cues, Cooperative Learning, Metaphors (Similes), Notemaking (Quotes) and Summarizing
Lesson Length	2 sessions
Purpose	The purpose of this lesson is to read a fictional text, visualize, identify sensory imagery, and compose a persuasive paragraph.

Objectives

After reading *Owl Moon*, students will be able to

1. Utilize their senses to vicariously experience an (unfamiliar) event.

2. Identify and record the senses used by the characters.

3. Analyze the text for the author's use of figurative language.

4. Synthesize information in order to compose a persuasive paragraph that uses evidence and figurative language from the text.

5. Self-assess their persuasive paragraphs using a rubric.

Resources, Materials, and Equipment

Owl Moon, by Jane Yolen, illustrated by John Schoenherr (multiple copies for student partners)

www.owling.com

Graphic Organizers: Admit Slip (Web Supplement 4H), Category Matrix (Web Supplement 4I), Sample Persuasive Paragraph (Web Supplement 4J), Persuasive Paragraph Rubric (Web Supplement 4K)

Train whistle

Overhead, data projector, or interactive whiteboard

Collaboration

Educators work with the entire class to model the tasks. Both educators support students as they partner-read, visualize, and analyze a text. Educators conduct conferences to support students' individual persuasive paragraph writing.

Assessment

Category matrixes are evaluated for completeness. The students' individual persuasive paragraphs are evaluated with a rubric.

Standards

Reading keywords: comprehend; vocabulary; determine the meaning of figurative language (similes)

Writing keywords: write persuasive text; paraphrase information; use literal and figurative language; use evidence from a text

Listening and speaking: effectively listen and speak

Information literacy keywords: recognize the need for information; develop and use successful strategies for locating information; organize for practical application; use information ethically; integrate information into one's own knowledge

Process

Day 1

Motivation

Cues: Play a recording of the call of an owl from the multimedia section of www.owling.com. Distribute one copy of the owling Admit Slip (Web Supplement 4H) to each student. (Put students into teams of two to prepare for partner-reading during the guided practice.) Project the admit slip and conduct a shared reading of this informational text about owling. Review the five senses.

In *Owl Moon,* the characters use three senses: sight, hearing, and touch. On the admit slip, each student records a prediction about which sense the characters in the story will use most as they search for an owl on a winter night and why they think that.

Student-Friendly Objectives

1. Read *Owl Moon* with a partner.
2. Identify and use tally marks to record the senses used by the characters.
3. Identify and quote similes and metaphors that relate to each sense.

Presentation

Educators use the similes on the first page of the story to review figurative language: "trees stood like giant statues" (sight) and "a train whistle blew, long and low, like a sad, sad song" (hearing). Determine the dominant sense in each simile. Convert each example into a metaphor: "The trees were giant statues" and "The long and low train whistle was a sad, sad song." The author uses similes and metaphors to help readers comprehend the owling experience. How does figurative language impact the reader's sensory experience of the text?

Project the Category Matrix (Web Supplement 4I). Distribute one matrix to each team.

One educator reads while the other closes her eyes to visualize. Ask the students to close their eyes as well. The listeners' job is to imagine the events in the story in their minds. The adult reader begins by blowing a train whistle and reading the first page. After the first page is read, the students and the other educator open their eyes. The adult listener tells the reader what she visualized. Make tally marks for the sensory images used in the print and record similes and metaphors in quotation marks next to the dominant sense on the category matrix. Discuss the ethical use of ideas and information.

Read the print on the second double-page spread and repeat this process. Students continue reading and recording with their partners. Let the students know that their category matrix will be their prewriting for a persuasive essay.

Student Practice Procedures

1. Take turns reading one page at a time and listening/visualizing the story.
2. Take turns recording senses used by making tally marks.
3. Take turns quoting simile/metaphor quotes on a shared graphic organizer.

Guided Practice

Both educators monitor students' reading, visualizing, and record keeping. They also facilitate cooperative learning. (One way to ensure that partners are collaborating is to have each student use a different-colored pen or pencil as she/he records on the graphic organizer.)

Closure

Ask students to tally their marks for each sense. Share some of the similes and metaphors from the text. Let students know that in the next lesson they will be composing persuasive paragraphs.

Day 2 ### Motivation

What is the purpose of writing a persuasive paragraph? The audience for your paragraphs will be students in another class. They will hear the book *Owl Moon* and then vote for the most persuasive paragraphs related to the primary sense used in owling.

Student-Friendly Objectives

1. Compose a persuasive paragraph that uses evidence from the text and quoted or original figurative language.
2. Self-assess with the rubric.

Presentation

The educators role-play a discussion of the predominant sense used in owling. Educators review the rubric with students and emphasize that evidence from the text is an important aspect of persuasive writing. They also mention that similes and metaphors can be used to strengthen an opinion. Writers can quote the author's figurative language or create similes and metaphors of their own. The educators share a Sample Persuasive Paragraph (Web Supplement 4J) and lead the class in assessing it using the rubric (Web Supplement 4K).

Student Practice Procedures

1. Review your category matrix.
2. Discuss the senses used in owling with your partner.
3. Compose an individual persuasive paragraph that uses evidence from the text and similes or metaphors to convince the reader that one sense is predominantly used in owling.
4. Self-assess the paragraph using the rubric.

Guided Practice

Both educators monitor students' paragraph composition and conduct writing conferences as needed. They support students in completing their individual assessment rubric.

Closure

Divide students into small groups and ask them to share their paragraphs. Vote as a class as to which sense is most important in owling. Conduct the reflection.

Reflection

How did closing our eyes help us visualize? What are some techniques writers use to help readers visualize? How does figurative language increase the effectiveness of sensory imagery? How can we use visualization to help us comprehend text?

Further Collaboration

Collaborate with another teacher and classroom. Bring both classes together. Divide students into groups of eight (four students from each class). Project and read the Admit Slip (Web Supplement 4H). Let students in the partner class know that, after hearing the book *Owl Moon*, they will listen to student-authored persuasive paragraphs related to which sense is most important when owling. Discuss the idea behind a persuasive paragraph. The students in the partner class decide which paragraph is most persuasive of the four shared in their group.

Extension Students can compose poems. One possibility is to do this in the style of prose poems in *The Important Book* (Brown/Weisgard). Example: "The important thing about owling is you must . . . / When you go owling, you will see . . . / hear . . . / feel . . . / But the most important thing about owling is. . . ." Students can illustrate their poems and publish a class book in hard copy or electronically.

5

Reading Comprehension Strategy Three
Questioning

The secret to wisdom is to be curious—to take time to look closely, to use all your senses to see and touch and taste and smell and hear. To keep on wandering and wondering.

—From *The Wise Woman and Her Secret,*
by Eve Merriam, illustrated by Linda Graves

Activating Background Knowledge

Using Sensory Images

Questioning

Making Predictions and Inferences

Determining Main Ideas

Using Fix-Up Options

Synthesizing

Although we first learn about our world nonlinguistically through our senses, once we have acquired a level of proficiency with language we continue constructing our knowledge by asking and answering questions. Young children go through a stage in this exploration when their speech is punctuated by question marks more often than by periods. They ask how? who? what? where? and when? and to every response from a more knowledgeable peer or adult, they ask the eternal question, why?

Questioning is among the social competencies that children bring with them to their schooling. But when they enter school, many children begin to think of questions in terms of answering the teacher's questions rather than asking and answering their own. "It is somewhat ironic that while parents will often complain about the number of questions that children expect them to answer, the opposite is true in schools. In schools, it is the teachers who ask the questions and children who are expected to provide the answers" (Whitebread 2000, 70).

As children progress through the grades, this phenomenon becomes even more pronounced. Studies have shown that the most common discourse pattern in U.S. classrooms is "IRE," in which the teacher initiates a question, one student responds, and the teacher evaluates the answer (Wells 1986). Teacher-initiated questions are usually asked after students are exposed to new information; they are less often used before or during students' encounters with texts. Teacher-initiated questions are most often at the knowledge level; they require only that students recall information. These questions are useful for fact testing because they can for the most part be correctly answered by the "right" response, but they do not develop students' abilities to ask their own questions or to think critically.

The questioning required to deepen reading comprehension is significantly different in purpose and in application. Unlike IRE questions, "questions that assist learning provoke in the child a way of thinking that he or she may not be able to produce alone" (Whitebread 2000, 70). When educators scaffold engagements with text by questioning before, during, and after reading, they must keep in mind that the goal is for readers to ask and answer their own questions, a reading skill practiced unconsciously by proficient readers (for an excellent resource about stimulating curiosity and understanding questioning across the curriculum, see Koechlin and Zwaan 2006).

As we approach this investigation into using questioning strategies to teach reading comprehension, educators must remember that all questions are not alike. Educators must strive to support students' thinking by modeling questioning that does not end with knowledge-level questions. They must model questioning that stretches readers beyond the facts found "on the line" (in the print or illustrations), to think between the lines, to think through and beyond the text. Higher-level questions require that students analyze, synthesize, or evaluate information. Teacher-librarians will recognize that information literacy standards such as using information critically, competently, and creatively as well as achieving excellence in knowledge generation are effectively supported through higher-order questioning.

McKenzie (1997) identified eighteen different kinds of question, including a category called "strategic questions," which raise the reader's awareness of his own thinking. When educators model with think-aloud strategies, they reveal their own meta-

cognition and use it as a tool for students to emulate. In this process, students learn that *how* one learns is as important as *what* one learns. Strategic questions posed throughout a reading and used for reflection at the end of a literacy experience help learners focus on learning how to learn.

Like the little girl Jenny who closely examines a coin in *The Wise Woman and Her Secret* (Merriam/Graves), readers can be encouraged to recapture the sense of wonder and curiosity of their early childhoods.

> "Would you like to keep it?" Jenny asked.
>
> "My dear child, it belongs to you." The wise woman opened her hand and held the coin out to Jenny.
>
> Jenny took the coin and held it close to her eyes the way the wise woman had. She peered at one side and then at the other. "Why," she wondered aloud, "does it look green instead of copper-colored? And what are the Latin words? How do they fit into such a small place? What do the numbers mean? Why did they put the face on the coin? What kind of building is that on the other side?"
>
> The wise woman laughed, and listened. "My dear child, you have found the secret. . . . The secret of wisdom is to be curious. . . ."

Educators can model and students can practice using the simple sentence starter "I wonder. . . ." Questions that can be answered in the text, questions that require thinking or research beyond the text, and questions that seem to have no answers at all can invite the reader to enter into the story or informational source. Questions can frame the reader's exploration. Questions awaken the mind.

The strategy highlighted in this chapter uses questioning the way elephants utilize their tusks to explore and probe their environment. Asking and answering questions before, during, and after reading helps readers establish, develop, and maintain an internal conversation while engaging with text. In her Newbery Medal acceptance speech for *The Midwife's Apprentice,* Cushman remarked:

"Writing for me is us feeding each other—writer and reader—fifty-four-year-old me and the young people who pick up my books. Me whispering in their ears and them talking back" (1996, 414). Questions support an internal dialogue between the reader and the author, the illustrator, or the text. Questioning keeps readers engaged. The metaphor of the elephant's tusks reminds readers to use questions to be active participants, rather than passive spectators, in the meaning-making process.

How to Teach the Strategy

Researchers have found that cueing and questioning account for as much as 80 percent of what happens every day in a classroom. If this is true, then being conscious of how they use cues and questions can help educators improve their practice. After carefully selecting texts, educators can offer cues and questions as previews to what will be important in the literacy engagement. This helps students' minds begin to focus and prepare for the literacy event to come. This information is used to frame the listening or reading experience. Often these introductions help students to remember and connect with what they already know about a topic, theme, author, or illustrator. These cues and questions, then, are linked to the background knowledge strategy discussed in chapter 3.

Educators are often skilled at using questions as cues to preview read-aloud selections. After reading the title and the author's and illustrator's names, adult readers usually ask questions to invite students to consider the meaning of the title, to make predictions based on the cover illustration, or to connect the story listeners' background knowledge. Connections to previously shared texts on this topic or theme or to other texts written or illustrated by this author or illustrator help prepare the listeners for what is to come.

Introductory questioning is important but, as comprehension builds, asking questions during the reading is likely more important and more challenging to teach and to learn. Educators who have worked in preschool or primary grades may be familiar with the practice of *dialogic reading*. This strategy involves story readers asking story listeners both closed- and open-ended questions about the text during the reading. Closed-ended questions seek the "right" answer and can be answered with single words or phrases. (It is important that these questions not be answered with a simple "yes" or "no"; one of the goals of this strategy is to build vocabulary.) Open-ended questions have no right or wrong responses and support children's language development because they invite elaboration and engage the child in higher-level thinking (Christie, Enz, and Vukelich 2003). Engaging in questioning while reading helps children learn to think about print and illustrations in ways proficient readers think about them. Dialogic reading is designed for the one-on-one experience; the adult can follow the interests of the individual child and provide him with immediate feedback (for more information on dialogic reading, see Arnold and Whitehurst 1994).

K–6 classroom teachers often struggle to create time for one-on-one reading opportunities with students. Although it is important to use dialogic reading strategies when reading with individual students and important to teach parents and reading tutors to utilize dialogic reading strategies as well, this strategy is not effective in the small group or whole-class setting. The benefit to children who have experienced this strategy is, however, significant, because they begin to think of reading in terms of interacting with texts through questioning.

Cultivating the thinking that follows "I wonder" is one sure way to teach this strategy. The following list gives examples of additional question starters that can guide educators as they model questioning and prompt students as they practice it.

- I wonder . . .
- Who . . . ? What . . . ? Where . . . ? When . . . ?
- How come . . . ?
- Why . . . ?
- What does that mean?

- What does that make you think of in your own life experience, in another text, or in the world?
- Does that question make you think of another question?

Lists like these can be used to create a classroom and library poster for readers' reference during individual and group engagements with texts. Educators and students can add their own question starters to expand on these possibilities.

In addition to "I wonder," educators often ask students to question by using the "five Ws"— "Who," "What," "Where," "When," and "Why"— along with "How." At the knowledge level, these clarifying questions situate the reader in the story or informational text and are basic aids to comprehension. Creating a category matrix to note questions that are raised before, during, and after the reading may serve as a guide for story listeners to emulate when they are reading and posing their own questions. Educators can begin by recording questions on a class-sized matrix (figure 5-1). During and after questioning, they can guide students in noting and coding specifics about the questions. Was the question answered "on the line" in the text (code with *), or did the reader use his own background knowledge to infer the answer "between the lines" (code with **)? If the question wasn't answered (code with ***), how can an answer be found, or is there an answer to this question? Thinking this way about the five Ws and How helps readers understand that these fundamental questions can be used to delve deeper into a text and can lead to sophisticated questioning and thinking.

FIGURE 5-1
Questioning Matrix

	BEFORE READING	DURING READING	AFTER READING
Who?			
What?			
Where?			
When?			
Why?			
How?			

*Answered "on the line" (in the text)
**Answered "between the lines" (by connecting information with own knowledge)
***Unanswered questions (may require research)

Educators can provide category matrix graphic organizers such as this one for student use as they read texts and practice questioning strategies in small group, partner, or individual learning situations. Organizers such as this can prompt students to remember to ask questions throughout the reading process.

Figure 5-2 illustrates educators' use of think-alouds to model questioning that begins with the cueing strategy framed by a book's cover, continues throughout the reading of the book, and extends beyond the reading. With this strategy, questioning propels the reader through the story, creating a dialogue among the characters, the author, the illustrator, the text, and the reader himself. The act of asking and answering questions motivates the reader to turn the page in order to ask and to answer more questions. This level of engagement with texts helps the reader achieve comprehension and offers a window into the deeper meanings associated with accessing the author's and illustrator's message or theme and the personal meanings made by the story reader himself; see Moreillon (2003) for development of this strategy as a foundation for an online, integrated language arts, fine arts, and technology unit.

Questioning must also be practiced with texts in content areas for which students are often asked to answer literal, inferential, and evaluative questions. Ouzts (1998) notes that one way to approach questions is to study question-answer relationships (QARs). In this model, students are asked to classify questions by the source of their answers. Is the question literal; is it found "on the line"? The answers to these questions may be found on a specific page in the text, or they may require that readers synthesize information found at various points in the text. Is the question inferential (see chapter 6); is it found "between the lines" by combining the information in the text with the reader's background knowledge? Is the question evaluative; does it require readers to make a judgment or state an opinion? Categorizing their own questions by type and answers by their sources helps students understand the ways questions support comprehension.

Becoming proficient at identifying QARs can also help students negotiate standardized test questions and answers.

The advanced sample lesson in this chapter focuses on the QAR strategy. Other questioning models are also available for teaching questioning as a reading comprehension strategy. Reciprocal questioning, or "ReQuest" (Manzo 1969), involves the class reading the text silently before the educator gives a prompt question such as "When does the story take place—in the past, present, or future?" Students then respond by asking related questions such as "Does the story begin with 'A long time ago when dinosaurs roamed the earth'?" Another strategy, questioning the author, or "QtA" (Beck et al. 1997), challenges students to pose questions in order to determine what the author means. These questions are targeted to expose the author's assumptions and to clarify the intended meaning. Through collaborative planning, educators can match challenging and appropriate texts with these strategies as well.

Making Literature Connections

Which texts lend themselves to exploring questioning strategies depends on the context in which they are used. Texts that prompt questions for some readers may or may not prompt questions for others. The usefulness of particular texts to teach this strategy is dependent on the students' prior knowledge and their connections to particular texts. As a result, it is hard to make specific recommendations of literature that supports this strategy. Teaching questioning strategies is one of many areas of the curriculum for which collaboration between classroom teachers and teacher-librarians is critical. Bringing together the teacher's more intimate knowledge of the students and their background knowledge and experiences and the teacher-librarian's extensive knowledge of literature and access to resources makes fertile ground for nurturing readers who become proficient at asking and answering questions while they read.

FIGURE 5-2
Questioning Before, During, and After Reading

Text: *An Angel for Solomon Singer*, by Cynthia Rylant, illustrated by Peter Catalanotto

Before Reading: Questions Related to the Cover, the Frontispiece, and the Title Page

One teacher reads the title of the book and the author's and illustrator's names. The other teacher asks himself questions aloud. After the questioner has shared his thinking about the cover (A), the reader turns to the frontispiece (B), and then to the title page (C).

A: I'm thinking about the title of the book. Is the main character named Solomon Singer? Is the man on the cover in the foreground the main character? I wonder who his "angel" is. Why does he need an angel?

When I look at the cover, I wonder about the tall, yellow-brown grass that the illustrator painted in front of the largest character. Why is this man standing in the grass? It seems odd to me that grass is growing right up to the window of the Westway Café. Where is the café? The man in the café probably works there. Is he a cook or a waiter? What is the relationship between the two men on the cover?

B: I can see part of the word "hotel." I think the main character from the cover lives in a hotel. I wonder why his face is downcast. The illustrations are watery and sad in tone. Is this man sad to live in a hotel? Why does he live there instead of in a house or in an apartment? What is the red writing under the window?

C: The man is going up the stairs, probably to his room in the hotel. His face is in shadow. I wonder if he lives alone. I wonder if the illustrator wants us to feel sad when we look at this page in the book. This man does not seem happy.

During Reading: Example from the First Few Pages

The reader begins and stops at the end of each double-page spread so the listener can answer and ask questions. Before resuming reading, the reader asks the listener why or how posing questions supports his understanding of the text.

I was correct. His name is Solomon Singer, and he does live in a hotel. The hotel is in New York City. The author wrote, "The hotel had none of the things he loved." I wonder what Solomon Singer loves. I notice he's eating his canned soup from a skillet and that his cup has a broken handle. Is he going to eat alone? I wonder if Solomon Singer is poor.

Now I know what he would love to have: a balcony, a fireplace, a porch swing, a picture window, a cat or a dog, and a wall painted yellow or purple. The illustrator paints in the man's favorite things. Does this page show Solomon Singer's imagination? Does it show him dreaming about his favorite things? I wonder if it's difficult to have these things because he lives in a hotel in New York City.

I answered my question from the title page. Solomon Singer is unhappy about where he lives. He wanders on the streets. I wonder what it's like to wander at night on the streets in New York City. I see the red writing from the frontispiece is on the hotel door and that there's more writing on the walls outside the hotel. Is this graffiti?

The listener continues to provide this think-aloud dialogue with the text as the reader continues reading and questioning the listener about the benefits of this process.

After Reading: Reflection and Further Questions

I think the author wants to tell us that friends are like angels. I think that's true. Friends keep us from feeling too sad. They help us feel at home wherever we are.

Asking and sometimes answering my questions as I read helped me become part of the story. I was there with Solomon and Angel at the Westway Café. Now that Solomon has a smile on his face and a friend named Angel, I wonder if Solomon will make other friends.

I think the author and illustrator worked together to create a beautiful story about the importance of friendship. Have Cynthia Rylant and Peter Catalanotto worked together on other books?

Some informational books utilize a question-and-answer format that can model a line of thinking as one reads on a topic of curricular or personal interest. The Don't Know Much About series frames inquiry in this manner on topics related to social studies. In *Don't Know Much about the Pioneers*, author Kenneth Davis begins by asking who the pioneers were and defining them as "trailblazers." This prompts him to ask these follow-up questions: "Weren't there people already living in the West 150 years ago?" and "Did pioneers call themselves 'pioneers'?"

In the social studies and science curricula, a series such as I Wonder Why also uses the question-and-answer format to lead students on a guided inquiry into a topic. A science example is *I Wonder Why Volcanoes Blow Their Tops* (Greenwood). Beginning with lightning, a weather phenomenon with which most readers have firsthand knowledge, and progressing through forest fires, wind, tornadoes, and more, the author builds readers' knowledge of natural disasters and their impact on people and nature. In addition to answering the main questions asked on each page, the author adds sidebars, which may answer more questions or prompt readers to ask additional questions. Texts such as these can be read to model questioning as a strategy that engages the reader in an ever-deepening spiral of understanding of the topic under investigation.

Informational texts for which students do not have a vast store of background knowledge can also be used to prompt questions. For example, if students are studying the Pilgrims and are unfamiliar with the food, the clothing, the ship *Mayflower,* or other artifacts related to Pilgrim culture and their arrival in North America, then it is natural for students to generate questions while reading about them. For readers who are cutting their reading teeth on early chapter books such as *Thanksgiving on Thursday* (Osborne), the nonfiction companion book *Pilgrims* (Osborne and Boyce/Murdocca) may create an ideal combination of texts. While reading the fiction story, students can use sticky notes to record questions as they read. They can note which questions were answered and which were not before bringing their questions to a reading of the nonfiction companion text, which condenses research from several sources.

To further explore the topic of the Pilgrims, which is prominent in social studies curricula in the elementary grades, informational books can also bring previously held knowledge into question and thereby prompt the reexamination of long-believed "facts." *Mayflower 1620: A New Look at a Pilgrim Voyage* (Plimoth Plantation) is one such book. Were all the people on board the *Mayflower* "Pilgrims"? Who were the others on the ship? Were there tensions and disagreements among the passengers and between the passengers and crew? Was the Mayflower Compact a democratic document, or was it something else?

Biographies and historical fiction can also lend themselves to practicing questioning strategies. As with historical information books, the readers' lack of background knowledge can prompt them to ask authentic questions before, during, and after reading. Instead of building a great deal of prior knowledge, educators can support students in developing questioning strategies by explicitly stating that readers' background knowledge is not yet developed and that questioning is a useful tool when confronting challenging texts on unfamiliar topics. Textbooks in all content areas can also be used effectively to teach and practice questioning.

Fictional texts of all types, both poetry and prose, can also be effective in teaching this strategy. Fantasy or science fiction texts, which by definition present alternate realities, can prompt numerous questions about the unfamiliar story elements presented—but make sure your students are sophisticated enough to distinguish fantasy and science fiction from realistic fiction. In choosing texts, the most important considerations are students' background knowledge and connections and their interest in the topics, themes, or story elements presented in the texts.

Summary

Questioning, a lifelong skill, can and should be taught across the curriculum. Questioning is an essential component of reading comprehension, of conducting research, and of critical thinking. In short, questioning is a key to learning. In the rapid pace of change of our information-rich 21st century, questioning may be more important than ever by providing readers with a path to follow. Instead of being overwhelmed by information, students can focus on asking and answering questions that are germane to their purposes. In the context of classroom-library collaboration, asking and answering questions while reading texts related to curriculum as well as texts of personal interest are essential to developing information literacy.

Through collaboration, teacher-librarians and classroom teachers can effectively design, implement, and assess lessons that demonstrate the use of questioning to engage readers with texts in order to make meaning. Educators can support one another by identifying texts that lead students to ask questions—whether questions inspired by the students' lack of background knowledge or by their motivation to explore the topic or theme of the text. By lowering the student-to-teacher ratio at the point of instruction, educators can better monitor the students' questioning and thinking as well as their participation in cooperative learning. Working together, classroom teachers and teacher-librarians can remind students to ask and answer questions in all curriculum content areas as well as when they read for pleasure.

Children's Literature Cited

Starred titles are used in the lesson plans.

Amelia and Eleanor Go for a Ride, by Pam Muñoz Ryan, illustrated by Brian Selznick

Amelia Earhart, by Jonatha A. Brown

An Angel for Solomon Singer, by Cynthia Rylant, illustrated by Peter Catalanotto

The Day of Ahmed's Secret, by Florence Parry Heide and Judith Heide Gilliland, illustrated by Ted Lewin

Don't Know Much about the Pioneers, by Kenneth C. Davis, illustrated by Renée Andriana

Eleanor Roosevelt, by Jonatha A. Brown

I Wonder Why Volcanoes Blow Their Tops, by Rosie Greenwood

Mayflower 1620: A New Look at a Pilgrim Voyage, by Plimoth Plantation, illustrated by Sisse Brimberg and Cotton Coulson

More Than Anything Else, by Marie Bradby, illustrated by Chris K. Soentpiet

Pilgrims: A Nonfiction Companion to Thanksgiving on Thursday, by Mary Pope Osborne and Natalie Pope Boyce, illustrated by Sal Murdocca

Thanksgiving on Thursday, by Mary Pope Osborne

Tomás and the Library Lady, by Pat Mora, illustrated by Raúl Colón

The Wise Woman and Her Secret, by Eve Merriam, illustrated by Linda Graves

Lesson Plans

In these strategy lessons, classroom teachers and teacher-librarians divide the class to lower the student-to-teacher ratio. This allows educators to maximize individual student's experience with this strategy and increase student-teacher or student-student interaction. Educators provide think-aloud strategies to demonstrate how to utilize questioning to comprehend new texts before, during, and after reading. Although graphic organizers are provided for recording questions, students can use large sticky notes to record their questions and place them on the book covers or pages of the text where they posed the questions.

Strategic questions that focus on learning how to learn are interjected throughout the lessons. The lessons at the higher levels of development build on the previous one by adding a more sophisticated analysis of questioning strategies. Advancing students may benefit from experiencing the emerging lesson with the same or a different text, and advanced students may benefit from engaging in all three lessons in sequence with the texts utilized in the examples or with different texts.

READING COMPREHENSION STRATEGY
Questioning

Reading Development Level	Emerging
Instructional Strategies	Cues and Questions, Categorizing, and Comparing
Lesson Length	1 session
Purpose	The purpose of this lesson is to record questions posed before, during, and after reading a text and to utilize a Venn diagram to compare questions.
Objectives	After reading *The Day of Ahmed's Secret,* students will be able to

1. Pose before, during, and after questions using key vocabulary words.

2. Compare questions asked by two groups and identify unanswered questions.

Resources, Materials, and Equipment	*The Day of Ahmed's Secret,* by Florence Parry Heide and Judith Heide Gilliland, illustrated by Ted Lewin (two copies)

Egypt Pathfinder: http://storytrail.com/Impact/Egypt.htm

Graphic Organizers: Questioning Category Matrix—Emerging Lesson (Web Supplement 5A), Venn Diagram (Web Supplement 5B), Question Evaluation Graphic Organizer (Web Supplement 5C)

Materials: Photographs of modern-day Cairo, Egypt, and rose water. (Make rose water in the spring with fresh rose petals or purchase it from a Middle Eastern market.)

Data projector or interactive whiteboard

Collaboration	Educators divide the class in half. Each half of the class reads the same book and completes a class-sized questioning category web. Both educators facilitate as the groups compare their questions using a Venn diagram and complete the question evaluation graphic organizer.
Assessment	Educators monitor students' ability to pose questions and to identify similarities and differences in their questions. The Venn diagram shows the comparison, and the question evaluation sheet shows which question most influenced each student's comprehension.
Standards	*Reading keywords:* answer or pose questions; culture; comprehension; vocabulary; compare events of characters and conflicts in literary selections from a variety of cultures to their experiences

Writing keywords: prewriting; organize ideas using webs, maps, or lists (Venn diagram); generate topics

Social studies keywords: geography; places have distinct physical and cultural characteristics; communities

Information literacy keywords: organize information for practical application; evaluate information

Process	*Motivation*

Working with the entire class, distribute small cups of rose water. Let the students know that this kind of water is sold on the streets in Cairo, Egypt. Ask students to smell, taste, and drink the water slowly and describe its smell and taste to a partner.

Cues and Questions: What gives this water flavor? Rose water is made by putting rose petals in hot water (steeping). Do you think you would find someone today on the street in downtown _____ (your city/town) selling rose water for people to drink? People who live in different communities have different traditions; they have different cultures. They do some things differently and some things the same as people do in our community. Define culture as a community's special foods, music, holidays, celebrations, and religion. When we ask questions about an unfamiliar culture, we use what we know about our own culture to think about similarities and differences.

Use the Egypt pathfinder, posters, photo prints, or books to show students images of modern-day Cairo. Use the visual aids to introduce the key vocabulary words: *culture, community, transportation, rose water, cart, caravan, fuel, camel, butagaz* (which is defined on the verso of the title page), and *lantern*. Using the key vocabulary words, discuss and ask questions about this information.

Student-Friendly Objectives

1. Ask before, during, and after questions.
2. Use key vocabulary words.
3. Compare questions asked by two groups.
4. Identify unanswered questions.
5. Choose the most important question.

Presentation

Divide the class in half. Each student sits with a partner. Each educator reads *The Day of Ahmed's Secret* with half the class. Read the title and the author's and illustrator's names. Show the double-page spread book jacket. Ask students to describe what they see to a partner.

The educator models asking questions based on the book jacket. What is Ahmed delivering with his donkey cart? Do all the people in Cairo use animals for transportation? Is Ahmed working? Could this story take place today? How do we know? What is Ahmed's secret? Will he tell his secret to someone? Invite students to ask questions as well. Using one color of marker, record several of these or other questions in complete sentences on the "before reading" section of the class-sized Questioning Category Matrix—Emerging Lesson (Web Supplement 5A).

Conduct a bookwalk and think aloud. Model asking questions and, when answers are found in the illustrations, model answering questions from evidence in the paintings. Note the expressions on the characters' faces as well as other details in the images. (Do not share the last three pages or reveal Ahmed's secret.)

Begin reading the print. While reading the first half of the book, think aloud and use another color marker to record the educator's (or students') questions in the "during reading" section of the category matrix. The educator records the questions as complete sentences in the appropriate column on the matrix and records the answers, if found, in parentheses as notes. Review the types of notes (figure 2-1 or Web Supplement 2A).

In the second half of the book, stop at the end of each double-page spread. Ask students to think-pair-share and prompt them to ask questions as complete sentences and suggest notes for answers when found. The educator records questions and answers on the graphic organizer.

Student Participation Procedures

1. Think-pair-share possible questions.

2. Ask questions as complete sentences.

3. Suggest answers as notes.

Guided Practice

Monitor students as they pose questions. Remind students to focus on asking rather than answering questions. Provide additional modeling as needed.

Closure

With a third color marker, pose and record "after reading" questions. Use the same student participation procedures. Review all of the questions posed. Which were answered in the text? Which remain unanswered? Reach consensus on one final burning question.

Bring the two groups together. Use a class-sized Venn diagram to record (in notemaking format) the groups' similar and different questions (Web Supplement 5B).

Guide students as they complete the Question Evaluation Graphic Organizer (Web Supplement 5C). In addition to the bibliographic information, the students report which question helped them most in understanding the story. Share each group's final burning question.

Reflection

How did questioning keep us engaged in the story? How did it help us understand the story? Did we all ask the same questions? Did we all find the same questions useful? Do we have the same final burning question?

Extension Conduct an inquiry based on the students' final burning questions. This extension can be conducted with both educators facilitating. It can also be conducted in the library with a small group or with half the class, giving the classroom teacher the opportunity to work with the other students in the classroom.

Questioning

Reading Comprehension Level	Advancing
Instructional Strategies	Cues, Classifying, and Cooperative Learning
Lesson Length	2 sessions
Purpose	The purpose of this lesson is to record questions before, during, and after reading and note how questions can be asked and answered to propel readers forward through the text.
Objectives	After reading *Tomás and the Library Lady* and *More Than Anything Else,* students will be able to

1. Pose and record before, during, and after questions on a category matrix.

2. Evaluate questions and determine their relative importance in comprehending the text.

Resources, Materials, and Equipment

Tomás and the Library Lady, by Pat Mora, illustrated by Raúl Colón (two copies)

More Than Anything Else, by Marie Bradby, illustrated by Chris K. Soentpiet (multiple copies)

Graphic Organizers: Teacher Resource: Questioning Category Matrix (Web Supplement 5D), Questioning Category Matrix—Advancing Lesson (Web Supplement 5E), Question Evaluation Graphic Organizer (Web Supplement 5F)

Materials: Markers in three colors for educators and fine markers in the same three colors for students

Overhead, data projector, or interactive whiteboard

Collaboration

To maximize students' engagement in the questioning strategy, each educator works with half the class. With the second text, students work in small groups with both educators monitoring.

Assessment

The students' group questioning matrix assesses their ability to pose questions before, during, and after reading. Educators must establish criteria for the quality of completed matrices. Students complete a question evaluation graphic organizer for the second text, *More Than Anything Else.*

Standards

Reading keywords: ask relevant questions in order to comprehend text; generate clarifying questions to comprehend text; describe the historical and cultural aspects of literature

Social studies: use stories to describe past events and cultures; identify examples of individual actions, character, and values

Information literacy keywords: organize information for practical application; evaluate information

Process
Day 1

Motivation

Cues: With each educator working with half the class, share the book jacket of *Tomás and the Library Lady.* Read the title and author's and illustrator's names. Share questions with students: Why is there a mark over the "a" in Tomás's name? Record these questions in the appropriate categories (Who? What? Where? When? Why? How?) using one color of marker in the column labeled "before reading" on a class-sized Questioning Category Matrix—Advancing Lesson (Web Supplement 5E). Periodically, ask students what additional questions they have about the title and the book jacket. Ask students to identify the question category and record. (Web Supplement 5D is a completed teacher resource.)

Tell the students that both the educator and the students will pose questions throughout and after the reading. The educator records the questions as complete sentences in the appropriate column on the matrix and records the answers as notes. Review the types of notes (figure 2-1 or Web Supplement 2A).

Student-Friendly Objectives

1. Ask questions before, during, and after reading.
2. Decide the question category.
3. Evaluate the questions.

Presentation

Read *Tomás and the Library Lady*. While reading, pose and record questions in the "during reading" section of the matrix using another color of marker. Educators use think-alouds as they determine questions. Encourage students to ask questions and probe students for the category of their questions. The educator records the questions in complete sentences and record answers, when learned, as notes.

Student Participation Procedures

1. Raise hand to stop reading.
2. Ask question and determine the category.

Guided Practice

Periodically pose strategic questions: How does asking questions get us excited, keep us engaged, and so on while reading this book?

Closure

After reading the book, select the third color of marker and follow the same procedures to pose and record questions in the "after reading" column of the category matrix. Review the questions. Which questions helped us better understand the story? Ask students to vote for one most important question in each column. Project the Question Evaluation Graphic Organizer for *Tomás and the Library Lady* (Web Supplement 5F) and work as a group to fill out this example.

Day 2   ### Student-Friendly Objectives

1. Ask questions before, during, and after reading.
2. Decide the category and record questions as complete sentences.
3. Record answers (when learned) as notes.
4. Evaluate the importance of the questions.

Presentation

Review the previous day's category matrix and question evaluation graphic organizer for *Tomás and the Library Lady*.

Divide the entire class into small groups of three or four students to read multiple copies of *More Than Anything Else*. Students decide how to read the book: one person reading, or rotating with each person taking a turn by reading a page. They pose and record questions on the small group Questioning Category Matrix—Advancing Lesson (Web Supplement 5E) and evaluate the questions for their usefulness in helping them understand the text on the Question Evaluation Graphic Organizer (Web Supplement 5F).

Student Practice Procedures

1. Make a group decision about how to read the book.
2. Pause after reading each page.
3. Ask questions before, during, and after reading. (Use three different-colored markers.)
4. Determine question categories.
5. Take turns writing the questions on the group category matrix.
6. Discuss questions as a group.
7. Record answers as notes.
8. Complete an individual question evaluation graphic organizer.

Guided Practice

Educators monitor students' ability to read the text. They support struggling readers as well as monitor students' ability to pause the reading to pose, to categorize, and to record questions.

When students have completed their small group matrices, educators monitor students' discussions about the most useful question in each category. Students record their individual choices for most useful questions on the Question Evaluation Graphic Organizer (Web Supplement 5F).

Closure

Combine students from two groups into one. Share questions. Did groups ask the same questions before, during, and after reading? Which question was most useful for each reader in each category?

Reflection

How did questioning help us comprehend the text? Did both groups ask the same questions before, during, and after reading? Did we all agree on the most useful question in each category?

Extensions Conduct an inquiry based on the students' unanswered questions. This extension can be conducted with both educators facilitating. It can also be conducted in the library with small groups, giving the classroom teacher the option to work with the other students in the classroom.

Provide students with lessons that prompt them to engage in asking before, during, and after questions while learning with other media. Films and websites on science and social studies topics may be especially effective.

READING COMPREHENSION STRATEGY
Questioning

Reading Development Level Advanced

Instructional Strategies Cues and Questions and Classifying

Lesson Length 3–5 sessions

Purpose The purpose of this lesson is to use questioning before, during, and after reading a historical fiction picture book, to prompt a deeper investigation into two historical figures, and to continue to use questioning strategies while reading biographies in order to understand the lives and contributions of these two people. Rather than concentrating on answering questions per se, recording questions and coding them for "on the line" answers, "between the lines" answers, or "unanswered" questions is the focus in this QAR (question-answer relationships) lesson.

Objectives After reading *Amelia and Eleanor Go for a Ride* and a biography, students will be able to

1. Pose questions before, during, and after reading a historical fiction text.

2. Code question-answer relationships during and after reading.

3. Identify primary source documents.

Resources, Materials, and Equipment *Amelia and Eleanor Go for a Ride*, by Pam Muñoz Ryan, illustrated by Brian Selznick

Amelia Earhart, by Jonatha A. Brown

Eleanor Roosevelt, by Jonatha A. Brown

Graphic Organizers: Teacher Resource: QAR Category Matrix (Web Supplement 5G), QAR Category Matrix (Web Supplement 5H)

Materials: Highlighters of three different colors for students and educators

Overhead, data projector, or interactive whiteboard

Collaboration While one educator reads the historical fiction book, the other records questions before, during, and after reading on a category matrix. After recording questions, one educator reads the author's note. The educators then code the questions based on the location of the answers ("on the line," "between the lines," or "unanswered"). A completed sample QAR matrix is provided.

Educators divide the class in half and continue to practice questioning and categorizing questions while reading brief biographies. Students code the questions and determine what questions are unanswered. Educators facilitate a discussion comparing the two groups' QAR category matrices and unanswered questions.

Assessment The students' category matrices show their use of questioning to achieve comprehension. Educators must establish criteria for the quality of completed matrices.

Standards *Reading keywords:* ask relevant questions in order to comprehend; locate facts in response to questions about expository text

Social studies keywords: use primary source material; retell stories to describe past events

Information literacy keywords: select information appropriate to the problem or question at hand; organize information for practical application

Process

Day 1

Motivation

Cues and Questions: Have women in our country always been able to do the same things men do? Brainstorm a list of things men can do in the United States, such as driving cars, flying airplanes, voting, and being elected president. Can women do these things too? When do you think these activities were commonplace for women? What about being elected president? When do you think that might happen?

Student-Friendly Objectives

1. Pose questions before, during, and after reading.
2. Code for question-answer relationships during and after reading.
3. Discuss how to answer unanswered questions.

Presentation

Review the definition of historical fiction and identify *Amelia and Eleanor Go for a Ride* as a historical fiction book. Provide cues before reading by utilizing questioning to explore the book covers. (Web Supplement 5G is a completed QAR category matrix.) One educator reads the book while the other records before, during, and after questions on the class-sized QAR Category Matrix (Web Supplement 5H).

Both educators pose questions using a think-aloud process, identify the question category, and code the answers as "on the line," "between the lines," or "unanswered." While reading and recording questions, the educators model discussing how questioning helps readers become actively involved in understanding the text. If educators feel it is important to record the answer as well, they record the answers in parentheses as notes. Review the types of notes (figure 2-1 or Web Supplement 2A).

Closure

Review the questions asked and codes and note unanswered questions. Ask how readers can learn more about Amelia Earhart and Eleanor Roosevelt.

Day 2

Divide the class in half. Each half is responsible for posing questions while listening to a brief biography about Amelia Earhart or Eleanor Roosevelt. Students record questions on individual QAR Category Matrices (Web Supplement 5H).

Motivation

Cues: What is the difference between historical fiction and biography? Identify the text as a biography. Read the table of contents. Conduct a bookwalk with a focus on viewing and discussing the illustrations and reading the captions. Notice and define the primary source documents contained in the text.

Student-Friendly Objectives

1. Pose questions before, during, and after reading an informational text.
2. Categorize and record questions before, during, and after reading.
3. Code questions during and after reading.
4. Discuss how to answer unanswered questions.

Presentation

Read the information on the back of the book cover. Project the QAR Category Matrix (Web Supplement 5H). Ask students to provide their own cues before reading by asking questions to prepare themselves to read the text. Categorize the questions and record on the matrix. Students copy questions in the appropriate category on their individual QAR category matrices. As the educator reads the text, students continue asking questions, categorize them, and record them on their individual matrices.

If necessary, educators use the think-aloud process to review and model questioning and categorize the questions during and after the reading. If more support is needed, the educator can also record questions for students to copy.

Student Practice Procedures

1. Raise hand to pause the reading and ask a question.
2. Categorize and record questions on QAR category matrix during and after reading.

Guided Practice

Educators monitor students' questioning and their identification of categories.

Closure

After reading, review the questions posed before, during, and after reading.

Day 3 ### Motivation

Bring both groups together. Pose questions: Do you always find the answers to questions stated "on the line" in a text? Are some answers found "between the lines"? What does that mean? What do we do with "unanswered" questions? Why is it important to know the source of the answer to a question? How does this help you find answers to specific questions?

Student-Friendly Objectives

1. Use highlighters of three different colors to code questions by relationship to the answer.
2. Tabulate the number of each type.

Presentation

Using examples from the "before reading" questions, the educators use think-alouds to identify and circle questions that were answered "on the line" with one color highlighter, questions that were answered "between the lines" with another color, and "unanswered" questions with a third color. Students copy the educators' work by appropriately highlighting questions in the "before reading" category on their own matrices. Tabulate the number of questions in each category and note it at the bottom of the page.

Student Practice Procedures

1. Circle "on the line" questions with one color of highlighter.
2. Circle "between the lines" questions with another color.
3. Circle "unanswered" questions with a third color.
4. Tabulate the number of each type of QAR.

Guided Practice

Students code "during" and "after" reading questions on their own. Educators monitor for correct identification of QAR.

Presentation

Pair the students, one from each biography group. To demonstrate partner work, educators model taking turns sharing one "before," one "during," and one "after" question and telling where the answer was found, if it was found. Then they tell the most important thing they learned and one unanswered question about Amelia Earhart or Eleanor Roosevelt.

Student Participation Procedures

1. Take turns.

2. Share one before, one during, and one after question.

3. Share where, or if, the answer was found.

4. Share one important new idea.

5. Share one unanswered question.

Closure

Review the characteristics of historical fiction and biographies. What is a primary source document? Discuss the use of QAR as support for comprehension, for conducting research or inquiry projects, and as a valuable test-taking skill.

Reflection

How did asking questions before, during, and after reading keep us engaged with the text? How did questions help us comprehend these texts? What can readers do with the unanswered questions?

Extensions   Working with a classmate from the other group, students can work in pairs to write a historical fiction dialogue between these two women. Fold a sheet of lined paper in half; each student writes on one half. The students take turns asking and answering each other's questions as well as sharing ideas based on the information they learned from hearing these texts. This procedure can be done electronically as well by setting up a document with a two-column table and multiple rows. Students can then keyboard their dialogues, each using one of the columns.

Provide students with additional lessons that prompt them to ask questions before, during, and after learning from multimedia resources. The Library of Congress's American Memory Project provides lessons by themes, topics, disciplines, and eras. Several may be particularly engaging for advanced readers: Artifact Road Show, Journeys West, American Dreams, and Voices for Votes: Suffrage Strategies. Access them at http://memory.loc.gov/learn/lessons/theme.html.

6

Reading Comprehension Strategy Four
Making Predictions and Inferences

When the fox opened the door, there stood a delicious-looking piglet.
"Oh, no!" screamed the piglet.
"Oh, yes!" cried the fox. "You've come to the right place."

—From *My Lucky Day,* by Keiko Kasza

Activating Background Knowledge

Using Sensory Images

Questioning

Making Predictions and Inferences

Determining Main Ideas

Using Fix-Up Options

Synthesizing

As they read and pose questions, readers often find themselves answering their own questions with predictions about what will happen next or with inferences drawn from the author's or illustrator's creations. The "on the line" strategy of predicting and the "between the lines" strategy of inferring prompt readers to turn the page to find out if their hypotheses are correct. Predictions are educated guesses about what will happen next based on what is known from reading the text; prediction can also involve readers' background knowledge. Inferences require that readers go beyond literal meaning; they use the print and illustrations plus their prior knowledge and experience to interpret the text. Through these processes, readers find clues or connecting points, make predictions or inferences, and draw conclusions. These conclusions or interpretations are a critical part of reading comprehension. Readers who make predictions and inferences before, during, and after they read are actively engaged in the meaning-making process.

Accomplished authors and illustrators of well-constructed picture books, chapter books, and novels have respect for the knowledge readers bring to the literary experience. They leave clues for readers to lead them on throughout the reading journey. They rely on readers to flesh out their texts by making connections between clues and readers' own background knowledge, values, and beliefs. The importance of prediction and inference in reading comprehension stems from the transactional nature of the reading event. If we understand reading as a transaction between a text, a reader, and the context in which the work is experienced, then the literal denotation of the words on the page and the content of the illustrations are only part of the story. For the transaction to occur, the reader must interpret the text. The unique interpretation of each reader is then an essential component of comprehension. As Meek suggests, "What is happening to the reader is as important as the text itself" (1988, 37).

This perspective honors the role of the reader in making meaning. It suggests that unique interpretations are valued and invaluable. When designing literature engagements, educators foster personalized interpretations by using a reading transaction framework that allows for multiple interpretations. As students immerse themselves in the deeper "between the lines" meanings of texts, they come to think of reading as a "lived-through" experience (Rosenblatt 1995). Just like a trip to the park or to a museum, reading a book is an event to be experienced, an event on which one can reflect and from which one can learn.

By sharing their unique responses to what they read, students who discuss their reading with partners or within literature circles learn that there are multiple perspectives that can mirror and enrich, or contradict or contrast with, their own interpretations of a work. A collaborative social context for talking about books gives readers a place for engaging in discussions and sharing interpretations. Book discussions can become a central part of life in the classroom and in the library (on facilitating literature circles, see Short and Pierce 1990).

Teaching inference strategy can be quite personally rewarding for both students and educators. Readers are often asked to interact with the literal meanings on the pages, but inference requires that each reader consider her own beliefs, values, and experiences before drawing conclusions. "To push beyond the literal text, to make it personal and three-dimensional, to weave it into our own stories—that is to infer" (Keene and Zimmermann 1997, 152). Readers must take the information provided by the author or illustrator and pass it through their own worldviews in order to determine what makes sense for them. By definition, inference requires that each reader construct a meaning that makes the text a reflection of her experience. In this way, the text becomes integrated into a reader's schema or background knowledge and holds the potential to change that schema. Readers who excel at inference may actually experience a sense of rewriting the text as they read. What better way could there be to feel co-ownership along with the author and illustrator? Through this deep comprehension process, a reader's newly made meanings are more personal, more personally valued, and longer remembered.

Figure 6-1 uses the book *My Lucky Day* (Kasza) to show educators demonstrating prediction and inference that engage and propel the reader through the entire plotline of a text. Fiction, which allows for a wider variety of interpretations than informational texts, provides rich fodder for exploring and practicing this strategy. All genres of fiction including fantasy, science fiction, historical fiction, and realistic fiction, mysteries in particular, can be selected to support teaching and learning prediction and inference.

As we teach inference strategy, we first model and then invite readers to connect profoundly, rather than superficially, with texts. Like an elephant using its head, we ask readers to use all of their mental faculties to think between the words and to think between the lines and through the images offered on the page or screen. Before they can make predictions or inferences, readers must bring together the text and the sum total of their prior knowledge. They must use their heads to their fullest potential.

How to Teach the Strategy

We can think of making predictions and inferences as specific types of questioning strategies. Predicting

FIGURE 6-1

Predicting and Inferring Before, During, and After Reading

Text: *My Lucky Day*, by Keiko Kasza

Before Reading: Predictions and Inferences Related to the Front and Back Covers

One educator reads the title of the book and the author-illustrator's name. The other educator makes inferences and predictions based on the front (A) and back covers (B) of the book.

A: I'm thinking about the title of the book. Whose "lucky day" is it? The fox has a "lucky" look on his face, but so does the pig. My background knowledge tells me that when foxes (or wolves) and pigs get together, it's the pigs who get eaten. I can infer that the pig doesn't fully understand the situation.

B: On the back of the book, there's a painting of the fox that makes him look exhausted. It may be difficult for him to get the pig, but, in the end, I predict the pig is going to get eaten by the fox.

During Reading: Predictions and Inferences from the First Few Pages

On the first page, the fox is sharpening his claws. He's reading a book that's opened to a page entitled "Hunting A-Z." He hears a knock at the door. I predict it's the pig. The fox can't eat the pig at the very beginning of the story so something unpredictable will happen.

On the wall, there are paintings of the fox holding different types of captured prey. I can infer from this that he is a successful hunter. Whoever is knocking on the door thinks a rabbit lives here. The fox says he would have eaten rabbits for breakfast. Author-illustrator Keiko Kasza wants us to infer that the fox will eat whoever is knocking on the door.

The author writes that the pig is "delicious-looking." She paints the pig with a surprised expression and with fright or sweat pouring off his head. The fox grabs the piglet and hauls him inside. Keiko Kasza wants us to think the fox will eat the pig.

The fox says pig roast is his favorite dinner. The pig's in trouble. I predict the pig will get eaten.

But the pig talks the fox into giving him a bath first. I'm wondering if my prediction is correct.

The fox ties up the pig while he prepares the bath. When the fox is scrubbing the pig, the pig compliments the fox. There's a boat floating in the tub. These two things make me think this story might not turn out the way most fox and pig stories do. I can infer that the pig is "outfoxing" the fox. He's getting the upper hand in this situation.

Ending and After Reading: Inference and Reflection

The piglet did have a lucky day. He got a bath, a dinner, and a massage. I can infer that he had planned this all along.

On the last page, the pig is eating a cookie the fox baked for him. He's looking at his address book to decide which animal to "visit" next. He's already crossed off the fox and the coyote; the wolf and bear are still on his list. The piglet did plan his visit to the fox. I predict he will visit the wolf next.

Ooops! He visits the bear next. The piglet looks scared, but the bear is awfully big. I wonder if the pig will be able to outsmart the bear.

Keiko Kasza surprised us by creating a story in which our predictions and inferences don't pan out the way we think they should. About halfway through the story, we realize that the piglet is very smart, and we change our predictions and inferences to make the piglet come out on top. At the end, she throws us off again, because we just can't be sure that a small piglet can really outsmart a huge bear.

By making predictions about what will happen next and using our background knowledge about pig and fox stories and by reading between the lines, we began to infer a different outcome. We were like detectives using the clues in the story. Our predictions and inferences made it fun to read on to find out if we were able to predict the outcome of the story correctly. The ending leaves us wondering if this story will repeat with the piglet coming out the winner or if the pig will get eaten by the bear this time.

---

and inferring can be at the word level, can be practiced at the sentence, paragraph, page, or chapter level, or can be accomplished through reflection at the end of a text. A variety of statements and questions can be used to prompt readers' explorations with prediction and inference:

- I predict that . . .
- My guess is that . . .
- I suspect that . . .
- I think this clue means that . . .
- I knew this would happen next because . . .

- I conclude that . . .

- What clues did the author or illustrator give readers?

- What do I see in my mind's eye that's not on the page?

- Why did that happen? What will happen next?

- What will happen next? Was I correct?

- What makes sense?

- What was the author trying to say in this story?

- What was the illustrator trying to show?

Educators can support students' practice of this strategy through the use of graphic organizers that require students to record their thinking. By providing evidence from the print or illustrations, students can "see" their own and their classmates' thought processes on paper. In figure 6-2 a category matrix specifies the evidence from the words and illustrations, the connecting background knowledge, and the resulting prediction or inference.

Some children's picture book authors and illustrators have created texts that in fact require readers to make predictions or inferences. *Once There Was a Bull . . . (frog)*, written by Rick Walton and illustrated by Greg Hally, is one such book. The

FIGURE 6-2
Locating Evidence in the Text for Predictions and Connecting Evidence
and Background Knowledge for Inferences

Text: *Two Bad Ants,* by Chris Van Allsburg

TEXT PROMPT	EVIDENCE (E) OR BACKGROUND KNOWLEDGE (BK)	PREDICTION (P) OR INFERENCE (I)
Crystals, queen ant loves taste, makes her happy	The white color and crystal shape suggest sugar. (E) Eating sweets makes people—and ants—happy. (BK)	Ants have discovered sugar. (I)
Boiling brown lake, tastes bitter	There is a spoon stirring a brown liquid. (E) Coffee is brown and bitter; people use sugar to make it sweeter. (BK)	Ants are in a cup of coffee. (I)
Cave	Nostrils and an upper lip are in the illustration. (E) A mouth is like a cave. People drink coffee. (BK)	Ants may be swallowed. (P)
Hiding place, red light, getting hotter, popped up, flying	A toaster is found in a kitchen; it's hot inside and toast pops up. (BK) Ants are being thrust out of a toaster. (E)	They will land somewhere in the kitchen. (P)
Waterfall, shiny surface, rushing water	A kitchen faucet has these features. (BK)	Ants may be swept into the sink, down the drain. (P)
Chamber, with wet food, frightening sounds, spinning	A kitchen garbage disposal has these features. (BK) The illustration shows pieces of things flying through the air. (E)	Ants could have been chopped up and were lucky to escape. (I)
Dark cells, force shot through wet ants	The illustration shows an electrical plug. (E) Water near electricity is dangerous. (BK)	Ants could have been electrocuted. (I)
Footsteps, got in line	The illustration shows the smiling ants following a fellow ant into a hole in the ground. (E) When you have a close call, you aren't likely to do that behavior again. (BK)	The two bad ants won't risk any more adventures. (P) It's safer to travel in a group and to follow the rules. (I)

Making Predictions and Inferences

print on each page ends with the first half of a compound word that is completed on the next page. Sometimes the illustration provides clues to the second half of the word. Sometimes the illustration on the second page repeats a visual feature of the preceding page, which can be revisited if the reader wasn't able to predict correctly. For instance, the first page of the book ends with "bull . . ." The illustration on the next page includes a frog with a spiral-shaped tongue, reminiscent of the spiral-shaped tail of the bull on the first page. Sometimes a semantic cue plus background knowledge help the reader predict the next word. "He looked under a toad . . ." The word "under" helps the reader predict that the next page will begin with the word "stool"—since "under a toadstool" makes sense. Students can be invited to author and illustrate piggyback texts that use compound words to challenge their classmates' abilities to make predictions based on visual or semantic cues.

One simple way to help children understand the meaning of the words *predict* and *infer* is to use three- or four-panel cartoons. Visual images with a few or no words can help readers gain experience with logical sequences of thought and plot that characterize much of the reading they will do in their lives. Educators can share highly predictable cartoons such as those offered in figure 6-3. They can help readers identify the evidence in the image or words or their background knowledge that leads to the next frame—this is one way to have fun while practicing the basics of this strategy. Students can also be invited to create their own cartoons to test their ability to convey plot logically.

The smaller student-teacher ratio afforded by collaboration and coteaching greatly supports teaching and learning this strategy. Modeling for a whole group followed by small group mini-lessons and small group guided practice provides educators with insight into students' thinking or struggles with making inferences. The advanced sample lesson in this chapter suggests that small group practice be facilitated by the teacher-librarian or classroom teacher who can help students know when to stop and infer.

Making Literature Connections

Predicting

Predictable texts are a logical choice to build students' confidence in their ability to predict individual words or story elements. Rhyming poems and picture books offer readers opportunities to predict the word at the end of the next rhyming line. Educators can share texts students have not previously read to show them how the author or poet has constructed a predictable pattern through the use of rhyme. This can be fun for students, whether or not their hypotheses agree with the original. Educators can share their thinking as they model this important cognitive process. Mary Ann Hoberman and Michael Emberley have collaborated to create three eminently predictable and fun two-voice poetry titles based on readers' background knowledge of literacy experiences, fairy tales, and Mother Goose rhymes; each title begins with *You Read to Me, I'll Read to You*. To find rhyming fiction titles or rhyming poetry, conduct library catalog searches for "stories in rhyme" or "rhyming poems."

Books that count up such as *One Cow Moo Moo!* (Bennett/Cooke) and books that count down such as *Cha-Cha Chimps* (Durango/Taylor) or *Thunder Cake* (Polacco) also provide a pattern that story listeners and readers can soon identify. Books that follow predictable sequences, such as the seasons in *The Seasons of Arnold's Apple Tree* (Gibbons) or the days of the week in *Today Is Monday* (Carle), provide predictable patterns for readers who have this cultural knowledge. *Tomorrow's Alphabet* (Shannon/Crews) invites readers to play with the alphabet and challenges them to think and predict at the word level. By covering the right-hand page, readers can predict the surprises on every other page: "A is for seed—tomorrow's apple."

Patterned language books also provide support for predicting at the word or phrase level. Books like *Fortunately* (Charlip) and *That's Good, That's Bad* (Cuyler/Catrow) quickly establish a pattern to help readers anticipate the unfolding of the plot. Web Supplement 6A is a selected bibliography of timeless classics and newer patterned language books

FIGURE 6-3
Using Cartoons to Make Predictions or Inferences

Illustrations by Lauren Cleff

categorized as folktales, picture books, and songs. Cumulative stories, one type of patterned language book that builds as it repeats phrases, offer repetition that supports listeners and readers as they participate in read-alouds and then reread these texts on their own; *The Napping House* (Wood/Wood) and *The Parrot Tico Tango* (Witte) are two excellent examples. In addition, books with predictable plots and patterned language offer readers excellent writing prompts for composing piggyback texts.

Texts in which the illustrations provide clues to help readers predict the plot sequence offer critical support for this strategy. In classics such as *Rosie's Walk* (Hutchins) and *Come Away from the Water, Shirley* (Burningham) and newer titles such as *The Mitten* (Brett) and *Officer Buckle and Gloria* (Rathmann), the illustrations supply visual story lines that parallel or extend the authors' words. These texts simply cannot be understood without interpreting the images as well as the print.

Inferring

Inference, which allows readers to make their own meanings based on limited clues in the text, requires more sophistication than does prediction. Inferring meaning at the word level requires a significant amount of language experience. For students who are English speakers, books that include terms in other languages offer practice at inferring word meaning; students who are proficient speakers or readers of other languages can furnish the definitions after their English-dominant classmates have made their inferences. Beginning readers are both challenged and supported to infer the Spanish words in the Eight Animals series (Elya/Chapman). The Chato books (Soto/Guevera), which integrate Spanish words and Mexican American culture, are featured in the advancing lesson in this chapter. *The Boy Who Loved Words* (Schotter/Potter) challenges experienced readers to use visual and semantic cues to discover the meanings in Selig's rich word choices: "Selig stayed on the outskirts, always

on the *periphery*—listening and collecting delicious words."

Using Picture Storybooks to Teach Literary Devices (Hall 2002) provides an annotated list of books that stretch readers with their use of foreshadowing and inference. One excellent example is the Caldecott Award–winning classic *Where the Wild Things Are* (Sendak). Readers can infer the connection between Max's mischief and the "wild things" he tames; some readers will make connections to their own misbehavior and the resulting consequences. Even though his mother sent him away without his supper, readers can assume that Max is loved because someone brings his supper to his room. Surely it was his mom. Readers can also infer that Max's adventure to the land where the wild things are was just a brief imaginative journey, because when he returns his supper is still warm. Authors and illustrators that stretch readers to make inferences give them opportunities to achieve the satisfaction that comes from thinking deeply about texts as they engage in making meaning.

Identifying the theme of a story is arguably the ultimate inference. Unless specifically stated, readers must infer the author's or illustrator's intended message; Hall (2002) also provides annotated examples for the study of theme. A theme is an overall meaning that is left with the reader; as such, themes can be uniquely expressed. Sometimes themes are described as lessons, but many times the theme of a story is much more allusive. For example, *Fly Away Home* (Bunting/Himler) is a moving story about a homeless boy and his father who live in an airport. The book could prompt students to generate themes related to social topics such as homelessness, to life skills such as perseverance, to moral concepts such as fairness, or to human desires such as hope, among others. Asking students to flesh out these topics and to express themes in one complete sentence (figure 6-4) helps them specify the emotional impact of a particular text. Conversations around theme present readers with ideas for rich discussions.

The Mysteries of Harris Burdick (Van Allsburg) is perhaps one of the most sophisticated picture books that students can use to practice inference. Each double-page spread provides readers with a title, a couple lines of print, and an illustration that all beg to be interpreted. Readers can write entire stories based on the clues in the text. They can also be asked to justify their stories by identifying the clues in the print and illustrations plus the background knowledge that led them to their unique interpretations. Instead of or in addition to writing, students can be invited to draw the next picture or sequence of pictures in the story as they imagine them.

Cartoons are another format that supports readers' use of prediction and inference to achieve comprehension. The antics of Jim Davis's *Garfield* and Charles Schulz's *Peanuts* characters have long been popular with young readers. Like their comic book cousins, stand-alone books such as *No Friends* (Stevenson) and *Meanwhile . . .* (Feiffer) also draw readers into anticipating and predicting the event in the next frame of the story. With the rise of the graphic novel for older students and adults, this genre is ever more widely available in elementary school and public libraries. Like the examples in figure 6-3, educators can use published comics to support students in practicing making predictions.

FIGURE 6-4
Examples of One-Sentence Themes

Text: *Fly Away Home,* by Eve Bunting, illustrated by Ronald Himler

TOPIC	ONE-SENTENCE THEME
Homelessness	Every person deserves to have a home.
Perseverance	No matter how difficult your life seems, never give up trying to improve your situation.
Fairness	Unfortunately, life can be unfair.
Hope	If you keep hope in your heart, you may find a way out of an unhappy situation.

Conduct a word search for "cartoons and comics" in the online catalog.

Summary

Predicting and inferring before, during, and after reading are comprehension strategies that can appeal to readers' sense of adventure and challenge. Some authors and illustrators have created texts that capitalize on these aspects of reading. Educators have a critical role in identifying exemplary texts that help students practice these strategies. When readers read on to test their hypotheses, their motivation, level of engagement, and enjoyment of texts can increase significantly. One important aspect of teaching prediction and inference is recognizing that whether readers' logical predictions or inferences match the authors' and illustrators' intentions is not as significant as the readers' active interaction with the text.

Through collaboration, educators can effectively design, implement, and assess lessons that demonstrate the use of prediction and inference. By lowering the student-to-teacher ratio at the point of instruction, educators can better monitor the students' thinking processes as well as their successful participation in cooperative learning strategies. These sophisticated strategies can best be practiced and learned via small group mini-lessons and small group guided practice. Working together, classroom teachers and teacher-librarians can effectively support students as they predict and infer both when they read and when they incorporate print and visual clues into the craft of their own writing and illustrating.

Children's Literature Cited

Starred titles are used in the lesson plans.

The Boy Who Loved Words, by Roni Schotter, illustrated by Giselle Potter

Cha-Cha Chimps, by Julia Durango, illustrated by Eleanor Taylor

*Chato and the Party Animals, by Gary Soto, illustrated by Susan Guevera

*Chato Goes Cruisin', by Gary Soto, illustrated by Susan Guevera

*Chato's Kitchen, by Gary Soto, illustrated by Susan Guevera

Come Away from the Water, Shirley, by John Burningham

Eight Animals Bake a Cake, by Susan Middleton Elya, illustrated by Lee Chapman

Eight Animals on the Town, by Susan Middleton Elya, illustrated by Lee Chapman

Eight Animals Play Ball, by Susan Middleton Elya, illustrated by Lee Chapman

Fly Away Home, by Eve Bunting, illustrated by Ronald Himler

Fortunately, by Remy Charlip

*Freedom Summer, by Deborah Wiles, illustrated by Jerome Lagarrigue

*Goin' Someplace Special, by Patricia McKissack, illustrated by Jerry Pinkney

*If You Give a Moose a Muffin, by Laura Numeroff, illustrated by Felicia Bond

*If You Give a Mouse a Cookie, by Laura Numeroff, illustrated by Felicia Bond

*If You Give a Pig a Pancake, by Laura Numeroff, illustrated by Felicia Bond

*If You Take a Mouse to School, by Laura Numeroff, illustrated by Felicia Bond

Meanwhile . . . , by Jules Feiffer

The Mitten, by Jan Brett

My Lucky Day, by Keiko Kasza

The Mysteries of Harris Burdick, by Chris Van Allsburg

The Napping House, by Audrey Wood, illustrated by Don Wood

No Friends, by James Stevenson

Officer Buckle and Gloria, by Peggy Rathmann

Once There Was a Bull . . . (frog), by Rick Walton, illustrated by Greg Hally

One Cow Moo Moo! by David Bennett, illustrated by Andy Cooke

The Parrot Tico Tango, by Anna Witte

Rosie's Walk, by Pat Hutchins

The Seasons of Arnold's Apple Tree, by Gail Gibbons

*Teammates, by Peter Golenbock, illustrated by Paul Bacon

That's Good, That's Bad, by Margery Cuyler, illustrated by David Catrow

Thunder Cake, by Patricia Polacco

Today Is Monday, by Eric Carle

Tomorrow's Alphabet, by George Shannon, illustrated by Donald Crews

Two Bad Ants, by Chris Van Allsburg

*The Unbreakable Code, by Sara Hoagland Hunter, illustrated by Julia Miner

*Voices of the Alamo, by Sherry Garland, illustrated by Ronald Himler

Where the Wild Things Are, by Maurice Sendak

You Read to Me, I'll Read to You: Very Short Fairy Tales to Read Together (in Which Wolves Are Tamed, Trolls Are Transformed, and Peas Are Triumphant), by Mary Ann Hoberman, illustrated by Michael Emberley

You Read to Me, I'll Read to You: Very Short Mother Goose Tales to Read Together, by Mary Ann Hoberman, illustrated by Michael Emberley

You Read to Me, I'll Read to You: Very Short Stories to Read Together, by Mary Ann Hoberman, illustrated by Michael Emberley

Lesson Plans

Predicting and inferring are similar to questioning in that students must be given opportunities to explore fully their individual thinking and connections. A smaller student-to-teacher ratio allows educators to maximize interaction before, during, and after reading. Educators provide think-aloud strategies to demonstrate how to utilize reading comprehension strategies to improve their own understanding of text. Although graphic organizers are provided for recording predictions and inferences, students can also use large sticky notes to record their ideas and place them on the book covers or pages of the text where they found evidence, made connections, and made their predictions or inferences.

Each sample lesson focuses on a different aspect of prediction and inference. The emerging lesson is based on making logical predictions. The advancing lesson focuses on inferring the meanings of Spanish words as well as making predictions about plot development. In the advanced lesson, which uses historical fiction picture books from the Thematic Text Set (Web Supplement 3A), students have the opportunity to infer themes. Students reading at the advanced and advancing levels may benefit from participating in the lessons designed for less developed readers.

READING COMPREHENSION STRATEGY
Making Predictions

Reading Development Level	Emerging
Instructional Strategies	Nonlinguistic Representation and Cooperative Learning
Lesson Length	2 sessions
Purpose	The purpose of this lesson is to practice making predictions while reading a text, to record predictions in picture format on a storyboard, and to retell the story in sequence.
Objectives	After reading at least two books from the Numeroff/Bond series, students will be able to

1. Make logical predictions based on the information presented in the text.
2. Record their predictions as nonlinguistic representations in storyboard format.
3. Retell the story in sequence using their own predictions, which may or may not match those found in the original text.

Resources, Materials, and Equipment	*If You Give a Mouse a Cookie,* by Laura Numeroff, illustrated by Felicia Bond

If You Give a Moose a Muffin, If You Give a Pig a Pancake, or *If You Take a Mouse to School,* by Numeroff and Bond. Gather multiple copies of two of these titles. Note: Not all books in this series are ideal for this lesson.

Graphic Organizers: Using Cartoons to Make Predictions or Inferences (Web Supplement 6B), Teacher Resource: Storyboard for Numeroff/Bond Series (Web Supplement 6C), Storyboard for Numeroff/Bond Series (Web Supplement 6D), and Storyboard Self-Assessment Rubric (Web Supplement 6E)

Materials: 11" by 17" sheet of white construction or legal paper folded into sixteen rectangles, pencils, and crayons

Overhead, data projector, or interactive whiteboard

Collaboration	Educators model for the entire class. Then they divide the class in half and into partner groups as students practice making and recording predictions and retelling the stories.
Assessment	Students self-assess their predictions (storyboard) and retelling using a rubric.
Standards	*Reading keywords:* predict; sequence a series of events; relate information in a text-to-life experience

Writing keywords: draw a picture or storyboard to show a sequence of events

Listening and speaking keywords: use effective vocabulary and logical organization to relate or summarize ideas, events, or information

Information literacy keywords: organize information for practical application; produce and communicate information and ideas in appropriate formats

Process	*Motivation*
Day 1	Project the Web Supplement 6B cartoons. Cover the final frame when presenting each cartoon. Ask the students: What do you think will happen next? Conduct a think-pair-share to predict the last frame of each cartoon. Then show the last frame. Discuss how readers make predictions on the basis of information in the text as they read.

Student-Friendly Objectives

1. Make predictions from the information in the text.
2. Draw predictions on the storyboard.
3. Retell the story using the storyboard.

Presentation

Read the title and examine the front cover of the anchor book, *If You Give a Mouse a Cookie.* (Use a big book if one is available.) Make a prediction about who the main character is in the story. Read the book from beginning to end. Review the book and discuss the logical sequence of the "gifts" the boy gives the mouse. Note that this is a circle story, one that begins and ends in the same way. Define the term *prediction* and talk about how readers can make predictions as they read in order to be active readers.

Choose another Numeroff/Bond text from those listed in the resources section. Record the book title in the first frame of a class-sized Storyboard (Web Supplement 6D). Using the title and book jacket illustration, make a prediction about the main character and record/draw the character in the second frame. (Supplement 6C is a completed teacher resource for four Numeroff/Bond titles.)

One educator reads the book. Cover the right-hand side of each page with a piece of paper before reading the print on either side of the page. The other educator records one prediction for each double-paged spread on a class-sized storyboard graphic organizer.

Before turning each page, think aloud about what the next gift could be. Talk about how readers use their background knowledge to make predictions. Record the prediction before turning the page. Ask: Did the prediction make sense? (For instance, in *If You Give a Mouse a Cookie,* apple juice is as valid a prediction as a glass of milk.) In the third frame, record the first "gift" both in print and as a nonlinguistic representation. Read the next two-page spread, think aloud to predict, record the prediction, and check the prediction.

After a few pages, involve the students in making predictions.

Student Participation Procedure

1. Think-pair-share.
2. Raise hand to share a prediction with the class.
3. Ask: Does this prediction make sense?

Guided Practice

If students are unable to make a prediction, turn the page with the right-hand side covered. Read the left-hand side and attempt another prediction. If no prediction seems logical, read the introductory phrase or introductory sentence on the right-hand page and then attempt a prediction. Once a prediction is made, draw or record it on the class-sized storyboard. Continue this process throughout the reading. (It is important to demonstrate predictions that don't match the text as well as ones that do.)

Closure

After reading the entire book, one educator uses the storyboard to retell the class version of the story, which may or may not match the published version. Then project the Storyboard Self-Assessment Rubric (Web Supplement 6E). Assess the storyboard and the retelling using the rubric.

Day 2   *Presentation*

Review the class-sized storyboard from the previous day. Discuss how predictions were made from background knowledge plus information in the text.

Divide the class in half. Divide the students into partner groupings. Give each group one of two remaining Numeroff/Bond titles, a piece of paper to cover the right-hand side of each double-page spread, and a storyboard for each student (Supplement 6D).

The educator reads the book. She stops at the end of each two-page spread to allow students to work with their partners to make and record predictions. Students must wait to turn the page and cover the right-hand side of each page before turning the page. Explain the practice procedures.

Student Practice Procedures

1. Record the title in the first frame.
2. Record the main character in the second frame.
3. Record the first gift in the third frame.
4. Make predictions by whispering to your partner.
5. Record your prediction by drawing or writing.
6. Move the cover sheet to the next page.
7. Wait until the teacher says to turn the page.
8. One finger up if prediction matched the one in the book. Two fingers up if it did not match.

Guided Practice

Educators monitor students' predictions and ask them questions related to the logic of their predictions.

Closure

Bring the two groups back together. Form an inside-outside circle with a group that read one book on the inside and the group that read the other book on the outside. Students retell their stories using their storyboards. Ask new partners to tell how to make a prediction while reading. If appropriate, rotate one circle to the left or right for additional retellings.

Students self-assess their storyboards and retellings (Web Supplement 6E).

Reflection

How do we make predictions when we read? Did we all make the same predictions? How did predicting help us stay interested in the story?

Homework

At the completion of this lesson, students may take home their storyboards and retell the story to a sibling, parent, or caregiver. As they retell the story, they can engage listeners in making predictions about what comes next. The educators should review this process just before students take home their storyboards.

Extension   Students can compose piggyback texts based on the Numeroff/Bond stories. They can challenge classmates to use a storyboard graphic organizer to make predictions about each others' student-made texts.

Making Predictions and Inferences

Reading Development Level	Advancing
Instructional Strategies	Cues, Notemaking, and Cooperative Learning
Lesson Length	2 sessions
Purpose	The purpose of this lesson is to infer the meanings of Spanish words and to make predictions about plot while reading a predominantly English text.
Objectives	After reading two or more books from the Chato series, students will be able to

1. Infer Spanish word meanings from their context and compare their inferences with the definitions found in the glossary.

2. Combine evidence in the text with their own background knowledge to make and record predictions as they read the text.

3. Record evidence or predictions as notes.

Collaboration	The educators model the strategy and then divide the class in half for the guided practice. If multiple copies of the book are available and students are able to read the texts independently, students can conduct the guided practice in small groups with both educators monitoring.
Resources, Materials, and Equipment	*Chato's Kitchen, Chato and the Party Animals,* and *Chato Goes Cruisin',* by Gary Soto, illustrated by Susan Guevera (Multiple copies of *Chato and the Party Animals* for partner work)

Graphic Organizers: Teacher Resource: Vocabulary Cues and Predictions/Inferences Graphic Organizer (for *Chato's Kitchen*) (Web Supplement 6F), Vocabulary Cues and Predictions/Inferences Graphic Organizer (for *Chato's Kitchen*) (Web Supplement 6G), Teacher Resource: Vocabulary Cues and Predictions/Inferences Graphic Organizer (for *Chato and the Party Animals*) (Web Supplement 6H), Vocabulary Cues and Predictions/Inferences Graphic Organizer (for *Chato and the Party Animals*) (Web Supplement 6I)

Overhead, data projector, or interactive whiteboard

Assessment	The students' partner work assesses their ability to make predictions and inferences before and during reading. Educators should set criteria for assessing the completeness of graphic organizers.
Standards	*Reading keywords:* make or draw inferences; use context to determine the relevant meaning of a word; locate specific information by using organizational features of text (glossary); describe the cultural aspects found in cross-cultural literature

Social studies: use stories to describe past events and cultures; examples of individual actions, character, and values

Information literacy keywords: organize information for practical application; derive meaning from information presented creatively in a variety of formats

Process	*Motivation*
Day 1	Show the book jacket of *Chato's Kitchen,* the anchor book for this lesson. *Chato* rhymes with *gato. Gato* is a Spanish word that means "cat." How can one infer that the cat is the main character is this book? Define the word *inference* as clues

or evidence in the text plus background knowledge. Look at the back jacket of the book. Notice the words written on the signs. Are these English words? Where do you see Spanish words? If you do not speak, read, or write in Spanish, how do you know what Spanish words mean?

Discuss the idea of using clues plus background knowledge or experience like a detective uses clues and prior experiences to solve crimes. Ask students to think of themselves as word detectives as they infer the meanings of Spanish words and draw inferences about the meaning between the lines or make predictions about what will happen next in the story. (Educators can dress as detectives to dramatize this connection.) Post this formula: Stop + Examine Clues + Connect to Background Knowledge = Make Inferences or Predictions.

Student-Friendly Objectives

1. Infer Spanish word meanings from their context.
2. Compare inferences with definitions found in the glossary.
3. Make and record predictions about what will happen next while reading.

Presentation

Cues: Project and read through the Spanish words on the Vocabulary Cues and Predictions/Inferences Graphic Organizer (Web Supplement 6G). Ask students to guess the meanings of the words by relating them to English words. (If there are Spanish speakers/readers in the class, give them the opportunity to share the meaning of each word during the reading.) Record students' guesses as notes. Review the types of notes (figure 2-1 or Web Supplement 2A). Open the book to the glossary and Chato's menu. Notice there is a list of Spanish words and their English translations. (Web Supplement 6F is a completed teacher resource for this text.)

While reading, infer the meaning of the Spanish words by their context, how they are used in the sentence and in the story. (Do not consult Spanish-speaking classmates or the glossary until after students have attempted inferences. If the temporary meaning suffices, ask listeners to wait until the end of the reading to consult the Spanish-language experts or the glossary.) Also make predictions about what will happen next while reading the story.

One educator reads *Chato's Kitchen* while the other records inferences about Spanish words and predictions about the story on a class-sized graphic organizer (Web Supplement 6G). Educators use think-alouds to model inferring Spanish word meanings. (If there are other words unknown to the listeners, model the process of inferring their meanings and add them to the graphic organizer.)

Stop to think aloud and make predictions about the story plot. Think aloud about why this is a good time to make a prediction. Clarify the connections among evidence in the text, background knowledge, and making a prediction. Record evidence, background knowledge, and predictions in notemaking format on the class-sized graphic organizer.

Closure

After reading, revisit the Spanish words. Ask Spanish-speaking students to provide the meanings of words they know, or consult the glossary. Compare the inferred meanings with the definitions given by classmates or those found in the glossary. Review the predictions. Were they logical?

Day 2 *Presentation*

Divide the class in half. Partner students and give each team a Vocabulary Cues and Predictions/Inferences Graphic Organizer (Web Supplement 6I). Each educator works with half the class to read *Chato and the Party Animals*. The educator reads aloud or, if students can read this text on their own, provide them with a copy for every team of two. (Web Supplement 6H is a completed teacher resource for this text.)

Review the process used by word and story detectives: Stop + Examine Clues + Connect to Background Knowledge = Make Inferences or Predictions. If necessary, review the types of notes (figure 2-1 or Web Supplement 2A). Review the following practice procedures.

Student Practice Procedures

1. Read the Spanish words and infer their meanings before reading.

2. Read the story and stop at Spanish words.

3. Think-pair-share and take turns recording the inferred meanings on the graphic organizer.

4. Make predictions while reading and record them as notes on the graphic organizer.

5. Review Spanish words and record definitions from classmates or from the glossary.

Guided Practice

Educators monitor students' ability to infer the meanings of Spanish words and make predictions by combining evidence in the text and their own background knowledge. Educators make sure that partners are taking turns as they record their inferences. They also monitor students' ability to know when to pause the reading to make predictions about the plot.

Closure

Regroup the entire class of students in groups composed of two partner teams. Students compare their inferences and predictions. When did readers first suspect that the mice would one-up the cat?

Reflection

How do readers make inferences about the meanings of words in texts? Does this apply only to non-English words? How do readers make predictions? How do inferences and predictions help readers comprehend texts?

Extension   Using the same process, educators can challenge students to use inferences and predictions while reading the third title in the Chato series, *Chato Goes Cruisin'*. In addition, this book includes three-panel cartoons. Use sticky notes to cover all or part of the third panel. Ask students to record predictions on the sticky notes before reading or viewing the third panel.

Making Predictions and Inferences

Reading Development Level	Advanced
Instructional Strategies	Cues, Advanced Organizers, and Notemaking
Lesson Length	2–4 sessions
Purpose	The purpose of this lesson is to make inferences during and after reading historical fiction, biography, or informational picture books in order to determine individual themes for the story by combining evidence in the text with readers' background knowledge.
Objectives	After reading *Freedom Summer* and a historical fiction picture book from a thematic text set, students will be able to

1. Determine when to pause the reading to make an inference or prediction.
2. Combine specific evidence from the text with their background knowledge to make inferences.
3. Record evidence, background knowledge, and inferences in preparation for crafting original one-sentence themes.
4. Use notemaking format when appropriate.
5. Craft one-sentence themes.

Resources, Materials, and Equipment	*Freedom Summer,* by Deborah Wiles, illustrated by Jerome Lagarrigue
	Goin' Someplace Special, by Patricia McKissack, illustrated by Jerry Pinkney
	Teammates, by Peter Golenbock, illustrated by Paul Bacon
	The Unbreakable Code, by Sara Hoagland Hunter, illustrated by Julia Miner
	Voices of the Alamo, by Sherry Garland, illustrated by Ronald Himler
	Graphic Organizers: Anticipation Guide (Web Supplement 6J), Teacher Resource: Evidence–Background Knowledge–Inference Category Matrix (Web Supplement 6K), Evidence–Background Knowledge–Inference Category Matrix (Web Supplement 6L)
	Overhead, data projector, or interactive whiteboard
Collaboration	While one educator reads the anchor book, the other records both educators' evidence and inferences during and after reading on a class-sized category matrix. After reviewing the evidence, background knowledge, and inferences, each educator proposes a theme for the book. Although both educators can jointly monitor students' partner or small group guided practice, sending one or two small groups at a time to the library is the ideal organization of instruction for monitoring the sophistication required for learning this strategy.
Assessment	The students' category matrices show their use of evidence, background knowledge, and inferences to construct themes that indicate deep comprehension. Educators should set criteria for assessing the completeness of graphic organizers.
Standards	*Reading keywords:* make inferences; predictions; analyze for story elements (theme)
	Social studies keywords: recognize the relationship of events and people; discuss the connections between current events and historical events

Information literacy keywords: select information appropriate to the problem or question at hand; organize information for practical application

Process

Day 1

Motivation

What is a theme? Brainstorm possible themes for stories with which students are familiar. The following are two possible examples.

Story Title	*Possible Theme*
"Little Red Riding Hood"	Heed the warnings of your elders.
	Don't talk to strangers.
"The Tortoise and the Hare"	Slow and steady wins the race.
	You haven't won until you cross the finish line.

It is quite rare that an author writes, "The theme of this book is . . ." If the author does not tell the reader the theme, then the reader must read "between the lines" to discover a theme for herself. How do readers determine themes? Is there only one possible theme for every book? Collaboratively construct a definition of *theme.* (Example: A theme is the deeper meaning that a reader gives to a story.)

Distribute the Anticipation Guide (Web Supplement 6J). Ask students to read the possible one-sentence themes suggested for the book *Freedom Summer.* Under the "before reading" column, circle whether they agree or disagree with each statement. Let students know that they will reread and reassess the validity of the statements after reading the book as well.

Student-Friendly Objectives

1. Decide when to pause to make an inference or prediction.
2. Combine specific evidence from the text with background knowledge to make inferences.
3. Record evidence, background knowledge, and inferences as notes (when possible).
4. Craft a one-sentence theme at the end of the reading.

Presentation

Project a class-sized Evidence–Background Knowledge–Inference Category Matrix (Web Supplement 6L). Define each category. Evidence is "on the line" information; inferences are "between the lines" ideas. Discuss how inferences are constructed. Let students know that they will be using inferences to determine a theme for this book. (Web Supplement 6K is a completed category matrix.)

One educator reads the anchor book *Freedom Summer* while the other records evidence, background knowledge, and inferences. Pause the reading to make an inference or prediction. Ask: When do readers pause to make inferences? Readers pause to make inferences and predictions when they are unclear about the meaning of a word, phrase, or idea. Readers also pause when they think the author or illustrator has given them a clue to what will happen next. Educators think aloud to share why they paused the reading. They make notes on the matrix to record evidence in the text, their background knowledge, and their inferences. Review the types of notes (figure 2-1 or Web Supplement 2A).

At the end of the reading, each educator shares how he used the evidence in the text and his own background to make an inference and suggest a one-sentence theme. The other educator records the process on the matrix.

Ask the students to revisit the Anticipation Guide (Web Supplement 6J). Reread it. Did any event or the experiences of any character cause them to change their mind? Circle *agree* or *disagree* in the "after reading" column.

Students then prepare to compose a one-sentence theme for *Freedom Summer*. They can work individually or with a partner.

Student Practice Procedures

1. Select a piece of evidence from the text and record it on the graphic organizer.

2. Connect the evidence with background knowledge and record a note about it.

3. Restate one of the possible themes or compose an original one-sentence theme based on the inference.

Closure

Students share their themes in small groups or with the entire class. Read the author's note found at the beginning of the book, which explains her motivation for writing this story.

Booktalk the historical fiction titles from the text set. Ask students to record their first- and second-choice books.

Day 2   ### Student-Friendly Objectives

Same as previous.

Note: Depending on the number of books available, divide the class into partners or small groups based on their preferences and the educators' judgments about cooperative groupings. Although the educators can cofacilitate students' guided practice, it is ideal to send one or two small groups at a time to the library to work with the teacher-librarian while the classroom teacher works with the remainder of the students in the classroom on another inference lesson or other content as needed.

Presentation

Distribute books and provide an individual Evidence–Background Knowledge–Inference Category Matrix (Web Supplement 6L) to each student.

Review ideas about when readers pause in their reading to make inferences and predictions. Review how inferences are made. Review the class-sized Evidence–Background Knowledge–Inference Category Matrix (Web Supplement 6L). Ask students to list the steps for making an inference and put them on the overhead or board for students' reference.

Student Practice Procedures

Same as previous.

Guided Practice

Educator(s) monitor students' reading, pausing to make inferences and record information on the category matrix. Monitor for comprehensible notes and notemaking format. After students complete the reading, educator(s) support them in crafting themes.

Closure

After reading, ask students to share the process of making inferences and developing one-sentence themes. Students can share their themes in small groups or with the entire class unless educators decide to engage students in the extension of this lesson.

Reflection

How did making inferences during and after reading keep us engaged with the text? How did inferences help us craft one-sentence themes? Do all readers make the same inferences? Do all readers come away from a text with the same theme?

Extension   Students can use their one-sentence themes to create an anticipation guide and exchange it with a group that has not yet read the book they explored. The groups can be paired and then repeat the process of this lesson. After reading, inferring, and crafting themes, both groups can come together to share their interpretations of the texts.

7 Reading Comprehension Strategy Five
Determining Main Ideas

But the important thing about a spoon is that you eat with it.

—From *The Important Book,* by Margaret Wise Brown,
illustrated by Leonard Weisgard

Activating Background Knowledge

Using Sensory Images

Questioning

Making Predictions and Inferences

Determining Main Ideas

Using Fix-Up Options

Synthesizing

As information specialists, teacher-librarians are acutely aware of the challenges students face when they are confronted with an excess of information. It isn't easy for proficient adult readers to sift through the daily barrage of data to determine what is important; for children it can be truly daunting. Today's students, "millennials" who were born into the Information Age, may not be aware of the distinctions that can and should be drawn between data, information, knowledge, and wisdom. To be useful, data must be organized into something accessible as information. Information is only a set of facts until someone determines its importance, internalizes it, and turns it into knowledge through use. And though we may not all agree on the manifestations of wisdom, we do know it requires an accumulation of knowledge and the ability to discern connections and relationships. Sorting out these distinctions is critical for students, for workers, and for citizens of this century. It is important that educators scaffold students' formal experiences with mining information so they can transfer this knowledge to outside-of-school experiences.

Main ideas are always dependent on the purpose of a reading. If students are reading fictional texts and exploring story elements, then characters, setting, plot, and theme are the main ideas; figure 3-3 shows a matrix for studying story elements using

Cinderella variants. Although there may be correct answers for some story elements in a narrative frame, we noted in chapter 6 that themes are inferred main ideas. When different readers interpret the text, they may determine different themes. Although students must be taught to look for main ideas as defined on standardized tests, there is rarely one absolute main idea for any given text. Distinguishing what is most important from what is somewhat or less important requires readers to pass new information through their prior understandings. Readers must determine what can be forgotten and make judgments about what should be remembered and integrated into their schemas.

The reader's purpose for a reading lies at the center of this process. If someone is reading an informational text for the latest, most unusual scientific discovery to satisfy his own curiosity, he will most likely focus on a different main idea than if he were conducting research for a five-page report or studying for a science exam. If reading to find the main idea in a passage on a standardized test, the reader will look for the best answer from the test maker's perspective. While practicing and applying this strategy, readers have the opportunity to use evaluation, a higher-order thinking skill.

Main ideas can be determined at the whole text, chapter, page, passage, paragraph, or sentence (word) level. In *Mosaic of Thought,* Keene and Zimmermann (1997) discuss *considerate* and *inconsiderate* texts in the context of readers searching for main ideas. A considerate text is one that provides support or scaffolds readers' access to the important parts; inconsiderate texts do not. In many fictional texts, clearly presented story elements offer such a framework. There are main and minor characters. There is a setting that includes time and place. There is a plot that rises and falls with a clear beginning, middle, and end. There is a conflict and some sort of resolution. There is a central theme that ties the story together. When readers understand the narrative frame that gives these texts structure, they are able to use it as a guide to determine the main ideas. Story maps and character maps are two graphic organizers that can help readers develop a strong sense of narrative structure. (Readers use these tools in the advancing lesson in this chapter.)

Whereas fiction texts are structured around story elements, expository texts may be built around a dominant theme, concept, or key idea. Some informational texts for children are written with a narrative frame that supports readers as they apply their background knowledge about how stories work, which they developed while hearing oral stories and reading fiction. More traditional informational texts include other considerate structures that help readers determine the main ideas from the author's (or book designer's) point of view. Text features such as tables of content, indexes, timelines, and glossaries point the way to main ideas. Graphics, including illustrations, photographs, charts, maps, tables, captions, and labels, support readers as they decide what is important. Headings and subheadings, font variations, and other print effects signal relationships and relative importance among the pieces of information presented.

Both fictional and informational texts use varying font size or style to alert readers to important ideas and concepts. Some texts of both kinds use predictable text structures such as sequencing, question and answer, cause and effect, or problem and solution to guide readers. Signal words indicate which structure is being used. For example, these are some words that indicate sequencing: *first, next, then,* and *finally.* Once students become aware of these reader supports, they can incorporate them into their own student-authored texts. In fact, use of these structures in their own writing may be one of the best ways for students to practice and demonstrate mastery of text structures.

In *The Important Book,* author Margaret Wise Brown tells readers the most important thing about a spoon and provides details, the less important things, as well.

> The important thing
> about a spoon is
> that you eat with it.
> It's like a shovel,
> You hold it with your hand,
> You can put it in your mouth,

It isn't flat,
It's hollow,
And it spoons things up.
But the important thing
about a spoon is
that you eat with it.

Brown devotes each double-page spread to daisies, rain, grass, and more, repeating the pattern of sharing the important thing, giving other details, and restating the important thing at the end of each entry. This poetic treatment of main ideas and supporting details can be an aid to educators when they first explain this strategy to students.

In school-based learning experiences, educators who clearly establish learning objectives for literary engagements provide a scaffold that supports students in determining main ideas. In teacher-directed lessons, educators give students clear purposes for reading. Educators must also demonstrate that, as the purpose for reading changes, the reader's focus changes as well. Reading a fictional text in order to study characterization requires a different focus from reading the same text to determine a theme. (All of the sample lessons in this chapter include extensions that suggest a different purpose for reading the same texts.) Making underlying decisions visible, such as the purposes for reading, is especially important for English language learners. It is also critical to give students, at all grade levels and levels of reading proficiency, opportunities to determine and to set their own purposes for reading, a lifelong learning skill.

As we teach determining the main ideas, educators model, then invite readers to make judgments about which ideas are most important and which are less important. Main ideas are the foundation on which the details rest. Like an elephant that must bear its significant weight on strong legs, we ask readers to think of main ideas as the base that holds up the supporting details. Readers must learn how to prioritize information as an essential skill in reading comprehension as well as in information literacy. They can use main ideas to develop their schemas and to shore up their ability to store and recall information.

How to Teach the Strategy

Teacher-librarians will recognize the connection between determining main ideas and information literacy, defined in *IP2* as "the ability to find and use information" (AASL and AECT 1998, 1). Readers cannot and should not try to record, remember, or integrate every bit of information they see or read into their schemas. Main ideas give learners the opportunity to pass judgment on the value of information and use it effectively. Standard 1 of the "Nine Information Literacy Standards for Student Learning" is to access information "efficiently and effectively." Learners must read and understand what they read in order to use a text effectively.

Information Literacy Standards 2 and 3 involve evaluating information and using it accurately. Helping students acquire these skills is a core component of the teacher-librarian's teaching responsibilities. Teacher-librarians who teach the Big6 information literacy model will also note that main ideas are a critical part of the Big6's category 4, extracting relevant information (Eisenberg and Berkowitz 1990). Working in collaboration with classroom teachers, teacher-librarians offer specific knowledge and experience in teaching these vital 21st-century skills.

While mining for relevant information, readers must distill the essential from a sentence, an image, a passage, a paragraph, a chapter, or an entire text. At the sentence level, students may be inferring and learning the meaning of new vocabulary while determining main ideas. At the paragraph level, students may be learning about the academic English discourse pattern, in which the topic sentence presents the main idea and the concluding sentence restates it. With opportunities to practice this strategy at all of these levels of complexity, students can build their abilities to separate main ideas from supporting details. Here are a few of the questions that can help students determine main ideas:

- What was my purpose for reading?
- What new ideas or facts did I learn?
- What do I want to remember from this text?
- What will I do with this information?

- What was the author's or illustrator's purpose in writing or illustrating this text?

Determining main ideas requires that readers discard some information. With a clear purpose in mind, a reader can decide what information to disregard. Such information may be superfluous to his purposes, or it may be information he already knows and therefore does not need to record. As he evaluates this new information, the reader may choose to substitute a new word with a more familiar term from his prior knowledge vocabulary in this content area. Finally, he will be in a position to consider the remaining information that meets his purposes and determine a main idea or ideas to record and store in his memory, a main idea that may modify or change his schema on this topic. His main idea is a judgment; he should be able to defend his opinion (figure 7-2 below shows an example of this process).

Students who are comfortable with the narrative frame may need extra support when interacting with expository writing. Guidelines for reading informational texts can be posted in the library and in the classroom. Educators can model the following sequence and give students many opportunities to practice these strategies:

- Set a purpose for reading.
- Preview the covers and inside book flaps; bookwalk to read the illustrations.
- Preview the text features (main ideas): titles, subtitles, captions, charts, maps, timelines, and graphs.
- As you read, slow down when you meet new vocabulary or difficult concepts.
- Use the glossary.
- Stop to talk about your reading, make notes, and write about what you are learning.
- Reread or use other fix-up options when the meaning isn't clear.

A critical part of working with main ideas involves recording significant learning while reading or viewing. Educators can post a notemaking chart such as figure 2-1 (or Web Supplement 2A) in both the library and classrooms to remind students of the goal of notemaking and the types of notes. The school library literature is rich with models for making notes. In *Classroom Instruction That Works: Researched-Based Strategies for Increasing Student Achievement* (Marzano, Pickering, and Pollock 2001), notemaking is highlighted and elaborated with different formats: teacher-prepared notes, informal outlines, webbing, and a combination of outline and webbing. A variation of teacher-prepared notes is a skeleton outline, which provides a scaffold for students by leaving blanks for them to fill in as they listen, read, or view. The "trash-n-treasure" notemaking method, offered by Barbara A. Jansen, is one that begins with skimming for keywords to answer researchable questions (http://www.big6.com/showarticle.php?id=45). *Tools for Teaching Content Literacy* (Allen 2004) offers a graphic organizer for the Cornell Note-Taking System. The English Companion website is one source for a wide variety of notemaking formats (http://www.englishcompanion.com/Tools/notemaking.html).

Shared notemaking is one way to start students on the path of making effective notes. Educators should use think-alouds to demonstrate how they distill the main ideas from a passage and then show students their process for recording notes that clearly reflect what they learned. Students should have many experiences working with partners and in small groups to talk about texts, determine main ideas, and then record notes on group or individual notemaking sheets.

The next step after making notes is to use them to summarize learning. By definition, summaries focus on main ideas. Again, educators can first model summarizing as they review group notes and then compose whole-class summaries of the main ideas found in the notes. Practice in writing partner and small group summaries helps student prepare to summarize independently. When conducting long-term inquiry or research projects, readers can be asked to summarize their learning at the end of notemaking sessions. These summaries serve as formative assessments of students' progress toward understanding the topics under investigation.

Using an excerpt from *Wild Dogs: Past and Present* (Halls), figure 7-1 shows an example of the notemaking and summarizing process. The purpose for reading is clearly stated at the beginning. The learner first reads through the entire excerpt, then reviews the purpose for reading and reads through the excerpt a second time. During the second reading, he deletes information that is already known or facts that don't fit the purpose for reading. Next, he can make substitutions that explain vocabulary or concepts. In this example, the page number for the taxonomy chart was added. What remains of the

FIGURE 7-1

Deleting, Substituting, Notemaking, Determining Main Ideas, and New Questions

Text: *Wild Dogs: Past and Present,* by Kelly Milner Halls

Purpose for Reading

To learn general information about wild dogs and choose one for further research

Excerpt

"When scientists group an organism, they follow a system that describes it in a general-to-specific manner. The system is called a taxonomy. All dogs—wolves, foxes, jackals, dingos, wild dogs, and domesticated dogs—are in the Canidae family.

"Being in the same family means that in the most basic ways, all dogs are alike. They are mammals, which means they give birth to live young, nurse their young with milk, and are covered with fur or hair. They are carnivores, or meat-eaters. (Some also eat plants when they are hungry, but meat is their primary food.) They are four-footed animals that walk on their toes and do not (usually) have retractable claws. They have well-developed teeth specialized for cutting and tearing. Up to this point, a dog is a dog is a dog.

"Beyond the basics, though, dogs begin to differ. That is where the taxonomy gets more specific. The genus and species together form the scientific name for each different kind of animal.

"For example, the gray wolf's scientific name is *Canis lupus,* Latin for 'wolf dog.' The coyote is *Canis latrans,* Latin for 'barking dog.' The red fox is *Vulpes vulpes,* Latin for 'fox fox.' That means that the gray wolf and coyote are more genetically alike than either of them is to the red fox" (p. 12).

~~Deletions~~ and [Substitutions]

"~~When scientists group an organism, they follow a system that describes it in a general-to-specific manner. The system is called a~~ **taxonomy. [Chart on page 13] All dogs**—~~wolves, foxes, jackals, dingos, wild dogs, and domesticated dogs—are~~ in the **Canidae family.**

"~~Being in the same family means that in the most basic ways, all dogs are alike. They are~~ mammals, ~~which means they~~ ~~give birth to live young, nurse their young with milk, and are covered with fur or hair.~~ They are **carnivores,** ~~or meat-eaters. (Some also eat plants when they are hungry, but meat is their primary food.) They are four-footed animals that walk on their toes and~~ **do not (usually) have retractable claws.** ~~They have well-developed teeth specialized for cutting and tearing. Up to this point, a dog is a dog is a dog.~~

"~~Beyond the basics, though, dogs begin to differ. That is where the taxonomy gets more specific.~~ The **genus and species together form the scientific name** ~~for each different kind of animal.~~

"~~For example, the gray wolf's scientific name is *Canis lupus,* Latin for 'wolf dog.' The coyote is *Canis latrans,* Latin for 'barking dog.' The red fox is *Vulpes vulpes,* Latin for 'fox fox.' That means that the gray wolf and coyote are more genetically alike than either of them is to the red fox~~" (p. 12).

Notes

Taxonomy—p. 13

All—Canidae family—common characteristics

Carnivorous mammals (usually no retractable claws)

Scientific name = genus + species—shows relationships and dif. char.

Main Ideas

All dogs are in the Canidae family and have common characteristics. The genus and species (scientific names) show how they are related to each other and how they are different from other wild dogs.

New Questions

Which wild dogs have retractable claws?

What is the scientific name for my pet dog?

excerpt are the main ideas. Students can practice this process on photocopies of texts, deleting unimportant information by striking it through with a pencil, adding substitutions with pen, and using highlighters to flag main ideas.

After engaging in this process, the reader then uses the main ideas to make notes in his own words. These notes are in the formats listed on the notemaking chart (figure 2-1 or Web Supplement 2A). From the notes, he can compose a summary in his own words and in complete sentences. Students are also encouraged to record their questions as they make notes or summarize. These questions help guide learners as they read on. In this example, the student may decide to focus his study on a wild dog with retractable claws. When he conducts further research, he will learn that some foxes have semi-retractable claws and can leave clawless footprints.

Notemaking and summarizing are often referred to as *study skills,* but they are two of the most powerful skills students can develop to identify the main ideas of their learning (Marzano, Pickering, and Pollock 2001, 48). Teacher-librarians must become expert teachers of writing in whatever writing process or method is used by the classroom teacher colleagues in their schools. When a school is in the process of exploring or adopting new strategies, it is paramount that the teacher-librarian be part of the discussion and participate in or provide professional development in the area of writing. Reading and writing are the two sides of the literacy coin; one cannot and should not be separated from the other.

Making Literature Connections

Any text related to the curriculum or to students' interests can be useful in teaching main ideas. As students are developing this strategy, educators should provide them with clear purposes and objectives for reading and engage them with considerate texts that spark their curiosity. It is important to use informational books as read-alouds. Many elementary students do not get enough opportunities to hear fluent readers reading and modeling strate-gies with expository text. With added emphasis on content-area reading in middle and high school, especially in science and social studies, elementary educators must prepare students to be successful readers of informational texts.

Today's informational texts are not, however, all found in the nonfiction section of the library. Teacher-librarians must cast a wide net to collect and integrate resources from across the Dewey spectrum to support teaching the curriculum. Poetry and poetic prose embedded with science and social studies information, fictionalized biographies and well-researched historical fiction, and picture book stories based on facts can be used to teach this strategy. Keyword searching allows educators and students to pull together texts from various genres in support of teaching and learning.

Some picture books shelved in the fiction section clearly communicate information, such as *Water Dance* (Locker). And some effective informational texts make use of the narrative frame. Because the brain functions narratively, we most often record, remember, and retell information in story format rather than by listing facts. Sandra Markle and Seymour Simon are two informational book authors who excel at combining rich, informative narrative with compelling illustrations. Although their texts take advantage of the narrative frame, they do not offer readers the organizational support, such as subheadings and special fonts, offered by more traditional informational books. Informational books with narrative frames make compelling read-alouds and may provide a bridge between fiction and more traditional nonfiction books.

Still, when students are searching for main ideas to answer questions posed by educators or questions of their own making, the structural support found in high-quality informational books offers them a scaffold for locating and determining main ideas. Graphic organizers, such as the Informational Book Self-Monitoring Graphic Organizer (figure 9-1 and Web Supplement 9K), assist readers as they notice which features of a particular informational book best support their learning. Teacher-librarians should be aware of the structural features offered in expository texts as they build their collections. Many publishers offer these texts in series, which means that students can develop schemas for a particular text format and anticipate where and how to locate main ideas in all the titles of a particular series. The Discovery Library series published by Rourke, National Geographic's Reading Expeditions, and the Reading Quest series by Newbridge Publishing are some of the many considerate texts in series format available to elementary school libraries and classrooms.

A growing number of books published for children are multigenre books. The format of some of these texts can offer readers interesting insight into the main ideas (from the author's or illustrator's perspective). *Song of the Water Boatman, and Other Pond Poems* (Sidman/Prange) and *Night Wonders* (Peddicord) are two examples in which poetry and expository text are offered side by side. While the poetic print may elicit a more aesthetic response in the reader, the expository print provides the facts behind the expressive language used in the poems. Combined with stunning illustrations, these components clearly point to the main ideas on the page. Figure 7-2 shows an example from the print information in *Song of the Water Boatman, and Other Pond Poems.*

Any text can support teaching and learning this strategy, and it is important to mention that all types of text should be used. Although teaching strategies through children's literature is the focus of this book, effective support for this strategy can be found in magazine and newspaper articles, pamphlets and brochures, all forms of media, and textbooks. Whenever possible, text sets created to support learning this strategy should include all of these formats. Textbooks in particular can and should be used to teach determining main ideas. These texts are often written above students' proficient reading levels and do not always take readers' background knowledge into consideration. To provide scaffolds for reading these texts, educators can construct

FIGURE 7-2
Determining Main Ideas with Multigenre Text

Text: *Song of the Water Boatman, and Other Pond Poems,* by Joyce Sidman, illustrated by Beckie Prange

Purpose for Reading

To learn about pond ecology

Excerpt

Poem
"Here hunts the heron, queen of the pond,
    that spears the fish
    that swallows the frog
    that gulps the bug
    that nabs the nymph
    that drinks the flea
    that eats the algae, green and small,
in the depths of the summer pond."

Excerpt

Expository text—Food Chain

"Life in the pond begins with plants, which manufacture food from the sun. Plants become food for plant-eating (herbivorous) animals like the tiny water flea or the water boatman. These small animals and bugs are eaten by bigger bugs, which are eaten by meat-eating (carnivorous) animals like minnows and tadpoles. Bigger fish eat the smaller fish. And the heron, with its keen eyes and sharp beak, eats whatever it wants."

Notes

Sample pond food chain: heron→bigger fish→minnows→ bigger bugs→fleas→algae

Some bugs—herbivores (eat plants)

Some bugs—carnivores (eat smaller bugs)

Main Ideas/Summary

Plants, herbivores, and carnivores make a food chain in the pond. Pond plants and animals provide food for other animals.

Question

What eats the heron?

graphic organizers that help readers focus on the main ideas found in keywords, headings, subheadings, captions, and other supports before, during, and after reading. Teacher-librarians should consider their role in helping teachers teach and students learn to read content-area textbooks effectively and fluently. A textbook is, in fact, a reference book and can be integrated into research and inquiry projects along with other reference resources.

Summary

Determining the main idea may be one of the most valuable strategies a 21st-century reader can develop. Sorting out what is important in the deluge of information is key to making sense and using information to generate knowledge. This is a complex process. Main ideas are always dependent on the purpose for reading and the judgment of the reader. Educators should give students the opportunity to engage with the same texts for different purposes.

Through collaboration, teacher-librarians and classroom teachers can effectively design, implement, and assess lessons that help students develop their ability to judge importance. Determining main ideas, notemaking, and summarizing are interconnected strategies. By lowering the student-teacher ratio, educators are better able to offer students invaluable writing conferences. In addition to sharing their learning through writing, students can create mathematical representations, perform dramas, construct models, and use other sign systems to summarize what they have learned.

Children's Literature Cited

Starred titles are used in the lesson plans.

* *Carlo and the Really Nice Librarian,* by Jessica Spanyol

* *I Want to Be a Librarian,* by Dan Liebman

* *Imaginative Inventions,* by Charise Mericle Harper

The Important Book, by Margaret Wise Brown

* *The Inventor's Times: Real-Life Stories of 30 Amazing Creations,* by Dan Driscoll, James Zigarelli, and the staff of the *Inventor's Times*

* *The Kid Who Invented the Popsicle, and Other Surprising Stories about Inventions,* by Don L. Wulffson

* *The Kid Who Invented the Trampoline, and More Surprising Stories about Inventions,* by Don L. Wulffson

* *The Kids' Invention Book,* by Arlene Erlbach

* *A Mother's Journey,* by Sandra Markle, illustrated by Alan Marks

Night Wonders, by Jane Ann Peddicord

Song of the Water Boatman, and Other Pond Poems, by Joyce Sidman, illustrated by Beckie Prange

Water Dance, by Thomas Locker

Wild Dogs: Past and Present, by Kelly Milner Halls

Lesson Plans

These lessons focus on determining importance with increasing sophistication using different research-based instructional strategies. A purpose for reading is established for each lesson, and each extension changes the purpose for reading, which then changes the readers' focus. Whenever possible, the lessons should include conferencing with individual and small groups of students. It is important for educators to probe students' thinking in order to support their progress using the main ideas strategy. Because there is rarely one correct main idea in any given text, educators must respect students' judgments and give students opportunities to explain their rationale for their choices.

READING COMPREHENSION STRATEGY
Determining Main Ideas

Reading Development Level Emerging

Instructional Strategies Cues and Questions, Classifying, Summarizing (Orally)

Lesson Length 1 session

Purpose The purpose of this lesson is to determine the topic of a text set and to categorize fiction and informational books. In this case, determining if books are fiction or informational is the purpose for reading, and therefore these are the main ideas. Students transfer math and science vocabulary to the reading/language arts/library learning context. Combined with the extension, this lesson demonstrates that the purpose for reading makes a difference in what readers pay attention to while they read.

Objectives At the end of this lesson, students will be able to

1. Determine the topic of a text set.

2. Read for a specific purpose.

3. Categorize books as fiction or informational.

4. Create a graph to show classification and make notes on a graphic organizer.

5. Comprehend and use math-science vocabulary in the language arts/library context: *arrange, group, same, different,* and *category.*

Resources, Materials, and Equipment *Carlo and the Really Nice Librarian,* by Jessica Spanyol

I Want to Be a Librarian, by Dan Liebman

Topical text set on libraries and librarians—up to four in each category (fiction and informational books)

Topical text sets on high-interest topics, one for each small group—not more than four in each category (fiction and informational)

Graphic Organizers: Fiction and Informational Book Summary Sheet (Web Supplement 7A), Graph (Web Supplement 7B)

Materials: Sticky notes (1½" by 2" size, two different colors) and rocks of two colors, sizes, shapes, or types

Overhead, data projector, or interactive whiteboard

Collaboration The educators conduct the entire lesson as a team to model reading for a specific purpose. They also model how vocabulary used in one context can be transferred to another discipline and demonstrate collaboration and presentation skills. Educators cofacilitate small group work. Each educator facilitates small group oral presentations for half the class.

Assessment The students' group graphs and presentations to the class using the key vocabulary show their understanding of the main ideas for this lesson—determining topics and categories.

Standards *Reading keywords:* determine if a literary selection is fiction or informational; acquire and use vocabulary in relevant contexts

Listening and speaking keywords: use effective vocabulary and logical organization to relate or summarize ideas; present a report

Math keywords: number sense; make a model to represent a given whole number 0 through 100

Science keywords: analyze; organize (e.g., compare, classify, and sequence) objects, organisms, and events according to various characteristics

Information literacy: organize for practical application; integrate information into one's own knowledge

Process   *Motivation*

Show a group of rocks. How are they the same? How are they different? Choose a category (color, size, shape, or type) and arrange them into two piles.

Show the covers of the books from the libraries and librarians topical text set. How are these books the same? Define the word *topic*. All the books are about libraries and librarians. How are they different? Did you know that books are arranged on the library shelves in a special way to help children and teachers find them? Just like there are different categories of rocks, there are different categories of books. These categories help people locate the books they are looking for.

Student-Friendly Objectives

1. Name the topic.
2. Categorize books as fiction or informational.
3. Use sticky notes to label the categories.
4. Make a graph to show categories.
5. Use these words when presenting: *arrange, group, same, different,* and *category.*

Presentation

Show the two anchor books. One is a fiction book and one is an informational book. Note that we read different kinds of books for different purposes. Share the purpose for reading in this lesson: to determine if books are fiction or informational books.

Taking turns, one educator conducts a bookwalk of *Carlo and the Really Nice Librarian.* The other educator conducts a bookwalk of *I Want to Be a Librarian.* Project the Fiction and Informational Book Summary Sheet (Web Supplement 7A) and fill it in during the discussion of fiction and informational books. What are the characteristics of a fiction book? What are the characteristics of an informational book? Show the letters and numbers on the spine of each book. Note that the markings on the spine are categories, fiction (letters only) or informational (numbers before letters). Other characteristics of fiction books: sometimes include talking animals, made-up stories, illustrations, often drawings or paintings. Other characteristics of informational books: true information, real events, sometimes illustrated with photographs.

Using the titles, book jackets, illustrations, and spine labels, categorize the libraries and librarians text set with sticky notes of two different colors. Arrange the books into two piles. Project the Graph (Web Supplement 7B) and place the sticky notes on the graph. Think aloud and use the terms *arrange, group, same, different,* and *category.* Count the number of fiction books by writing numbers on the sticky notes. Do the same for the informational books.

Distribute one text set per table group. Tell the students that they will be working in small groups to determine the topic, categorize, and make a group graph of the text sets on their table.

Student Participation Procedures

1. Read the book titles.
2. Look at the covers and spine labels.
3. Bookwalk.
4. Name the topic.
5. Use sticky notes of two different colors to categorize the books into two groups.
6. Make a group graph and number the sticky notes.

Guided Practice

The educators support groups that need help reading the book titles. They ask students to hypothesize if the books are fiction or informational before looking at the spines. Educators support students as they group their books and create graphs.

Presentation

Educators model presenting their graph for the libraries and librarians text set. They follow the student presentation procedures.

Student Presentation Procedures

1. Decide on two presenters.
2. Name the members of the group.
3. Give the topic or main idea of the text set.
4. Read and explain the group graph.
5. Choose one book from each category and tell why it is fiction or informational.

Guided Practice

Educators help the groups rehearse their presentations.

Closure

Divide the class in half. Each educator facilitates a group. Groups present their graphs to half the class using the target vocabulary. Using the Fiction and Informational Book Summary Sheet (Web Supplement 7A), review the characteristics of fiction and informational books.

Reflection

What was our purpose for reading these books? How did the purpose help us determine the main idea—fiction or informational books? If we change the purpose for reading, would we notice different things in the texts?

Extensions   Divide the class in half. Establish a new purpose for reading. This time focus on the theme (another kind of main idea) of each book. One educator reads *Carlo and the Really Nice Librarian;* one reads *I Want to Be a Librarian.* Each group composes a group theme for the book they heard and shares it with the entire class.

In the library, practice resource location skills related to these two broad categories: fiction and informational books.

READING COMPREHENSION STRATEGY
Determining Main Ideas

Reading Development Level   Advancing

Instructional Strategies   Notemaking and Summarizing

Lesson Length   3 sessions

Purpose   The purpose of this lesson is to identify and make notes about the story elements in an informational book with a narrative frame. Students deepen their engagement with this text through a character study and by completing a character map and writing a character summary. (Note: The anchor text is shelved with fiction.)

Objectives   After reading *A Mother's Journey*, students will be able to

1. Determine story elements in an informational book and record them on a story map.

2. Conduct a character analysis and record characteristics and evidence on a character map.

3. Retell the information using the story map and the character maps as prompts.

4. Compose a character summary and self-assess with a rubric.

5. Dramatize the characteristics of the mother penguin or read the character paragraph.

Resources, Materials, and Equipment   *A Mother's Journey*, by Sandra Markle, illustrated by Alan Marks

Emperor Penguin Pathfinder: http://storytrail.com/Impact/Penguins.htm

Graphic Organizers: Teacher Resource: Story Map (Web Supplement 7C), Story Map (Web Supplement 7D), Teacher Resource: Character Map (Web Supplement 7E), Character Map (Web Supplement 7F), Sample Character Summary Paragraph (Web Supplement 7G), Character Summary Paragraph and Presentation Rubric (Web Supplement 7H)

Materials: Scratch paper and pencils for brainstorms

Overhead, data projector, or interactive whiteboard

Collaboration   The educators model determining main ideas and notemaking on a story map. They also model finding evidence from the text for a character study and collaborate to compose a sample character summary. Both educators facilitate students' small group work and conduct writing conferences with student partners.

Assessment   The students' story maps, character maps, character summaries, and summary rubric serve as assessments.

Standards   *Reading keywords:* identify the main idea and supporting details in expository text; sequence a series of events; story or literary elements

Writing keywords: record information; write an expository paragraph with a topic sentence, supporting details, evidence, or relevant information

Science keywords: life cycles; interactions of living organisms with their environment; adaptations of animals that allow them to live in specific environments

Theater keywords: research information for a dramatic scene; sequence a drama

Information literacy keywords: organize information for practical application; derive meaning from information presented creatively in a variety of formats

Process   *Motivation*

Day 1   Do not display the anchor book. Play audio of emperor penguins found as a link of the emperor penguin pathfinder. Ask students to guess what makes that sound. Show the brief video about emperor penguins (also a link from the pathfinder).

Show the anchor book and read the title and the author's and illustrator's names. What do students already know about emperor penguins? Think-pair-share in groups of four. Collect background knowledge orally. Let students know the purpose for reading this book: to determine main ideas from an informational book that is told as a story.

Student-Friendly Objectives

1. Determine the main ideas.

2. Record them on a story map.

3. Retell the story/information in the book using the story map as a guide.

Presentation

Project the Story Map (Web Supplement 7D). While one educator reads the book, one records the educators' and students' notes on the story map. (Web Supplement 7C is a completed teacher resource story map.) Teach or review types of notes (figure 2-1 or Web Supplement 2A). Reinforce note types while recording on the story map.

Read the first page of the book. Educators think aloud to process information and make notes about the character(s) and setting. Use different-colored markers to record notes for each story element.

Read to the page that ends: "But the closest food is in the open sea, more than 50 miles away." Ask students to determine the problem in this story. Record it on the story map.

Educators think aloud about the main ideas found at the beginning of the story. Review the story to this point by bookwalking through the pages read so far. On the board or overhead, web ideas about the beginning of the story. Circle the main ideas. Identify items not circled as supporting details. Number the main ideas in order of occurrence in the story. Record notes on the story map.

Read to the page that ends: "But it is a zig-zag course that never takes her too far from the ice edge." Conduct a bookwalk to review the middle pages of the book. Distribute story maps to each student (Web Supplement 7D). Students work in groups to web the main ideas of the middle of the story plot.

Student Practice Procedures

1. Web the main ideas on scratch paper.

2. Negotiate three to five main ideas and circle them.

3. Number the ideas in the order they happened in the book.

4. Record them on the story map.

5. Copy notes from the class story map.

Guided Practice

Educators monitor group work and help students negotiate main ideas from their brainstorms.

Presentation

Educators fill in the middle plot section of the class story map using the ideas from the Teacher Resource: Story Map (Web Supplement 7C). Continue reading until the end of the book. Repeat the procedure by bookwalking, brainstorming, circling, prioritizing, and recording on the class story map. Repeat the student practice procedures and the guided practice above.

Closure

Lead a group discussion about how the problem in the story was solved. Educators add the plot ending and solution to the class story map. Review the purpose for reading this text. Educators model retelling the story elements using the class story map.

Students use their individual story maps to retell the story of the mother emperor penguin to a partner. Remind students to keep their focus on the main ideas: character(s), setting, problem, plot (beginning, middle, and end), and solution.

Day 2 ### Student-Friendly Objectives

1. Determine four main characteristics of female emperor penguins.

2. Record two pieces of evidence from the text for each characteristic.

3. Write a one-paragraph summary describing the female emperor penguin.

Presentation

Students work with a partner. Distribute Character Maps (Web Supplement 7F) to each student. Facilitate a discussion about the main character in the book. Brainstorm behaviors and qualities of the female emperor penguin. Record and save on the board or overhead. (Use Web Supplement 7E as a character map teacher resource.)

The educators think aloud to complete one section of the character map. They choose one character trait from the brainstorm and cite two examples from the book of the mother penguin demonstrating that characteristic. Record ideas on the character map in notemaking format. Students then work with a partner to complete individual character maps for the female emperor penguin.

Student Practice Procedures

1. Write "female emperor penguin" in the center of the map.

2. Work with a partner to choose four characteristics.

3. For each characteristic, make notes on two examples from the book.

Guided Practice

Educators monitor students for accurate examples of each characteristic and for their use of different types of notes.

Presentation

Project the completed Teacher Resource: Character Map (Web Supplement 7E). Distribute the Character Summary Paragraph and Presentation Rubric (Web

Supplement 7H), one per partner group. Educators provide an oral summary of the character map and then model writing a one-paragraph character summary. (Web Supplement 7G is a sample summary paragraph.) Emphasize the sequence in the topic sentence and the order of the body sentences. Point out that the concluding sentence refers back to the main idea in the topic sentence.

Students work with a partner to write a one-paragraph character summary.

Student Practice Procedures

1. Practice an oral summary of the character map with a partner.
2. Compose a topic sentence with four characteristics.
3. Write one sentence that gives an example for each characteristic.
4. Keep the same order as the topic sentence.
5. Take turns writing with your partner.

Guided Practice

Educators monitor for cooperation and paragraph organization.

Day 3 ### Presentation

Project the Sample Character Summary Paragraph (Web Supplement 7G). Assess it with the Character Summary Paragraph and Presentation Rubric (Web Supplement 7H). Model the presentation to the class, with one educator reading the paragraph while the other dramatizes the four characteristics of the mother penguin in sequence.

Student Practice Procedures

1. Self-assess the draft using the rubric.
2. Revise and correct grammar, spelling, capitalization, and punctuation.
3. Each student writes a final copy of the paragraph.
4. Practice the presentation.
5. Each team turns in the character map, a draft and two final copies of the summary paragraph, and one rubric.

Closure

Divide the class in half, with each educator facilitating one group in order for student partners to share their presentations. Review the purpose for reading *A Mother's Journey:* to determine main ideas from an informational book written in story format.

Reflection

How does the purpose for reading influence what we pay attention to when we read? How do we determine main ideas when we read a story or an informational book told in story format? Can people determine different main ideas? What is a summary?

Extension Change the purpose for reading to collecting as many facts as possible about the emperor penguin. Provide access to a text set on emperor penguins, including websites. Students work in small groups and record facts in notemaking format on index cards. Groups meet to review their facts. Quiz groups on emperor penguin facts using the numbered-heads-together method. Pose the question: Does changing the purpose for reading change what readers pay attention to when they read?

Determining Main Ideas

Reading Development Level	Advanced
Instructional Strategies	Notemaking and Summarizing
Lesson Length	2 (or more) sessions
Purpose	The purpose of this lesson is to learn how to determine main ideas in a text with a problem-solution text structure and to change the purpose for reading in order to note the change in the readers' focus.
Objectives	After reading *The Kids' Invention Book* and researching inventors, students will be able to

1. Determine main ideas in a problem-solution text structure.
2. Record notes and maintain a bibliographic record.
3. Use the writing process to compose a summary.
4. Self-assess using a rubric.

Resources, Materials, and Equipment	*Imaginative Inventions*, by Charise Mericle Harper

The Inventor's Times: Real-Life Stories of 30 Amazing Creations, by Dan Driscoll, James Zigarelli, and the staff of the *Inventor's Times*

The Kids' Invention Book, by Arlene Erlbach

The Kid Who Invented the Popsicle, and Other Surprising Stories about Inventions, by Don L. Wulffson

The Kid Who Invented the Trampoline, and More Surprising Stories about Inventions, by Don L. Wulffson

Graphic Organizers: Teacher Resource: Bibliography and Notemaking Graphic Organizer (Web Supplement 7I), Bibliography and Notemaking Graphic Organizer (Web Supplement 7J), Sample Problem-Solution Summary Paragraph (Web Supplement 7K), Rubric for Problem-Solution Summary Paragraph (Web Supplement 7L)

Overhead, data projector, or interactive whiteboard

Collaboration	The educators model determining main ideas, recording a bibliography entry, and making notes. One or both educators monitor students' research and notemaking.
Assessment	The students' completed bibliography and notemaking graphic organizers, problem-solution summary paragraphs, and rubrics show if they can identify the main ideas.
Standards	*Reading keywords:* identify the main ideas and support details in an expository text; draw valid conclusions from information presented in an expository text

Writing keywords: write a variety of expository forms (summary); write an information report that uses main ideas and relevant details

Science keywords: propose a solution, resource, or product that addresses a specific human, animal, or habitat need; design and construct a technological solution to a common problem or need using common materials

Information literacy keywords: select information appropriate to the problem or question at hand; organize information for practical application

Process   *Motivation*

Day 1   Educators read pages 6 and 7 from *The Kids' Invention Book*. Think-pair-share: Have you ever invented anything? Ask for volunteers to share.

Educators take turns reading a selection of stories about inventions from *The Kid Who Invented the Popsicle,* such as the title story, "Ice-Cream Cone," "Sandwich," or "Velcro." Pair each reading with verse about the same inventions found in the book *Imaginative Inventions.* Let students know that they will be reading about different kid-made inventions. Students choose one inventor and invention to study and write a summary (optional: in preparation for creating their own solution to a common problem or need).

Student-Friendly Objectives

1. Read about a kid inventor.

2. Make notes on the problem and solution (main ideas).

3. Write a summary with the main ideas.

4. Self-assess the summary using a rubric.

Presentation

Project the Bibliography and Notemaking Graphic Organizer (Web Supplement 7J). (Web Supplement 7I is a teacher resource.) Think aloud while locating bibliographic information and fill in the blanks for *The Kids' Invention Book*.

Review notemaking goals and types (figure 2-1 or Web Supplement 7A). Read pages 8 and 9 in *The Kids' Invention Book*. Reread and make notes. Educators think aloud as they record notes on the sample graphic organizer. Stress noting the reference number and page number where the information was found.

Depending on the number of resources, divide the students into partners or small groups. If resources are scarce, this project can become a center rotation for students to come to the library to conduct their research with the teacher-librarian facilitating.

Students work with a partner or in small groups to choose an inventor, read, record bibliographic information, and make notes.

Student Participation Procedures

1. Skim the tables of contents or bookwalk through the resources to locate a few inventors/inventions of interest. Read about at least three.

2. Choose one to reread.

3. Fill out the bibliographic information.

4. Make notes.

Guided Practice

The educator(s) monitor students' completion of the bibliographic information, accurate recording of reference and page numbers, and use of note types.

Closure

Think-pair-share the most surprising information read. Ask for volunteers to share about these inventors and their inventions.

Day 2   *Presentation*

Educators model composing a problem-solution summary paragraph. (Web Supplement 7K is a sample for inventor Chester Greenwood.) First project the notes (Web Supplement 7I) and circle the problem and solution (main ideas). Next compose a summary paragraph. Use the Rubric for Problem-Solution Summary Paragraph (Web Supplement 7L) to guide the composition. Then assess the paragraph.

Students follow the writing process, compose with a partner, conference with a teacher or peer and revise, write an individual final copy, and self-assess individual paragraphs.

Student Practice Procedures

1. Circle the problem and solution (main ideas).

2. Review the rubric.

3. Compose a rough draft with a partner.

4. Conference with a peer or teacher.

5. Revise and edit the paragraph.

6. Make an individual final copy.

7. Self-assess using the rubric.

Guided Practice

Educator(s) monitor students' writing process and peer conferences and conduct writing conferences with students.

Closure

Form groups of four or five students who studied different inventors. Students read their paragraphs to their peers and share an illustration from the book they used for their research.

Reflection

How did we determine the main ideas in the problem-solution text structure? What makes a detail relevant?

Extensions   Change the purpose for reading. This time ask students to read and skim more widely and only make notes on all of the different kinds of materials kid inventors used to create their inventions. Collect kid problems or needs by asking for submissions from other classrooms in the building or in the greater cyber-community.

Form groups, gather everyday materials, and create inventions to solve a selection of these problems. Write summaries of each invention, using *Imaginative Inventions* (rhyming poems) or *The Inventor's Times: Real-Life Stories of 30 Amazing Creations* (newspaper articles) as models. Create a PowerPoint presentation of photographs of the students' inventions and their summaries to share with the students who suggested the problems and with families, or post on the school's website. Set up an invention museum in the library. Display the students' summaries alongside their inventions.

Reading Comprehension Strategy Six
Using Fix-Up Options

'Twas brillig, and the slithy toves
Did gyre and gimble in the wabe;
All mimsy were the borogoves,
And the mome raths outgrabe.

—From "Jabberwocky," in *Through*
the Looking Glass and What Alice
Found There, by Lewis Carroll

How does a reader know when she has lost comprehension? Monitoring her own meaning-making and getting back on track when she has lost her way may be the most difficult tasks for any novice reader. The fix-up strategy offers readers processes they can use to recover meaning, such as rereading, reading ahead, or figuring out unknown words. The tricky part is knowing when to use these options.

The first five reading comprehension strategies presented in this book, activating background knowledge, using sensory images, asking questions, predicting and inferring, and determining main ideas, can be used both in the recognition of a loss of comprehension and in the effort to recover it. When the reader is no longer making connections as she reads, she should begin to suspect that she has lost the thread of meaning. Texts quickly become boring when the reader fails to make text-to-self, text-to-text, or text-to-world connections. Without bringing her background knowledge and prior experience to bear, the distance between the author, the text, and the reader grows wider and can become a gap too wide to cross. A reader who strives to make meaning notices when the communication offered by connections is interrupted; the voice in her head becomes silent.

And what happens when the movie in her head pauses or the screen goes blank? The reader who can no longer visualize the story or information presented in the text has lost comprehension. With her senses turned off, the reader's imagination can no longer access the meaning behind the print on the page. Reading that does not engage the imagination does not touch the mind or the heart, and the lived-through experience or information is not stored in memory. The significance of the text is nowhere to be found.

Questioning, predicting, and inferring are activities that express curiosity. When the reader is not questioning the author or the text, when she is not seeking to ask and answer her own questions, she most certainly has lost interest and may have lost comprehension as well. Readers who predict what will come next are actively following a trail that leads them to information that may confirm or disprove their educated guesses. If the reader's interest wanes and she is no longer interested in reading on to find out more, chances are she is no longer finding significance in the reading. Making inferences also shows a commitment to teasing out the meaning in the text. When the thrill is gone, comprehension is often a victim.

Losing the ability to determine what is most important may also be a signal that comprehension is lost. When the reader cannot distinguish between main ideas and supporting details, it can indicate a state of being overwhelmed by the text. Without the ability to use her schemas for the narrative framework or for text structures in order to put the information presented into a hierarchy of importance, the reader can be quickly buried in meaninglessness. Not knowing what to pay attention to as she reads, the reader may become frustrated and quickly tune out.

What is a reader to do when it becomes apparent that she has lost comprehension? Why, use fix-up options, of course! Educators must teach readers to recognize the symptoms of lost comprehension and then provide them with tools for fixing up their meaning-making. In the figure 8-1 excerpt from Lewis Carroll's nonsense poem, the reader uses several fix-up options to recover comprehension. The complete poem and process are found in the advanced fix-up strategy lesson at the end of this chapter.

FIGURE 8-1
Sample Fix-Up Options

Text: "Jabberwocky," from *Through the Looking Glass and What Alice Found There,* by Lewis Carroll

	Fix-Up Options
	Reread the entire poem.
'Twas brillig, and the slithy toves	**Connect to background knowledge** (text-to-text): "'Twas" means "it was," as in the poem "'Twas the night before Christmas."
	Make an inference: "Brillig" sounds like the word "brilliant." Perhaps the events in the poem take place in the daytime.
	Look at sentence structure (BK): "Slithy" is probably an adjective that describes the toves.
	Make a prediction: The toves are animals.
Did gyre and gimble in the wabe;	**Look at sentence structure** (BK): "Gyre" and "gimble" are verbs.
	Make an inference: The wabe is the place where the toves live.
	Read ahead to the end of this verse.
All mimsy were the borogoves, And the mome raths outgrabe.	**Make inferences:** Borogoves and raths are also creatures that live in the wabe. "Mimsy" sounds like "whimsy," which suggests a pleasant, peaceful scene.
	Visualization: Imagine strange animals.
	Ask a new question: Are they living peacefully in a forest?

Like the elephant that uses its trunk to manipulate its environment, the reader can employ fix-up options to retrace her steps, to find where she lost her way, and to get back on the path of meaning-making once more. Fix-up options are tools that readers can rely upon to find their way home, to make sense of what they read. Learning to self-monitor for comprehension and then to use fix-up options when comprehension is lost gives readers responsibility for their own process, ownership that is critical for the success of their lifelong, independent reading. The fix-up strategy empowers readers to succeed.

How to Teach the Strategy

Think-alouds in which educators and more proficient readers model both their loss and their recovery of comprehension are essential in helping less proficient readers grasp the two-part process. Proficient readers must first model how to monitor comprehension and notice when it is lost, and then how to choose and use fix-up options to regain it. The questions in figure 8-2 can be posted in the classroom and the library to remind students of the symptomatic warning signs that they are not effectively using the active reading strategies they have learned.

FIGURE 8-2
Am I Still Actively Reading?
Questions to Monitor Comprehension

Am I making connections?

Am I visualizing and using all my senses as I read?

Am I asking questions?

Am I making predictions and inferring as I read?

Am I determining main ideas?

Can I summarize what I'm reading?

> If you cannot answer "yes" to these questions, then you may have lost comprehension.
>
> What can you do?
>
> Use fix-up options and get your comprehension back on track!

Students can develop their own metaphors for lost comprehension. Some readers may think of comprehension in terms of the "voice" inside their heads—is it lost or confused? Others may think in terms of a "video" showing the action on a screen inside their minds. Has the projector shut off? Others may think about staying on a path and notice if they wander off the trail. It is important to involve students in determining their own signals, because they alone can recognize the moment they lose the thread of a story or the core of an informative text.

In *Strategies That Work: Teaching Comprehension to Enhance Understanding*, Harvey and Goudvis offer a lesson to help readers monitor their own comprehension (2000, 85). This is an adaptation of the process they suggest. Students write a number and "Huh?" on a sticky note and place it on the text where they become confused. As they reread or read ahead, they pay close attention to the point at which their confusion is cleared up. Students can take another sticky note, record the number from the "Huh?" sticky note, draw a lightbulb on it, and place it in the text where they regained comprehension. This way, both students and educators can notice where students lose comprehension and where they get back on track. These are important steps toward eventual independence and using fix-up options automatically.

As this strategy lesson suggests, monitoring comprehension must be continuous throughout the reading. Readers who wait until they reach the end of the text before they realize they have no idea what it means have wasted time and effort by continuing long past their loss of comprehension. There is no simple way for readers to master self-monitoring. Modeling by educators or more proficient peers is a place to begin, but readers surely need a great deal of practice with a wide range of texts that present a variety of comprehension challenges. The three sample lessons at the end of this chapter include specific support for modeling and monitoring meaning-making.

Loss of comprehension can develop at the word, sentence, paragraph, chapter, or whole-text level. It seems natural for beginning readers to start investigating this phenomenon at the word level. When teacher-librarians work with classroom teachers to help students develop strategies for defining unknown words, they build continuity between classroom and library. Students often meet challenging words while reading library resources. Teacher-librarians, who are reference resource lovers, may be inclined to guide struggling students toward the dictionary or encyclopedia before encouraging them to use context clues. If classroom teachers are asking students to use context clues before turning to a reference resource, then teacher-librarians should as well. Shared classroom and library goals and objectives in the area of vocabulary and concept development are essential. If the teacher-librarian is using the same strategies and terms as the classroom teacher, students benefit. Through curriculum conversations and collaborative planning and teaching, educators can provide consistent support for students.

These are some of the steps readers take when learning new vocabulary. When attempting to read an unknown word, students learn to skip the word and read to the end of the sentence. They can then guess at the meaning or replace the unknown word with one that makes sense. They should then reread both the sentence before the one with the unknown word and the sentence in question with the substituted word to determine if it makes sense. Readers are encouraged to use context clues—the words around the unknown word and the images in illustrated texts—to figure out meaning. They can also look for parts of the unknown word with which they may already be familiar, such as *under* in *underneath.*

After pursuing these primary strategies, readers can choose to consult secondary resources. They can begin with text features such as the glossary or index. If these features are not available, they can consult a dictionary, thesaurus, or encyclopedia. They can also ask a peer. Educators should balance providing students with answers to their word-level questions with prompting them to discover the word's meaning on their own through one or more

of these options. It is important to remember that, in teaching all reading comprehension strategies, the reader's independence is the ultimate goal.

At the sentence, paragraph, chapter, and whole-text levels, students can use the sixteen fix-up options recommended by Zimmermann and Hutchins (2003, 163) and adapted in figure 8-3. The fix-up options are sequenced according to relative difficulty of application. In this chapter's three lesson plans, fix-up strategy self-monitoring sheets are provided in three stages so as not to overwhelm readers. Options 1–8 are used in the emerging lesson, options 1–12 are used in the advancing lesson, and all sixteen options are listed on the self-monitoring sheet at the advanced level. (See Web Supplements 2B, 2C, and 2D for reading comprehension strategy bookmarks; the fix-up options are on one side of the bookmarks.)

Offering a complete tool kit, these sixteen fix-up options present learners with a review of the reading comprehension strategies addressed in this book. Students at all developmental levels can be encouraged to use as many options as possible. Educators must explain and model the use of each option and of multiple options during the how-to strategy lessons. Readers should be clear that one option alone, such as rereading, may not be sufficient to recover meaning. Keeping a tally sheet is one way to review the various options and to notice which options readers are using.

Rereading and reading ahead are the most easily modeled and practiced fix-up options. Stopping to think is likewise easy to model, but students must be clear about what prompted the adult reader to reread, read ahead, or pause the reading in the first place. In think-alouds, educators should provide students with a broad range of possibilities, such as an unknown word or phrase or a difficult or new concept, a new character, a change in the speaker or in the point of view, or an inability to summarize what has been read. Visualizing, posing questions, and predicting are options that make direct connections to the reading comprehension strategies discussed in chapters 4, 5, and 6, respectively. Using an illustration (such as a chart) or a text

FIGURE 8-3
Fix-Up Options Self-Monitoring Sheet

OPTIONS	OPTIONS USED	OPTIONS NOT USED
1. Reread.		
2. Read ahead.		
3. Stop to think.		
4. Try to visualize.		
5. Ask new question.		
6. Make a prediction.		
7. Study the illustration or other text features.		
8. Ask someone for help.		
9. Figure out unknown words.		
10. Look at the sentence structure.		
11. Make an inference.		
12. Connect to background knowledge.		
13. Read the author's or illustrator's note.		
14. Write about the confusing parts.		
15. Make an effort to think about the message.		
16. Define/redefine the purpose for reading this text.		

Adapted from Zimmermann and Hutchins (2003).

feature (such as a bold glossary word) are options that readers should connect with the strategy of determining main ideas (chapter 7).

Asking someone for help is last, but not least, in the first set of fix-up options. When educators model getting help from someone, they should clearly articulate the kind of help they need. "I don't get it" is not enough. Readers must learn to be more specific about their loss of comprehension and the kind of help they seek. For example, a reader can ask for help understanding why a character acted in a particular way or how a graph illustrates the idea found in the print. Using precise language is an important part of modeling asking fix-up questions of peers and adults.

Four more options follow this initial set. Figuring out unknown words should be demonstrated using context clues first, as noted above. Sentence structure, or syntax, provides readers with important context clues about the part of speech of the unknown word. These options can be modeled, practiced, and reinforced with *cloze procedures,* in which educators think aloud and students fill in the blanks. Students hypothesize the part of speech required and use the context clues to suggest missing words (see the glossary for an example). Figuring out unknown words by reading between the lines is one type of inference. Students can make inferences about all story elements as well as root causes or resulting effects of information presented in expository texts (chapter 6). To make effective inferences, students must successfully use their background knowledge, which is the next option. The self-recognition that they do not have enough background knowledge is of course necessary before they can remedy it (chapter 3).

The final four options require a good deal of sophistication on the part of the reader. Authors and illustrators give readers insight into themes and meanings of texts from the creators' perspective when they explain their motivation for writing or connections to the story or topic. Some children may have difficulty comprehending authors' notes, which are sometimes written for adult readers. Writing has been called "thinking on paper." When readers make the time to write about their confu-

sion, they may be able to identify the source of their problem, or they may be able to work through their misunderstanding. Making a conscious effort to think about the message, moral, or theme of the text is a high-level inference (chapter 6). Combining conscious thinking and writing about confusion can be most effective. Students need to be prompted to use writing about their confusion as a fix-up option.

Redefining the purpose for reading in order to make sense of a text is an advanced option for educators to model and for which students can reach. As students learned when studying main ideas, the purpose for reading determines the reader's focus. The care with which readers pay attention to comprehension has a great deal to do with their purpose for reading and their commitment to meaning-making. With a low investment in the text, readers may decide to read on after comprehension is lost if they believe they can piece together what they missed or if what they are reading has little importance to their lives. If, on the other hand, a reader's main goal is to make meaning throughout the reading, then she will most likely retrace her steps and apply one or more fix-up options to regain comprehension.

Making Literature Connections

Texts that support monitoring comprehension and using fix-up options have one thing in common: they are confusing to the reader. Identifying texts to teach this strategy requires educators to be sensitive to the unique background experiences and reading development of the students in their charge. A text built around an unfamiliar text structure, such as cause and effect or problem solution, can also be bewildering to the reader. A text in content areas with new or specialized vocabulary or concepts can confound the reader. Texts that use idiomatic expressions and jargon can be confusing to students who are not insiders to a particular culture, who are new to a particular region, or who are learning a second language. Science fiction texts that require readers to keep an alternate reality with all of its imagined characteristics clearly in their minds can be mystifying. Poetic texts that use metaphors can pose challenges to students who lack the background or experience to make the necessary comparisons between literal and figurative meanings. When educators are selecting anchor texts for teaching fix-up options, they can look to every genre.

Ultimately, any and every text has the potential to leave a reader perplexed. It is up to the reader herself to recognize her loss of comprehension during the reading process. In addition to using children's materials, educators must model both the loss of comprehension and the use of fix-up options to regain it with texts written for adults. This helps students realize that using the fix-up strategy is a lifelong learning skill. The importance of recognizing the need for self-monitoring meaning-making is a prerequisite for teaching the fix-up options. Monitoring comprehension and using fix-up options are two sides of the same coin.

Summary

Using the fix-up strategy is one of the important tools students can develop to improve reading comprehension. Fix-up options are only as effective as readers' ability to monitor their own understanding of texts. Educators and students can share the many ways they realize when they have lost track of the meaning of something they are reading. Think-aloud strategies are essential in helping readers understand the cognitive processes behind this strategy. Using the active reading questions to monitor comprehension (figure 8-2) and the fix-up option terms (figure 8-3) in both the classroom and the library helps students strengthen their ability to achieve this high level of metacognition.

Students can develop the ability to recognize and remedy a loss of comprehension in a supportive learning environment. Learners must feel safe in order to take the risks implied in this strategy, and all classmates must be committed to everyone's success. It is educators' responsibility to create an encouraging atmosphere that can nurture students' exploration of fix-up options. One way to build that level of trust in the classroom and in the library is for adults to share their own struggles in comprehending challenging texts. In their collaborations, educators can show students that they too must take risks by acknowledging their confusion and sharing their efforts to achieve comprehension. Although fix-up options can be taught in formal lessons, the most effective way to teach this strategy is at teachable moments with authentic and troublesome texts.

Children's Literature Cited

Starred titles are used in the lesson plans.

*"Jabberwocky," in *Through the Looking Glass and What Alice Found There,* by Lewis Carroll (any illustrated version)

* *Rosa,* by Nikki Giovanni, illustrated by Bryan Collier

* *Voices in the Park,* by Anthony Browne

Lesson Plans

All three lesson plans include anchor books with formats, topics, concepts, or vocabulary that may be unfamiliar to students at each level of literacy development. Each lesson includes a teacher resource supplement that offers examples of ways to introduce readers to the fix-up options. These supplements may include more examples than educators would normally integrate into one lesson. Educators are encouraged to choose the options that seem most appropriate for their students. Ideally, educators will introduce and reinforce these strategies at teachable moments, when the need for a fix-up occurs spontaneously during a text reading.

In each of the lessons, educators ask students to brainstorm how they know when they have lost comprehension, when they no longer understand what they are reading or hearing. Record and save students' ideas. Use their ideas to create a class and library chart similar to figure 8-2. Remember that the fix-up options are only useful if readers are conscious of their loss of comprehension. In fact, monitoring the loss of comprehension, rather than the fix-up options themselves, may be the most important component of these lessons.

Using Fix-Up Options

Reading Development Level	Emerging
Instructional Strategies	Cues and Questions, Classifying, and Summarizing
Lesson Length	1 session
Purpose	The purpose of this lesson is to monitor comprehension and to use fix-up options to regain comprehension of a sophisticated picture book.
Objectives	At the end of this lesson, after reading *Voices in the Park,* students will be able to

1. Define eight fix-up options.

2. Determine when they have lost comprehension.

3. Use fix-up options to regain comprehension.

4. Evaluate which options were most useful with this particular text.

5. Participate in a shared-writing reflective paragraph about the experience of using the fix-up strategy.

Resources, Materials, and Equipment	*Voices in the Park,* by Anthony Browne
	Graphic Organizers: Teacher Resource: Fix-Up Options (Web Supplement 8A), Fix-Up Options Monitoring Tally Sheet (Web Supplement 8B), Sample Shared-Writing Paragraphs (Web Supplement 8C)
	Overhead, data projector, or interactive whiteboard
Collaboration	The educators divide the class in half. Each uses think-alouds to model recognizing a loss of comprehension and using fix-up options to recover comprehension. Each educator facilitates a shared writing, a reflective paragraph about using fix-up options.
Assessment	The students' participation (class tally sheet and shared writing) shows what they understand about recognizing a loss of comprehension and using fix-up options.
Standards	*Reading keywords:* predict using prior knowledge; confirm predictions; relate information to life experiences; interpret text
	Writing keywords: generate ideas through prewriting; participate in a group response to a literary selection; use the writing process
	Information literacy keywords: organize information for effective use; use information accurately and creatively
Process	*Motivation*

Divide the class in half. Each educator works with half the class. Booktalk *Voices in the Park,* the anchor book for this lesson.

Cues and Questions: Ask students to think about a time they visited a park. Who were you with? What did you do? If the other child or adult with you were to tell the story of that day in the park, would his story be the same as yours? Educators model asking and answering these questions. Then they ask the questions one at a time and involve students in a think-pair-share with a partner.

Bookwalk *Voices in the Park*. Show that the book is divided into four voices. Have students read books that are constructed like this one? Discuss how that type of construction may be confusing for a reader.

Lead a discussion: What can readers do when the words and ideas they are reading are not making sense?

To make meaning when we read, we need to understand what we are reading. How do we know when a text stops making sense? Ask students to brainstorm how they know when they have lost comprehension, when they no longer understand what they are reading or hearing. Record and save students' ideas. (Supplement brainstorm with ideas from figure 8-2 or some of these examples: "voice" in head is lost or confused; "projector" inside head shuts off; mind starts to wander; can't remember what was just read; characters suddenly appear or the reader has no memory of them; lost track of what's happening; bored!)

Student-Friendly Objectives

1. Notice when the book doesn't make sense.

2. Use eight fix-up options.

3. Count fix-up options used.

4. Decide which option helped most and which helped least.

5. Contribute to a shared-writing response to the book.

Presentation

Students sit with partners. Project the Fix-Up Options Monitoring Tally Sheet (Web Supplement 8B). Post this sign: READ, STOP AND THINK, TALK ALOUD, USE A FIX-UP OPTION, MARK TALLY SHEET, READ ON

An educator reads *Voices in the Park* and marks the class tally sheet. She uses think-aloud strategies to share a possible loss of comprehension and use of fix-up options. (Web Supplement 8A is a teacher resource.) After modeling with a few pages, stop periodically to conduct think-pair-share procedures. Invite students to suggest when there is a loss of comprehension and to recommend a fix-up option.

Students raise hands to stop the reading. The educator probes the student's confusion or suggests one of her own. (Stop after reading each double-page spread.) Continue to use think-alouds to determine the fix-up option to use to get unstuck. The educator marks the class tally sheet.

Student Practice Procedures

1. Raise hand when confused.

2. Explain your confusion.

3. Think-pair-share loss of comprehension.

4. Use one or more of the fix-up options.

5. Raise hand to share with the class.

Guided Practice

The educators monitor the students' contributions and cooperative learning.

Closure

Each half-class group tallies the fix-up options and notes which options were used most often and which were used least frequently. Think-pair-share a response to the story. Think-pair-share ideas about using fix-up options to make meaning.

Compose one shared-writing response to the story and one shared-writing reflection about using fix-up options to make meaning (Web Supplement 8C is a sample). Bring the groups back together as one whole class to share the writing pieces and conduct the reflection.

Reflection

When a book is difficult to understand, should we simply give up? What are some of the options we learned to help us understand challenging text? How do we know when to use fix-up options? How can we remember what the options are? If we are not making meaning, are we reading?

Extension To extend this lesson, repeat this process with other challenging texts, including poems, short stories, and informational texts. Continue to monitor which options are used most frequently and which new options are being added to the students' repertoires.

Using Fix-Up Options

Reading Development Level	Advancing
Instructional Strategies	Cues and Questions, Classifying, Metaphors, and Summarizing
Lesson Length	2 sessions
Purpose	The purpose of this lesson is to monitor comprehension and to use fix-up options to regain comprehension of an informational book.
Objectives	At the end of this lesson after reading *Rosa*, students will be able to

1. Define twelve fix-up options.
2. Determine when they have lost comprehension.
3. Use fix-up options to regain comprehension.
4. Evaluate which options were most useful with this particular text.
5. Define and use metaphors.
6. Compose a reflective paragraph about their experience using the fix-up strategy.

Resources, Materials, and Equipment	*Rosa,* by Nikki Giovanni, illustrated by Bryan Collier
	Graphic Organizers: Teacher Resource: Fix-Up Options (Web Supplement 8D), Fix-Up Options Self-Monitoring Tally Sheet (Web Supplement 8E), Sample Reflective Paragraph (Web Supplement 8F), Rubric for Reflective Paragraph (Web Supplement 8G)
	Overhead, data projector, or interactive whiteboard
Collaboration	The educators work as a team to model recognizing a loss of comprehension and using fix-up options to recover comprehension. They collaborate to model partner writing and reflective paragraph assessment.
Assessment	The students' self-monitoring sheet, reflective paragraphs, and rubric assessments show what they understand about recognizing a loss of comprehension and using fix-up options.
Standards	*Reading keywords:* predict using prior knowledge; confirm predictions; ask clarifying questions; use knowledge of word order (syntax); use graphic organizers; make connections to other texts or background knowledge; interpret text
	Writing keywords: summary or reflective paper that describes, explains, informs, or summarizes ideas and content; supports a thesis based on experience; prewriting; paragraph includes topic sentence, supporting details, and relevant information; use the writing process
	Social studies keywords: individuals (e.g., Rosa Parks and Dr. Martin Luther King Jr.) worked for and supported the rights and freedoms of others; identify traits of character (e.g., honesty, courage, cooperation, respect, trustworthiness, responsibility, citizenship) that are important to the preservation and improvement of democracy
	Information literacy keywords: organize information for effective use; use information accurately and creatively

Motivation

Cues and Questions: Rosa, the anchor book for this lesson, has earned many awards, both for the words (print) and for the illustrations. Many people believe this book is well written and beautifully illustrated. It also includes some words and concepts that may be difficult for students to understand.

Lead a discussion: What can readers do when the words and ideas on the page or on the screen don't make sense?

To make meaning when we read, we need to understand what we are reading. How do we know when a text stops making sense? Ask students to brainstorm how they know when they have lost comprehension, when they no longer understand what they are reading or hearing. Record and save students' ideas. (Supplement brainstorm with ideas from figure 8-2 or some of these examples: "voice" in head is lost or confused; "projector" inside head shuts off; mind starts to wander; can't remember what was just read; characters suddenly appear or the reader has no memory of them; lost track of what's happening; bored!)

Student-Friendly Objectives

1. Identify signs of lost comprehension.

2. Define and apply the twelve fix-up options.

3. Identify which fix-up options help most and least in comprehending this text.

Presentation

Students sit with partners. Each team has a copy of the Fix-Up Options Self-Monitoring Tally Sheet (Web Supplement 8E). Project a copy of the tally sheet. Post this sign: READ, STOP AND THINK, TALK ALOUD, USE A FIX-UP OPTION, MARK YOUR ORGANIZER, READ ON

One educator reads *Rosa.* The other educator takes responsibility for marking the class tally sheet. Both use think-alouds to share their loss of comprehension and use of fix-up options. (Web Supplement 8D is a teacher resource.) After modeling with a few pages, stop periodically to conduct think-pair-share procedures. Invite students to suggest when there is a loss of comprehension and to recommend a fix-up option.

The students work with a partner. They raise their hands if they lose meaning. (The educators fill in where students do not respond to a loss of comprehension.) Probe the student regarding her loss of comprehension. Educators facilitate the think-pair-share. Students offer fix-up options to regain meaning.

Student Practice Procedures

1. Raise hand when confused.

2. Explain your confusion.

3. Think-pair-share loss of comprehension.

4. Use one or more of the fix-up options.

5. Raise hand to share with the class.

6. Place a tally mark on the graphic organizer.

Guided Practice

The educators probe students to ascertain the source of their confusion. They clarify the students' fix-up option contributions.

Closure

As a class, tally the fix-up option marks. Note which options were used most often and which were used least frequently.

Day 2

Student-Friendly Objectives

1. Brainstorm metaphors for fix-up options.
2. Write a paragraph with a partner about losing comprehension and using fix-up options.
3. Include a metaphor in the paragraph.

Presentation

Define similes as comparisons between different things or ideas that use *like* or *as* and metaphors as comparisons that do not use *like* or *as*. Give some examples such as those found in figure 4-1. As a class, brainstorm some similes and metaphors for the concept of the fix-up strategy and using fix-up options, which the educators then record on the board or butcher paper. (Examples: tools from a reader's toolbox; needle and thread to stitch comprehension back together; a magnifying glass that helps readers focus and see where they went wrong; friends that help you when you get lost.) Let students know that they will be using a simile or metaphor in their reflective paragraphs.

Using the class tally sheet as a writing prompt, educators model the student practice procedures and compose a reflective paragraph to summarize what they learned about losing comprehension and using fix-up options (Web Supplement 8F). Use the Rubric for Reflective Paragraph (Web Supplement 8G) to assess the sample paragraph.

Students work with a partner to complete the tasks. Each student writes his/her own final copy of the reflective paragraph.

Student Practice Procedures

1. Review the class comprehension loss brainstorm.
2. Review your tally sheet.
3. Web three big ideas about losing comprehension.
4. Web three big ideas about applying fix-up options.
5. Compose a paragraph with your partner.
6. Check the rubric, revise, and edit.
7. Each person writes a final copy.
8. Self-assess as a team using the rubric.
9. Turn in web, draft, final copy, and rubric.

Guided Practice

Educators monitor students' writing process and conduct writing conferences when appropriate.

Closure

Discuss the reflection questions. Pose the final reflection question and ask students to think-pair-share. Invite volunteers to share their ideas with the class.

Reflection

When a book is difficult to understand, should we simply give up? What are some of the options we learned to help us understand challenging texts? How do we know when to use fix-up options? How can we remember what the options are? If we are not making meaning, are we reading?

Extensions *Rosa* is also an anchor text in the advancing synthesizing lesson in chapter 9. If educators do not facilitate that mini-unit, reread *Rosa* and make notes on the information in the text. Ask students to design a product to show what they learned about Mrs. Rosa Parks (see ideas from the advancing lesson in chapter 9).

To extend this lesson, repeat this process with other challenging texts, including poems, short stories, and other kinds of informational text. Continue to monitor which options are used most frequently and which new options are being added to the students' repertoires.

Using Fix-Up Options

Reading Development Level	Advanced
Instructional Strategies	Cues and Questions, Classifying, Metaphors, and Summarizing
Lesson Length	2 sessions
Purpose	The purpose of this lesson is to monitor comprehension and to use fix-up options to regain comprehension of a nonsense poem.
Objectives	At the end of this lesson, after reading and analyzing "Jabberwocky," students will be able to

1. Define all sixteen fix-up options.

2. Determine when they have lost comprehension.

3. Practice metacognition to apply their preferred options.

4. Evaluate which options were most useful with this particular text.

5. Define and use metaphors.

6. Compose a reflective paragraph about their experience using the fix-up strategy.

Resources, Materials, and Equipment	*Jabberwocky,* by Lewis Carroll, illustrated by Joel Stewart, or another illustrated edition of the poem "Jabberwocky," from *Through the Looking Glass and What Alice Found There,* by Lewis Carroll

Graphic Organizers: Teacher Resource: Fix-Up Options (Web Supplement 8H), Poem Graphic Organizer (Web Supplement 8I), Fix-Up Options Self-Monitoring Tally Sheet (Web Supplement 8J), Sample Reflective Paragraph (Web Supplement 8K), Rubric for Reflective Paragraph (Web Supplement 8L)

Overhead, data projector, or interactive whiteboard

Collaboration	The educators work as a team to model recognizing a loss of comprehension and using fix-up options to recover comprehension. Both monitor student partners as they practice this strategy. They collaborate to model partner writing and reflective paragraph assessment.
Assessment	The students' self-monitoring sheet, reflective paragraph, and rubric assessment show what they understand about recognizing a loss of comprehension and using fix-up options.
Standards	*Reading keywords:* predict using prior knowledge; confirm predictions; ask clarifying questions; use graphic organizers; make connections to other texts or background knowledge; interpret text

Writing keywords: summary or reflective paper that describes, explains, informs, or summarizes ideas and content; supports a thesis based on experience; prewriting; record observations on charts; paragraph includes topic sentence, supporting details, and relevant information; use the writing process

Information literacy keywords: organize information for effective use; use information accurately and creatively

Motivation

Cues and Questions: Have you ever read the poem "Jabberwocky" by Lewis Carroll? Cover the book jacket so students cannot see the cover illustration. Read an illustrated version but do not share the illustrations. Let students know this is intentional and designed to force them to make sense from the print alone. Does this poem make sense to you? Why not? What can readers do when the words and ideas they are reading don't make sense?

To make meaning when we read, we need to understand what we are reading. How do we know when a text stops making sense? Ask students to brainstorm how they know when they have lost comprehension, when they no longer understand what they are reading or hearing. Record and save students' ideas. (Supplement brainstorm with ideas from figure 8-2 or some of these examples: "voice" in head is lost or confused; "projector" inside head shuts off; mind starts to wander; can't remember what was just read; characters suddenly appear or the reader has no memory of them; lost track of what's happening; bored!)

Student-Friendly Objectives

1. Identify signs of lost comprehension.

2. Define and use the sixteen fix-up options.

3. Identify which fix-up options help most and least in comprehending this poem.

Presentation

Students sit with partners. Each team has a copy of the Poem Graphic Organizer (Web Supplement 8I) and the Fix-Up Options Self-Monitoring Tally Sheet (Web Supplement 8J). Post this sign: READ, STOP AND THINK, TALK ALOUD, USE A FIX-UP OPTION, MARK YOUR ORGANIZER, READ ON

Project the Poem Graphic Organizer (Web Supplement 8I). Reread the entire poem and then reread the first verse. To make sense of this nonsense poem, educators model pausing the reading, thinking aloud, using fix-up options to regain comprehension, making a note about it, and marking the tally sheet to indicate which strategy they used (Web Supplement 8J). (Use Web Supplement 8H as a teacher resource.) If necessary, review the types of notes (figure 2-1 or Web Supplement 2A). Through this process, review as many of the sixteen fix-up options as possible and clarify their meaning by giving examples from the first verse. Notice which options were not used and explain those.

Tell students to continue reading with their partners and to apply the process just modeled. Remind students that even partners' graphic organizers can be different. Readers often use different options for the same reading challenges.

Student Practice Procedures

1. Read aloud.

2. Stop at the end of each line.

3. Think aloud with your partner.

4. Use one or more of the fix-up options.

5. Make notes about how you used the option on the poem graphic organizer.

6. Place a tally mark on the tally sheet.

7. Read on.

Guided Practice

The educators monitor the groups' process and progress. Conference with groups about the tricky parts.

Closure

Did all of us use the same options? Ask students to tally their marks. Note which options were used most often and which were used least frequently. Reread "Jabberwocky" as illustrated by Joel Stewart and share the illustrations. Ask students if these were the images they visualized.

Day 2 **Student-Friendly Objectives**

1. Web ideas about losing comprehension.

2. Web ideas about using fix-up options.

3. Write a reflective paragraph with a partner about fix-up options.

4. Include a metaphor or simile in the paragraph.

5. Turn in partner web and draft and individual final paragraphs and rubrics.

Presentation

Define similes as comparisons between different things or ideas that use *like* or *as* and metaphors as comparisons that do not use *like* or *as*. Give some examples such as those found in figure 4-1. As a class, brainstorm some similes and metaphors for fix-up options, which the educators record on the board or butcher paper. (Examples: swords that slay the confusion dragon; tools from a reader's toolbox; needle and thread to stitch comprehension back together; a magnifying glass that helps readers focus and see where they went wrong; friends that help you when you get lost.) Let students know that they will be using a simile or metaphor in their reflective paragraphs.

Using a fictitious tally sheet as a writing prompt, educators web their ideas and then model composing a reflective paragraph to show what they learned about losing comprehension and using fix-up options. (Web Supplement 8K is a sample paragraph.) Include a simile or metaphor. Use the Rubric for Reflective Paragraph to assess the sample paragraph (Web Supplement 8L).

Students work with a partner to organize their prewriting and draft their paragraphs. They write individual final copies and complete individual self-assessments using the rubric.

Student Practice Procedures

1. Review the class comprehension loss brainstorm.

2. Review your tally sheet.

3. Web three big ideas about losing comprehension.

4. Web three big ideas about applying fix-up options.

5. Compose a paragraph with your partner and include a simile or metaphor.

6. Check the rubric, revise, and edit.

7. Write an individual final copy.

8. Self-assess final copy using the rubric.

9. Turn in partner webs and draft and individual final copy and rubric.

Closure

Ask students to share their similes and metaphors for fix-up options. Discuss the reflection questions. Pose the final reflection question and ask students to think-pair-share. Invite volunteers to share their thoughts with the class.

Reflection

How do we recognize when we have lost comprehension? What are some options we can use to recover our comprehension? Why is it important to make meaning from what we read? If we are not making meaning, are we reading?

Extensions Create a cloze procedure by deleting the unknown words in "Jabberwocky." Give students the opportunity to make up their own poem using real or nonsense words and then to illustrate it. Share the poems and illustrations and create an electronic or printed class book.

Collect a text set of illustrated versions of "Jabberwocky." Ask students to compare their own visual imagery with that of published illustrators of this poem.

To reteach the fix-up strategy lesson, repeat this process with other texts, including other poems, short stories, and informational texts. Continue to assess which options are used most frequently and which new options are being added to the students' repertoires.

9

Reading Comprehension Strategy Seven
Synthesizing

The Mouse Moral: Knowing in part may make a fine tale, but wisdom comes from seeing the whole.

—From *Seven Blind Mice*, by Ed Young

Activating Background Knowledge

Using Sensory Images

Questioning

Making Predictions and Inferences

Determining Main Ideas

Using Fix-Up Options

Synthesizing

Synthesizing is putting it all together; it is the whole elephant. Unlike a summary, which is just the facts and only the facts, synthesis goes a step farther. True, it is composed of the main ideas as selected by the reader, but through the selection process the reader analyzes the information he has gathered and filters it through his own interpretation. Synthesis sheds light on the significance of texts from the reader's point of view. Although it is possible to synthesize the information found in just one text, the more common practice of this strategy, particularly from a school library perspective, involves bringing together information from several sources. As readers synthesize, they sort and evaluate information. They may find agreement among texts, or they may encounter conflicting "facts." Synthesizing, like determining main ideas, requires that readers make value judgments.

Modeling and practicing this comprehension strategy is a natural activity for classroom-library collaboration. With a focus on information literacy, teacher-librarians are perfectly positioned to serve as teacher leaders with expertise in teaching synthesizing strategies. Teaching students to access information efficiently and effectively, to evaluate information critically and competently, and to use information accurately and creatively are part and parcel of the teacher-librarian's instructional role. If "synthesis is the process of ordering, recalling, retelling, and recreating [information] into a coherent whole" (Keene and Zimmermann 1997, 169), then surely the library with its rich array of resources is the perfect location for modeling and practicing this strategy. In fact, it may be in libraries of all types that students will continue to put this lifelong learning skill into practice.

Synthesizing requires that readers use the strategies offered in this book to read, to evaluate, and to use ideas and information. Synthesis requires longer-term, in-depth learning. When students are exploring curriculum-based subjects or independent inquiry topics, the teacher-librarian can offer expertise in teaching information literacy skills and strategies. The library collection, the Web, and interlibrary loan can supply the resources students and classroom teachers need to be successful. Keeping accurate bibliographic records and notemaking effectively, which are core information literacy skills, are even more critical when students are synthesizing information from multiple sources. Classroom teachers will appreciate teacher-librarians who can codevelop graphic organizers that help students maintain organization while gathering information.

With a library collection that is aligned with classroom curricula and the independent reading and research needs of the learning community, the teacher-librarian can support resource-based units of instruction. This is a pivotal professional task for teacher-librarians. Classroom-library collaboration supports educators in assessing the effectiveness of specific resources within a text set before, during, and after the lesson. Educators can note which titles generate the most interest among students. They can determine which resources present particular challenges to readers. Through resource evaluation at the point of practice, educators can collaboratively guide the library's collection development.

Supplementing the collection through interlibrary loan is a way to ensure that classroom teachers and students are successful in their research and inquiry projects. Interlibrary loan can be particularly valuable when educators need multiple copies of texts. District-level union catalogs help teacher-librarians locate and share resources. Bringing in resources from the public and college or university libraries may also be necessary. Pointing out to students that there are useful learning resources outside the school may help them connect with other institutions for homework or independent learning.

Units of study that focus on synthesis invite increased opportunities for interdisciplinary teaching and learning. Including other educators in synthesis collaborations can enhance student outcomes. Students benefit when specialists such as art or music teachers participate in designing, implementing, and assessing lessons. Teacher-librarians and classroom teachers can also increase their own knowledge in these domains as they learn alongside students. In addition, these broader partnerships have the potential to influence the level of collaboration throughout the school community. Everyone can profit from the resulting culture of shared responsibility for student learning.

As with all collaborative teaching, increasing adult support can offer students more individual assistance. Lowering the student-to-teacher ratio can also help students remain on task during extended learning periods, because they don't have to wait as long to receive help or redirection. Classroom-library collaboration to teach and practice synthesis is not just more effective, it's also more fun. With two or more educators to monitor student learning and adjust instruction, students may experience greater learning success, and educators may find more enjoyment in teaching long-term projects.

For students to synthesize information effectively and make it their own, they must first bring it all together. They must develop all of the reading comprehension strategies discussed in this book and use them to make meaning. They must merge the information found in various resources, interpret it, and put it back together into a transformed and coherent whole. Readers who can synthesize are like the white mouse in *Seven Blind Mice* (Young). They are able to consider the parts and to understand the whole elephant. Students who master this strategy are proficient at comprehending the texts they read, combining information from multiple sources, and passing that information through their own interpretations. It is through this process that learners generate knowledge that creates, develops, and revises their schemas. The persistent information overload of 21st-century life has made this skill more important than ever.

How to Teach the Strategy

Synthesizing requires that readers determine main ideas from multiple sources, summarize information, and add their own interpretations. Graphic organizers, such as the Informational Book Self-Monitoring Graphic Organizer in figure 9-1, can be developed to help readers record main ideas and surprising information as well as their connections, responses, and interpretations.

Bringing these strategies together helps readers see how comprehension strategies are related. The example in figure 9-1 includes a section to help readers be aware of the print and text features that present new information. This list also serves as a reminder to use all the features in informational resources.

Although a summary meets the criteria for learning at the comprehension level on Bloom's taxonomy (Bloom et al. 1956), synthesizing is a higher-order thinking skill. Synthesis is the process of learning from others' ideas and transforming those ideas through analysis and interpretation to offer a new meaning. Through synthesis, the learner makes information and ideas his own. Some examples of verbs associated with synthesizing are *construct, design, devise, formulate, imagine, invent,* and *propose.* Each of these actions suggests that the learner goes beyond the facts to suggest his own ideas, to offer his own interpretations.

Synthesis reminds educators of the importance of providing students with opportunities to express their responses to the texts they read. If, for example, students have been sharing, writing, drawing, and using other sign systems to respond to texts, then synthesizing is a natural outgrowth of their prior literacy learning experiences. A simple way to

express the components of synthesizing that may be particularly appropriate to younger readers is

Information + Response = Synthesis

Readers' responses to texts can be described in many ways. They can make personal or text-to-self connections that include their prior knowledge, experiences, and feelings. They can respond to specific story elements, such as the setting or theme. They can pose questions about concepts or topics and suggest "what if" scenarios. The important thing about a response is that it not be a restatement of the story or facts. A response is unique to the reader and demonstrates the central role of the reader in the reading transaction. Combined with information or evidence from texts, readers' responses are the other main ingredient in synthesis.

In a 1996 study of students in a tenth-grade advanced-placement American history class, researchers learned that, after reading a variety of online documents, students' opinion papers did not include evidence from the texts to support their opinions or perspectives. Nor did their descriptive papers explain conflicting information they had encountered in texts. The researchers concluded that explicit instruction on how to use and evaluate information from multiple sources should begin in elementary school (Stahl 2005, 189). Teaching the reading comprehension strategy of synthesis using multiple texts is a place to begin.

When more advanced readers interpret texts, they explain meaning in relation to their own beliefs, judgments, or circumstances. To that end, another way for students to conceive of synthesis is

Information + Interpretation = Synthesis

Unit design is one way to ensure that students incorporate their own interpretations into their synthesis projects. Assignments must require that students do more than cut and paste information and call it a "report." Designing instruction so that students are required to think about the ideas and information they read is fundamental. Involving students in asking authentic questions, analyzing information, and transforming it through synthe-

FIGURE 9-1
Informational Book Self-Monitoring Graphic Organizer

Student's Name: _____

Book Title: _____

Author/Illustrator: _____

1. I reread to better understand information about:

2. I made notes about the five Ws and the H:

   Who?

   What?

   Where?

   When?

   Why?

   How?

3. I found this new information the most interesting or surprising to me:

4. I learned that new information by reading:

   a. the print

   b. the illustrations

   c. the captions

   d. a graphic such as a map, chart, graph, or photograph

   e. other (Name it.)

5. What connections am I making? What do I think or feel about this information?
   What does this information mean to me?

sis means expecting them to do more than regurgitate facts. Loertscher, Koechlin, and Zwann's *Ban Those Bird Units: 15 Models for Teaching and Learning in Information-Rich and Technology-Rich Environments* (2004) is an exemplary resource for guiding classroom-library collaboration to help students achieve synthesis.

All of the print and electronic information-seeking skills can be taught during instruction focused on synthesis. Resource location skills and using the text features of informational books are tasks that may be required for students engaged in learning this strategy. Teaching students to use the online card catalog efficiently and effectively can be integrated into units of instruction in which students select their own text sets and materials. Skimming, scanning, and notemaking are sub-skills in the research process and can be taught or reviewed during synthesis lessons. When a savvy teacher-librarian shares expertise in searching Web-based and database resources, classroom teachers as well as students can further develop their electronic literacy skills. Teaching students how to evaluate resources, particularly websites, for authority, accuracy, and currency is easily integrated into synthesis lessons. For students, practicing synthesis requires them to master a valuable set of subskills and strategies, many of which can be taught most effectively through classroom-library collaboration.

Making Literature Connections

When choosing texts for the purpose of synthesizing ideas and information, educators can provide students with carefully selected text sets of resources at various reading levels, in multiple genres, and in a variety of formats, including websites and other technology sources. Developing text sets collaboratively can be a valuable learning experience for both classroom teachers and teacher-librarians, who may bring different strengths and perspectives to the table. One educator may be particularly knowledgeable in the area of print resources; the other may be savvy about websites. One may be more familiar with fiction titles; the other may be more versed in informational sources. Together, educators can develop engaging text sets for student explorations.

Ultimately, educators must give students the responsibility to develop their own text sets on a particular topic or theme. By collecting and evaluating resources, students can demonstrate what they have learned about the strengths of various genres in supporting research and inquiry projects. They can assess the works of favorite authors, illustrators, and Web-based resources for their usefulness in achieving their learning objectives. After classroom teachers and teacher-librarians have modeled collecting and using text sets, students are ready to assume responsibility for this aspect of the research process, and educators can then serve in an advisory role.

Summary

Classroom-library collaboration to teach and to support students as they practice synthesizing information offers young people the opportunity to practice 21st-century literacy skills. Although we cannot predict what the world will be like when today's elementary students graduate from high school, we can feel certain that their daily lives will include accessing, evaluating, and using information. By guiding students through the information literacy process and requiring that their process include their own interpretations of the ideas and information they read and view, educators can help students develop the critical-thinking skills they will need to negotiate the challenges of the future.

Each of the units of study in this chapter ends with an extension that involves the class authoring a shared-writing article to inform the learning community of their accomplishments. It is important for teacher-librarians to make their collaborative work known to colleagues, families, and decision makers in the school and beyond. Involving students in summarizing classroom-library collaborations gives them the opportunity to practice their writing skills while supporting classroom teachers and advocating the teaching role of the teacher-librarian and the importance of the library program in their learning.

Educators who coplan, coimplement, and coassess student outcomes are also modeling collaboration, one of the core competencies for 21st-century learning. In *Results That Matter: 21st Century Skills and High School Reform*, the Partnership for 21st Century Skills (2006) defines rigor for high school students that goes beyond learning core subjects to include mastery of learning and thinking skills, information and communications technology literacy skills, and life skills. Collaboration is among the learning, thinking, and life skills that students need to be successful in today's global economy.

It is never too early to begin connecting reading with meaning-making and connecting meaning-making with generating knowledge that can make a difference in the world. Educators at the elementary school level can set students on a course of learning that serves them well throughout their lives. Through collaborative teaching, information literacy skills and strategies can be seamlessly integrated with curriculum-based lessons and units of instruction so that students can use these tools in the service of their learning. As the Mouse Moral states, "Wisdom comes from seeing the whole." Classroom teachers and teacher-librarians who codesign, coteach, and coassess instruction that helps students see the connections among reading comprehension strategies and information literacy can help learners become more strategic readers who use these skills effectively over their lifetimes. They may even choose to use their knowledge to make the world a more humane and just place for all of us. Now that is maximizing your impact!

Children's Literature Cited

Starred titles are used in the lesson plans.

* *The Bus Ride That Changed History: The Story of Rosa Parks,* by Pamela Duncan Edwards, illustrated by Danny Shanahan

* *Camille and the Sunflowers: A Story about Vincent van Gogh,* by Laurence Anholt

* *The Other Side,* by Jacqueline Woodson, illustrated by E. B. Lewis

* *Remember: The Journey to School Integration,* by Toni Morrison, illustrated with photographs from the 1950s and 1960s

* *Rosa,* by Nikki Giovanni, illustrated by Bryan Collier

* *Rosa Parks,* by Michelle Levine

Seven Blind Mice, by Ed Young

* *This Is the Dream,* by Diane Z. Shore and Jessica Alexander, illustrated by James Ransome

* *Van Gogh: The Touch of Yellow,* by Jacqueline Loumaye, illustrated by Claudine Roucha, translated by John Goodman

* *Vincent's Colors,* by Vincent van Gogh

Lesson Plans

These lessons for teaching synthesis are units of instruction at three levels of literacy development. The language arts/visual arts mini-unit for emerging readers extends students' experience to making notes from several sources, responding to all the texts, writing a synthesis, and creating a painting inspired by Vincent van Gogh. After immersing students in information about Rosa Parks and racial discrimination, the advancing social studies/language arts unit gives students an opportunity to develop their own synthesis product. This unit gives students the open-ended choice to develop their own learning products. With lower student-to-teacher ratios, the benefit of more adult facilitation is particularly apparent. The advanced unit is the most interdisciplinary example offered in this book. It lends itself to a wider collaboration that includes art and music teachers as well as the classroom teacher and teacher-librarian. At the end of this unit, students synthesize their learning through expository and creative writing as well as by creating an illustration in Pablo Picasso's cubist style.

To synthesize from multiple resources, students need time to explore and immerse themselves in a topic, to investigate various resources in many formats, and to reorganize information and combine it with their own interpretations. Through classroom-library collaboration, educators are able to help students sustain the motivation and interest required to complete a long-term project. These valuable opportunities to go deeper set the stage for more independent research and inquiry projects that will be core schooling and lifelong learning experiences for students.

READING COMPREHENSION STRATEGY
Synthesizing

Reading Development Level	Emerging
Instructional Strategies	Categorizing, Notemaking, and Summarizing
Lesson Length	3–5 sessions
Purpose	The purpose of this mini-unit is to synthesize information from three sources and express learning through writing and visual art.
Objectives	At the end of this lesson, students will be able to

1. Categorize and make notes and record sources.
2. Synthesize the information from three sources.
3. Compose sentences and create artwork to show learning.
4. Self-assess with a rubric.

Resources, Materials, and Equipment

Camille and the Sunflowers: A Story about Vincent van Gogh, by Laurence Anholt

Van Gogh: The Touch of Yellow, by Jacqueline Loumaye, illustrated by Claudine Roucha, translated by John Goodman

Vincent's Colors, words and pictures by Vincent van Gogh

Graphic Organizers: Teacher Resource: Bibliography and Notemaking Graphic Organizer (Web Supplement 9A), Bibliography and Notemaking Graphic Organizer (Web Supplement 9B), Sample Letter to Vincent van Gogh (Web Supplement 9C), Teacher Resource: Prewriting Category Web (Web Supplement 9D), Prewriting Category Web (Web Supplement 9E), Sample Summary and Synthesis (Web Supplement 9F), Sample Artwork and Writing (Web Supplement 9G), Artwork Directions (Web Supplement 9H), Synthesis Sentences and Painting Rubric (Web Supplement 9I)

Materials: Poster, print, or online access to van Gogh's painting "Sunflowers," globe and map of Europe, and sunflowers and a vase (optional)

Art Materials: See Web Supplement 9H

Overhead, data projector, or interactive whiteboard

Collaboration

The educators both team and individually teach notemaking. They model synthesizing information from three sources. They both monitor students' artwork and writing and take dictation if needed. Collaboration with the art teacher may enrich this study.

Assessment

The students' bibliography and notemaking graphic organizers, sentences and artwork, and rubrics show the process and results of their learning.

Standards

Reading keywords: extract information and use graphic organizers to comprehend text; connect information and events in text to related text and sources

Writing keywords: use written language for a variety of purposes and audiences; functional writing (letters); paraphrase information from at least one source; write a simple report with a title and three facts

Visual arts keywords: use subjects in a work of art; use expressive qualities to create meaning in a finished work of art; compare the influences and experiences of the artist and viewer in relation to a particular piece of artwork

Information literacy keywords: organize for practical application; integrate information into one's own knowledge; use information creatively

Process   *Motivation*

Day 1   Display or project "Sunflowers" by Vincent van Gogh. Have students seen this painting before? Do they know the name of the painter who created it? Ask students to think-pair-share a response to the painting. Educators model responses that include emotions and ideas the painting evokes. They should also model responses related to van Gogh's artistic style and painting technique.

Student-Friendly Objectives

1. Identify painter van Gogh and his style.

2. Respond to artwork and book.

3. Share ideas for group notes.

4. Give ideas for a shared writing.

Presentation

One educator reads *Vincent's Colors* and the other records class notes. On a class-sized Bibliography and Notemaking Graphic Organizer (Web Supplement 9B), record the title/author/illustrator and read the first page of the book. Review the types of notes (figure 2-1 or Web Supplement 2A). Model notemaking with information from page 1. (Web Supplement 9A is teacher resource of completed notes for all three texts.) Use the globe and a map of Europe to show the location of the Netherlands, Paris, and Arles in southern France.

Continue reading. The students suggest notes and categories. An educator records notes.

Student Participation Procedures

1. Think-pair-share with partner.

2. Suggest a note.

3. Tell which category it fits.

Guided Practice

Educators encourage responses and monitor types of notes.

Closure

Students think-pair-share their initial responses to van Gogh's paintings and words. Ask a few students to volunteer to share their thoughts with the class.

Review the bibliography and notemaking graphic organizer with a focus on the responses. Educators lead the students in composing a shared-writing letter to van Gogh that expresses their responses to his paintings and words (Web Supplement 9C is a sample letter).

Days 2 and 3   *Presentation*

Divide the class in half. One educator reads *Camille and the Sunflowers*. The other shares the paintings and reads the captions in *Van Gogh: The Touch of Yellow*. Each group keeps a Bibliography and Notemaking Graphic Organizer (Web Supplement 9B). Notes can be written by the educator, or if students are more proficient writers they can make notes on their own graphic organizers.

Follow day 1 procedures.

Closure

Review the notes and think-pair-share one new idea about van Gogh. For Day 3, switch student groups and repeat this procedure.

Day 4   *Presentation*

Bring the whole class together. If an art teacher is involved, he takes the lead on this lesson. If not, display or project the painting "Sunflowers." Share the Sample Artwork and Writing (Web Supplement 9G). Follow the Artwork Directions (Web Supplement 9H).

Student-Friendly Objectives

1. Create artwork inspired by van Gogh.

2. Use bright colors, especially yellow, and thick paint.

Guided Practice

Monitor students' artwork for use of van Gogh's colors and thick dashes of paint.

Closure

Display students' artwork around the classroom or library. Think-pair-share responses.

Day 5   *Presentation*

Let students know that they will be writing sentences about van Gogh to accompany their artwork. Their paintings and writings will be displayed together.

Display the paintings around the room. Take a moment or two to admire them. Review all of the notes on van Gogh. Web at least three facts from the texts. Web at least three responses to the artwork. (Web Supplement 9D is a teacher resource. Web Supplement 9E is for student use.)

Project the Sample Summary and Synthesis (Web Supplement 9F). Cover the synthesis and read the summary. Ask: Does it summarize the ideas in the texts we have read? Uncover the synthesis and read it. Ask: What is the difference between these two paragraphs? Share the Synthesis Sentences and Painting Rubric (Web Supplement 9I). Discuss synthesis as bringing together information with students' own responses and interpretations.

Students work individually to complete a web and a synthesis.

Student Practice Procedures

1. Web three facts from the texts.

2. Web three responses to the facts or paintings.

3. Write sentences.

4. Conference with a teacher.

5. Self-assess the painting and the writing with the rubric.

Guided Practice

The educators support students' prewriting webs and conference with students about their writing.

Closure

Display and view the students' writing and paintings while conducting the reflection.

Reflection

What does it mean to synthesize information? When we synthesize our learning, is it enough to share only the facts?

Extensions   Revisit the three texts used in this mini-unit. *Vincent's Colors* contains primary sources, van Gogh's paintings, and quotes from his letters. *Van Gogh: The Touch of Yellow* is an informational book. *Camille and the Sunflowers* is historical fiction based on an actual event and real characters. Help students begin to develop schemas for these types of resource and genre.

Especially if working with an art teacher, students can create more paintings in the style of van Gogh. Invite students' families or other classrooms to view the students' artwork and writing.

After the display comes down, create a class book, print or electronic. Post students' work on the school's website. Compose a shared-writing summary of the unit for the library, school, school district newsletter, or local newspaper, radio stations, or television stations.

Synthesizing

Reading Development Level	Advancing
Instructional Strategies	Notemaking and Summarizing and Cooperative Learning
Lesson Length	6–8 sessions

Purpose

The purpose of this unit is to synthesize information from several sources, to distinguish primary from secondary sources, to self-select a product, and to self-assess it using a rubric.

Objectives

At the end of this unit, students will be able to

1. Define primary and secondary sources.
2. Make notes and record sources.
3. Synthesize the information from at least three sources.
4. Design a product to show what they have learned.
5. Self-assess with a checklist.

Resources, Materials, and Equipment

The Bus Ride That Changed History: The Story of Rosa Parks, by Pamela Duncan Edwards, illustrated by Danny Shanahan

The Other Side, by Jacqueline Woodson, illustrated by E. B. Lewis

Remember: The Journey to School Integration, by Toni Morrison, illustrated with photographs from the 1950s and 1960s

Rosa, by Nikki Giovanni, illustrated by Bryan Collier

Rosa Parks, by Michelle Levine

This Is the Dream, by Diane Z. Shore and Jessica Alexander, illustrated by James Ransome

Graphic Organizers: Teacher Resource: Informational Book Self-Monitoring Graphic Organizer (Web Supplement 9J), Informational Book Self-Monitoring Graphic Organizer (Web Supplement 9K), Sample Summary (Web Supplement 9L), Group Information Sheet and Synthesis Product Checklist (Web Supplement 9M)

Materials: One note card per student and one folder for each group

Overhead, data projector, or interactive whiteboard

Collaboration

The educators model synthesizing information from a variety of sources. They may both monitor students' research and product-making processes, or the teacher-librarian may take responsibility for supporting student research in library center rotations. Educators share responsibility for guiding and assessing students' learning products.

Assessment

The students' informational book self-monitoring graphic organizers, synthesis products, and checklists show the process and results of their learning.

Standards

Reading keywords: extract information and use graphic organizers to comprehend text; connect information and events in text to related text and sources

Writing keywords: record information related to the topic; write in a variety of expository forms; organize notes in a meaningful sequence; paraphrase information from at least one source

Listening and speaking keywords: effective vocabulary and logical organization to relate or summarize ideas; presenting a report

Social studies keywords: recognize that individuals worked for and supported the rights and freedoms of others; use primary source materials (e.g., photos, artifacts, interviews, documents, maps) and secondary source materials to study people and events from the past; identify traits of character (e.g., honesty, courage, cooperation, respect, trustworthiness, responsibility, citizenship) that are important to the preservation and improvement of democracy; discuss the branches of state and national government (judicial); retell stories to describe past events, people, and places

Information literacy keywords: organize for practical application; integrate information into one's own knowledge; use information ethically

Process

Day 1

Motivation

Display the recommended text set for this lesson so that students can view all the book covers. Show a selection of photographs from *Remember: The Journey to School Integration*. Discuss these photos as being primary source documents. Pair a few illustrations with paintings (secondary sources) from *This Is the Dream*. (Examples: *Remember,* page 52, with the opening illustration in *This Is the Dream; Remember,* page 66, with *This Is the Dream,* pages 29–30.)

The educators collaboratively read *This Is the Dream* by reading alternating lines/pages. Invite students to think-pair-share their initial responses to the photographs, paintings, and reading. Ask a few students to volunteer to share their responses with the class. Record and save.

Student-Friendly Objectives

1. Identify primary source and secondary source images.

2. Identify main ideas (five Ws and How).

3. Contribute ideas for group notes orally.

Presentation

Read the titles of the books in this mini-text set. Do students know who Rosa Parks was? Provide a bit of background if the students are unfamiliar with Mrs. Parks.

Create a class-sized Informational Book Self-Monitoring Graphic Organizer (Web Supplement 9K). (Web Supplement 9J is a teacher resource.) Review the types of notes (figure 2-1 or Web Supplement 2A). Record bibliographic information at the top of the self-monitoring sheet.

While one educator reads *Rosa,* the other records class notes on a class-sized self-monitoring sheet. (*Rosa* was the anchor text in the chapter 8 advancing fix-up strategy lesson. Ideally, this will be a second reading of this challenging text.)

Students suggest notes and categories for the class-sized informational book self-monitoring graphic organizer.

Student Participation Procedures

1. Listen for main ideas (five Ws and How).

2. Raise hand to pause the reading.

3. Share a main idea or an interesting detail.

4. Suggest a note.

5. Choose a category.

Guided Practice

Educators support students in suggesting succinct and clear notes and choosing categories for their notes.

Closure

Review the class notes. Think-pair-share a response to the information about Rosa Parks or the civil rights movement for equality among the races. Ask for a few volunteers and record students' ideas (Question 5 on Web Supplement 9K).

Day 2

Student-Friendly Objectives

1. Determine main ideas and supporting details.
2. Participate in group writing.

Presentation

Students sit in small groups. Reread the class notes from the Informational Book Self-Monitoring Graphic Organizer (Web Supplement 9K). Using the numbered-heads-together technique, students supply responses; educators record them. Ask: What are the main ideas? Circle them in one color. (Main ideas are noted in red on the teacher resource, Web Supplement 9J.) Ask: What are supporting details? Circle them in another color.

Student Participation Procedures

1. Number off.
2. Talk with your table group to determine if a note is a main idea or a supporting detail.
3. Answer for the group when the table and your number are called.
4. Contribute ideas to the summary.

Guided Practice

Educators monitor cooperative learning and facilitate a shared-writing summary. (Web Supplement 9L is a sample summary.)

Closure

Review the shared-writing summary. Read it chorally. Think-pair-share and orally review the information found in *Remember* and in *This Is the Dream*. What information from those two resources could be added to this summary of *Rosa*? Brainstorm some ideas using two different marker colors, one for each text. Refer to the students' personal responses that were recorded after reading the texts.

When we put information together from several sources and combine it with our own thoughts and opinions, we are synthesizing. Let students know that they will be reading one or two more books about Rosa Parks before they synthesize the information and design and produce a product to show what they have learned.

Day 3

Student-Friendly Objectives

1. Identify primary source and secondary source images.
2. Make notes and record book titles, authors, and illustrators.
3. Suggest new information for a summary.
4. Synthesize the information and create a product to show learning.
5. Self-assess the product.

Presentation

Divide the class in half. One educator shares *The Bus Ride That Changed History: The Story of Rosa Parks* with half the class. The other educator reads *Rosa Parks,* a biography, with the other half. Depending on the sophistication of the students, educators can record information on a class-sized informational book self-monitoring graphic organizer, or students can make their own notes as the book is read.

The educators or the students record bibliographic information and notes on Web Supplement 9K.

Student Participation Procedures

1. Listen for main ideas (five Ws and How).

2. Raise hand to pause the reading.

3. Share a main idea or an interesting detail.

4. Suggest a note.

5. Choose a category.

Guided Practice

Educators note main ideas and supporting details. They support students in suggesting different types of notes and choosing categories.

Closure

In half-class groups, review the Informational Book Self-Monitoring Graphic Organizer (Web Supplement 9K) for additional information. What new information from the book we just read could be added to our notes on the book *Rosa*? Circle new information on Web Supplement 9K. Conduct a shared writing or compose individual responses to Question 5.

Day 4   *Student-Friendly Objectives*

1. Identify and share new information.

2. Brainstorm text-to-text connections.

3. Brainstorm products that can show learning.

Presentation

Bring both groups together. Put them in mixed group partners. Ask students to share their Informational Book Self-Monitoring Graphic Organizers (Web Supplement 9K). (If class-sized graphic organizers were used, display them or make a copy for each student or share as a class.) What new information did we learn? What responses did we have? Educators model taking turns and sharing new information and responses.

Using their graphic organizers as prompts, students share orally with partners.

Student Participation Procedures

1. Take turns.

2. Share new information and responses.

Guided Practice

Monitor cooperative learning.

Closure

Read *The Other Side*. Compare the illustration of Clover and Annie holding hands to the final illustration in *Remember*. What text-to-text connections can you make among all of the books we have read about Rosa Parks and people of different races working together for equality? Brainstorm and record ideas. Discuss synthesis as information plus personal responses.

How can we synthesize this information? How can we show what we have learned? Brainstorm some different sign systems that students could use to share their learning, such as a skit, song, poem or story, mural, dance, report, or PowerPoint slide show. Record the name of the student who suggested each product.

Ask students to write their first and second choices on note cards. The educators form the groups and designate a communications person from each group before the next session.

Days 5–8   *Student-Friendly Objectives*

1. Keep all work in the group folder.

2. Synthesize the information and design a product to show learning.

3. Self-assess the product.

Presentation

The educators share the Group Information Sheet and Synthesis Product Checklist (Web Supplement 9M). Emphasize that a synthesis is more than a summary. To synthesize, students must add their own ideas, interpretations, and feelings to the information. Students complete the group information section and keep this document in their folders.

Distribute one group information sheet and checklist to each group. Provide groups with folders in which to keep their paperwork.

Guided Practice

Educators monitor collaboration among group members and provide students with any materials they need to achieve their goals for their learning products. They remind groups to review the checklist, particularly as it relates to assessing the synthesis of information in the final product.

Closure

Groups present and self-assess their learning products using the checklist. After each presentation, students are asked to share orally the sources of their information and the ideas they added to this information to synthesize this unit of study.

Reflection

What is it called if you only tell the facts that someone else has already written down? What must you add to the facts in order to synthesize? What does it mean to synthesize information?

Extensions   Some or all groups may decide to share their projects with other classrooms, with the larger school community, or with families. Compose a shared-writing summary of the presentations for the library, school, school district newsletter, or local newspaper, radio stations, or television stations.

READING COMPREHENSION STRATEGY
Synthesizing

Reading Development Level	Advanced
Instructional Strategies	Notemaking and Summarizing, Classifying, and Nonlinguistic Representation
Lesson Length	10–14 sessions
Purpose	The purpose of this unit is to make notes and to synthesize information from multiple sources and formats, to present learning creatively, and to self-assess using a rubric and a checklist.
Objectives	*Language arts objectives:* At the end of this unit, students will be able to

1. Hear and see patterns in literature, music, and visual art.
2. Make notes and record sources.
3. Synthesize information from multiple sources.
4. Follow the writing process.
5. Compose and assess three to five synthesis paragraphs.
6. Create art in the style of Pablo Picasso and use it as a creative writing prompt.
7. Self-assess with a rubric and a checklist.

Music objectives: At the end of this unit, students will be able to

1. Define terms such as *bebop, blues, dissonance, fusion, improvisation, jazz, ragtime, riff, syncopation,* and *tempo.*
2. Describe characteristics of various musical genres and cultures (jazz).
3. Communicate meaning through making music (extension).

Visual arts objectives: At the end of this unit, students will be able to

1. Apply subjects, themes, or symbols from various cultural or historical contexts to their own artwork (Picasso and cubism).
2. Communicate meaning through art.

Technology objectives: By engaging in the extension for this lesson, students will be able to

1. Keyboard their writing.
2. Scan or take digital photos of illustrations.
3. Make design decisions during production.
4. Publish and present.

Resources, Materials, and Equipment	Jazz Topical Text Set (Web Supplement 9N)
	Jazz Pathfinder: http://storytrail.com/Impact/Jazz.htm
	Music by Louis Armstrong, John Coltrane, Miles Davis, Duke Ellington, Dizzy Gillespie, and Charlie Parker
	Graphic Organizers: Build-Know-Wonder-Learn-Question Chart (Web Supplement 9O), Teacher Resource: Bibliography Graphic Organizer (Web Supplement 9P), Bibliography Graphic Organizer (Web Supplement 9Q), Teacher Resource: Jazz and Miles Davis Notes (Web Supplement 9R), Notemaking Graphic Organizer (Web Supplement 9S), Sample Synthesis (Web Supplement 9T), Synthesis Rubric (Web Supplement 9U), Teacher

Resource: Jazz Poem Category Web (Web Supplement 9V), Jazz Poem Category Web (Web Supplement 9W), Sample Art and Poetry Product (Web Supplement 9X), Artwork Directions (Web Supplement 9Y), Synthesis Product Checklist (Web Supplement 9Z)

Materials: Poster, print, or online access to Pablo Picasso's painting "Three Musicians" and highlighters of at least three different colors for students' use

Art Materials: See Web Supplement 9Y

Overhead, Internet access, and data projector, or interactive whiteboard, CD and video players

Collaboration The educators provide parallel as well as cotaught lessons. They model synthesizing information from a variety of sources in a variety of formats. They both may monitor students' research and product-making processes, or the teacher-librarian may take responsibility for supporting student research in library center rotations. Educators share responsibility for guiding and assessing students' learning products. This unit lends itself to extending the collaboration to include art and music teachers.

Assessment The students' bibliography and notemaking graphic organizers, synthesis paragraphs, artwork and poems, rubric, and checklist show the process and results of their learning.

Standards *Reading keywords:* extract information and use graphic organizers to comprehend text; connect information and events in text to related text and sources

Writing keywords: use written language for a variety of purposes and audiences; six traits of writing (ideas, voice, word choice)

Music keywords: describe characteristics of various musical genres and cultures; analyze how music is used to reflect particular moods and feelings; demonstrate a story utilizing the elements of music (extension)

Social studies keywords: use primary source materials (e.g., photos, artifacts, interviews, documents, maps) and secondary source materials to study people and events from the past

Visual arts keywords: identify cultural and historical symbols for their meaning past and present; apply subjects, themes, or symbols from various cultural or historical contexts to own artwork

Information literacy keywords: organize for practical application; integrate information into own knowledge; use information ethically and creatively

Educational technology keywords (extension): demonstrate functional operation of technology devices; design and create a multimedia presentation; publish and present

Process This is an outline rather than a detailed procedure. Depending on the time allotted and the level of collaboration with art or music specialists, this unit can expand or contract as needed.

Day 1 *Motivation*

Display the Topical Text Set (Web Supplement 9N). Educators and students collaborate to read *Jazz Cats* (Davis/Galey). One educator reads the verses; the other cues the students to say "jazz cats" and provides the jazz cats' adjective; it changes in each verse.

After reading, begin collecting jazzy terms on a vocabulary web. Ask students to share what they remember from this book: *swingin', swayin', groovin', wailin', far-out, hepcat, hip, cool daddy,* and so on. Add to this web throughout the unit of study.

Student-Friendly Objectives

1. Collect jazzy vocabulary.

2. Brainstorm what we already know about jazz.

3. Identify primary source and secondary sources.

Presentation

Read the titles and booktalk the books in this text set. Project a class-sized Build-Know-Wonder-Learn-Question Chart (Web Supplement 9O) and distribute individual charts to students. What do students know about the musical art form called jazz? Educators and students record ideas in the "K" section of the chart.

Define the words *improvised/improvisation, individual expression,* and *collaboration.* Share the first fifteen minutes of Ken Burns's *Jazz: Episode 1: Gumbo.* (Note: The musicians who are described but not named are Jelly Roll Morton, Duke Ellington, Benny Goodman, Billie Holiday, Charlie Parker, Miles Davis, and Louis Armstrong.) Stop the video when narrator Wynton Marsalis talks about gumbo. Which components of the video are primary source documents? Which are secondary?

Distribute file folders with Bibliography Graphic Organizers (Web Supplement 9Q) and Notemaking Graphic Organizers (Web Supplement 9S). Demonstrate a bibliographic entry and notemaking from the video clip. Review the types of notes (figure 2-1 or Web Supplement 2A). Students suggest and educators record the notes. Emphasize recording the reference number in each note box. (Web Supplements 9P and 9R are teacher resources with a focus on Miles Davis. The notes are color coded to match the sources; notes in black are personal responses and interpretations of the information.)

Students suggest notes and copy the bibliographic information and notes onto their individual graphic organizers.

Student Participation Procedures

1. Think-pair-share.

2. Share a main idea or an interesting detail with the class.

3. Suggest a note.

4. Record a reference number.

Guided Practice

The educators support students' contributions to the shared notemaking activity and monitor students recording of bibliographic information and notes on their individual notemaking graphic organizers.

Closure

Review the class notes. Think-pair-share something new that students learned about jazz. Think-pair-share responses to this information. Ask for volunteers to share with the class.

Discuss the unit. The class investigates jazz through language arts, music, and visual art. They research as a class, and then individuals determine a subtopic, a jazz musician, to research independently. At the end of the unit, students create art in the style of Picasso's cubist work "Three Musicians" and use their artwork as a prompt for composing a jazz poem.

Approximately days 2–7

Student-Friendly Objectives

1. Add jazzy words to the vocabulary web.
2. Determine notes and record.
3. Record bibliographic information.
4. Record personal responses and interpretations of information.
5. Analyze jazzy poems for word choice, rhythm, and themes.

Presentations

Throughout the unit, educators share poems from the Topical Text Set (Web Supplement 9N) throughout the week. Invite students to respond to the words, rhythm, and themes of these selections. Invite them to practice and read/recite these poems for the class. For fun, also share *Hip Cat* (London/Hubbard).

Educators share the six starred picture books from the topical text set. Titles can be read in both the classroom and the library. Educators can coteach these books, with one person reading and one person recording bibliography entries and students' notes on class-sized graphic organizers. The books can also be read by one or the other educator, or the class can be divided into smaller groups for the readings. If students are proficient readers, set up small group center rotations around each of the six books about jazz musicians. Provide a copy of *I See the Rhythm* (Igus/Wood) and *Jazz A-B-Z: An A to Z Collection of Jazz Portraits* (Marsalis/Rogers) for each center.

Before reading each book, play music by that particular musician. (In addition, pair the audiotape of *Charlie Parker Played Be Bop* [Raschka] with *Jazz for Kids: Sing, Clap, Wiggle, and Shake.*) Record bibliographic information and make class notes. Students copy bibliographic information and notes and keep their materials in their research folders. Add jazzy words to the vocabulary web. (If you are not working with a music teacher, begin to define jazz musical terms and add them to the vocabulary web. See music objectives.)

Student Practice Procedures

1. Suggest jazzy words for the vocabulary web.
2. Make notes and record bibliographic information.
3. Record personal responses and interpretations of information on notemaking sheets.

Guided Practice

Educators monitor students' notemaking and bibliography entries.

Closure

In addition to recording information, invite students to respond to each text by recording ideas, connections, feelings, or questions on their notemaking sheets. Continue this process until students have heard or read all six books.

When all the books have been read, project the Build-Know-Wonder-Learn-Question Chart (Web Supplement 9O). As a class, begin to fill in the "B" section with the background information students have gained. Ask students to read over their notes and complete the "B" section on their own.

Approximately Day 8	**Guided Practice**

Students choose one jazz musician and conduct independent research on that person. Students fill in what they wonder ("W") about a particular musician on their individual Build-Know-Wonder-Learn-Question Chart (Web Supplement 9O). Students can use the jazz pathfinder, reference books, or any other resources available to them. Individual research can be accomplished with the entire class in a computer lab or library setting, or through small group rotations through the lab or library, or as homework.

Approximately Day 10   **Student-Friendly Objectives**

1. Use the vocabulary web.
2. Web ideas for prewriting.
3. Write a three- to five-paragraph synthesis.
4. Follow the writing process.
5. Revise, edit, and make a final copy.
6. Self-assess paragraphs with the rubric.

Presentation

After students have completed their independent research, educators model synthesizing information. Review all class notes as well as the bibliography graphic organizer and additional notes on Miles Davis (Web Supplements 9P and 9R). Review the jazzy vocabulary web.

Project the Sample Synthesis (Web Supplement 9T). Discuss how information came from various sources as noted. (On their final paragraphs, students highlight each resource on the bibliography and information in their paragraphs from that source with the same color.) Emphasize how personal response to the information is included in the synthesis paragraphs. (Students can be asked to write three, four, or five paragraphs.) Assess the paragraphs using the Synthesis Rubric (Web Supplement 9U).

Students use their own notes to compose synthesize paragraphs and self-assess with a rubric.

Student Practice Procedures

1. Review the vocabulary web and notes.
2. Review the rubric criteria.
3. Web ideas for an introduction (about jazz in general).
4. Web ideas for body paragraphs (about the musician you studied).
5. Draft three to five paragraphs.
6. Revise and edit.
7. Conference with a teacher or peer.
8. Revise, edit, and make a final copy.
9. Highlight information from each source with a different color.
10. Do not highlight your own ideas, connections, or feelings.
11. Self-assess synthesis with the rubric.

Guided Practice

Educators conference with students. They monitor students' work based on the rubric criteria. They remind students of the synthesis goal for this work.

Closure

Students share their paragraphs with a partner who studied a different jazz musician. Students complete their individual Build-Know-Wonder-Learn-Question Chart (Web Supplement 9O) with what they learned ("L") and their remaining questions ("Q").

Presentation

If they have not yet shared them, educators share poems from the jazz topical text set. Project Picasso's "Three Musicians." If an art teacher is contributing, she takes the lead on this aspect of the unit. If not, define abstract art. Discuss cubism and analyze the painting for color, shape, and feeling/tone. Use the Artwork Directions (Web Supplement 9Y).

Model using the Jazz Poem Category Web (Web Supplement 9W) to gather ideas for both the artwork and the poem. (Web Supplement 9V is a teacher resource.) Complete only the musician and instrument at the center before composing a drawing in the cubist style. Cover the poem and share the Sample Art and Poetry Product (Web Supplement 9X). Assess the illustration with the Synthesis Product Checklist (Web Supplement 9Z).

Students create their artwork.

Student Practice Procedures

1. Decide on the name for an imaginary musician.

2. Choose a jazz instrument.

3. Record the musician and instrument in the center of the category web.

4. Compose an illustration in the cubist style of Picasso's "Three Musicians."

5. Self-assess using the checklist.

Guided Practice

Educators (including the art teacher) monitor students' use of color, shape, and expression.

Closure

Each student uses the checklist to assess his/her artwork. Can we use our artwork as a writing prompt for a jazz poem?

Final Day *Presentation*

Model using the sample illustration from the Sample Art and Poetry Product (Web Supplement 9X) as a writing prompt. Fill in the jazz poem category web based on that individual piece of art (Web Supplement 9W). Use jazz terms from the vocabulary web. Discuss alliteration as one way poets give their work rhythm.

Share the sample poem from the Sample Art and Poetry Product and use the Synthesis Product Checklist (Web Supplement 9Z) to assess the poem. Point out the alliteration in the poem.

Students compose individual poems and read them to a classmate.

Student-Friendly Objectives

1. Use your artwork as a prompt.

2. Review the vocabulary web.

3. Complete the jazz poem category web.

4. Compose a poem based on your artwork.

5. Assess the poem using the checklist.

6. Revise if necessary.

7. Read your poem to a classmate.

Guided Practice

Educators facilitate writing conferences.

Closure

Play jazz music. Share poems and display the artwork. Decide as a class how to share the artwork and poems with a larger audience.

Reflection

What does it mean to synthesize information? How do we let viewers or readers know where we got our information? Why is this important? After conducting research, what are some ways we can show what we learned?

Extensions Students can scan or take digital photographs of their artwork and keyboard their poems. They can create a slide show of their work for a print or electronic book. They can post their work on a website. Some or all students may decide to share their poems with other classrooms, families, or the larger school community. Students may set their poems to jazz rhythms or music. Compose a shared-writing summary of the unit for the library, school, school district newsletter, or local newspaper, radio stations, or television stations.

Glossary

admit slip. An admit slip helps establish a purpose for reading. It provides background information for students before they read the main text. An admit slip stimulates the reader's thinking by providing compelling facts or posing probing questions.

anchor text. An anchor text is one that is used to teach a strategy or concept and can be referred to later to help students access their schemas, make connections, and transfer their learning to new situations.

anticipation guide. An anticipation guide is a preview. It helps learners prepare by providing background information or posing questions to help them focus their thinking about the ideas and information to be presented in the lesson.

backward planning. This lesson design framework posits that effective instructional design begins with selecting student learning outcomes based on curriculum standards (Wiggins and McTighe 1998). Educators begin lesson planning by determining the learning tasks and criteria on which student work will be assessed as well as a tool with which to assess it.

Bloom's taxonomy. Developed in the 1950s by researchers headed by Benjamin Bloom, the taxonomy is commonly used to describe learning objectives. The taxonomy levels are knowledge, comprehension, application, analysis, synthesis, and evaluation. Depending on the learning tasks, different cognitive levels may be required.

booktalk. A booktalk is offered as an enticement to choose a particular text. It should include a hook to pique readers' curiosity. The booktalker gives a brief description of one or more of the story elements or reads a short passage without giving away too much. Educators and students can give booktalks to share the titles they have found intriguing.

bookwalk. Sometimes called a picture walk, a bookwalk is a cueing strategy. Readers preview or discuss the illustrations in a text (without disclosing the ending in a fiction selection) to prepare listeners or readers for the literacy engagement.

brain-compatible strategy. Neuroscientists have identified physiological processes that suggest that some instructional strategies are well matched with the way the brain processes and stores information. For instance, active, hands-on learning experiences that involve "practice by doing" provide multiple sensory input that is more likely to be retained because it engages both the body and the mind. For further reading, see Sousa (2001).

cloze procedure. A cloze procedure requires learners to use context clues to fill in the blanks with words that have been deliberately removed from a text. Example: "The library has _____, _____, and _____ to help students learn about geography." These blanks name something, so they must be nouns. Possible answers are *globes, maps,* and *atlases.*

considerate text. Considerate texts support readers' intellectual access. Considerate fictional texts present story elements clearly and follow a narrative frame. Considerate informational texts provide organizational features that offer support, such as subtitles, tables of contents, indexes, glossaries, and graphics. These text features signal the main ideas presented.

Dewitt Wallace–Reader's Digest Library Power Project. Library Power was a ten-year initiative that affected 700 schools serving more than 1 million students in high-poverty communities around the United States. The project was built on the principles outlined in AASL and AECT (1988). The goal of the project was to ensure that all learners in Library Power schools, both students and adults, had increased opportunities to become effective users of ideas and information. The project provided funding, resources, professional development support, and opportunities for teacher-librarians to become leaders in instruction in their schools through classroom-library collaboration.

differentiated instruction. In teaching with differentiated instruction, educators plan for groups of learners to conduct and demonstrate their learning in different ways depending on students' learning styles or strengths, as long as they achieve the same learning outcomes. Two goals of differentiated instruction are to increase student motivation and involvement in learning.

essential elements of instruction (EEI). Also known as the Madeline Hunter method, EEI is a lesson implementation sequence that includes the following steps: introductory or anticipatory set, statement of the lesson objectives, input, modeling, check for under-

standing, guided practice, independent practice, and closure, which includes assessment and a bridge to transfer learning to a new situation.

evidence-based practice. This movement in school librarianship is founded on the need for teacher-librarians to document their impact on student achievement (Todd 2001). Educators measure student outcomes by comparing pretest data to posttests and students' learning products.

flexibly scheduled library. In a flexibly scheduled library, teaching time in the library is booked after classroom teachers and teacher-librarians have coplanned a lesson or unit of instruction and determined the length of time the instruction and practice require. The teacher-librarian's schedule is based on the needs of students, teachers, and curriculum. This is the ideal arrangement for best practices in the school library.

genre. A genre is a particular category of book, one with a typical style, form, or content. Examples include realistic fiction, historical fiction, science fiction, fantasy, traditional literature (folktales, fairy tales, fables, and myths), biography, and informational texts.

higher-order thinking. Higher-order thinking often refers to the top three levels of Bloom's taxonomy: analysis, synthesis, and evaluation. At these levels, the answers to learning problems are not predetermined, and multiple solutions are possible. This level requires original thinking on the part of the learner.

illustration. Illustration is the graphic component of a text and can include images and artwork created with a variety of media. Charts, graphs, maps, and timelines can also be considered illustration. Authors and illustrators can also use font variations and variety to communicate information graphically; this can be considered illustration. Illustrations convey meaning.

inside-outside circle. In this arrangement, students are divided into two groups: one forms the inside circle, and the other forms the outside circle. People in the two circles face one another to create partners. Partners can then share information. By rotating one circle to the left or right, partners are changed and sharing is repeated.

literacy engagement. Literacy engagements are planned learning experiences that take into account students' motivation, level of comprehension, and enjoyment of texts. They incorporate reading authentic texts and writing for a purpose as well as fostering oral conversation and developing listening skills.

literature circle. In this text discussion framework, readers take the primary responsibility for guiding conversation. Going beyond summaries and retellings to reach for deeper understandings through reader response is one goal of literature circles. Educators can support literature circles by serving in different roles, such as facilitator, participant, mediator, or active listener.

metacognition. Metacognition is "thinking about thinking." It is a person's awareness or analysis of the cognitive processes she uses to think and to learn. Think-alouds are one way educators can demonstrate metacognition.

multigenre text. Multigenre texts have elements of more than one genre. Examples: a book that uses expository text to illuminate the references in a poem; a historical fiction picture book that has a narrative story line plus text boxes with expository information inserted in the illustration.

narrative frame. This framework is most often found in various types of fiction. It contains the story elements characters, setting, plot, conflict, and resolution. In a narrative frame, the main characters respond to an initiating event. As the plot unfolds, the consequences of their actions lead to some sort of resolution. In much of children's literature, readers can expect a linear narrative frame in which the plot has a clear beginning, middle, and end.

notemaking. Recording information in one's own words is what distinguishes notemaking from note taking. Notemaking requires that learners pass information through their prior knowledge and experience and determine what is important to record. Note taking is essential for recording quotes, but notemaking more clearly indicates what the student has learned or understood from the text.

numbered-heads-together. This is a whole-class question-and-answer participation strategy. Students sit in groups of equal number. Each student is assigned a number. For example, if there are six groups of four, six students have the number one, one student in each group. A question is posed and all groups have a set time to caucus on the answer. When time is up, each group is called on in a set rotation. A number is called at random, and the person in that group with that number answers for the group. If the answer is incorrect, the person with the same number in the next group is asked to provide her group's answer. Keeping score is optional.

open access. In an open-access school library, students can use the library any time during the school day. Students can check out and return materials or stay in the library to use materials, even when the teacher-librarian is teaching other students. Open access facilitates serving students at the point of need. Depending on the size of the facility, open access can also include whole-class access under the classroom teacher's supervision if the teacher-librarian is teaching other students.

pathfinder. An Internet pathfinder is a Web page with a list of links to online resources. The purpose of a pathfinder is to provide learners and educators with reliable, preselected websites so they can focus on accessing the information itself rather than spending time searching for appropriate resources.

piggyback text or song. A piggyback text or song is created when a writer imitates another work or uses the musical score of a song as the basis for a new story or new lyrics. This is one way writers can capitalize on the reader-singer's prior knowledge of the original.

print. Print is the words of a text.

QAR (question-answer relationships). In this model, students are asked to classify questions by the source of their answers. Questions can be answered "on the line" (literal), "between the lines" (inferential), or as readers' judgments (evaluative) (Ouzts 1998).

reader response. When readers respond to texts, they bring their prior experiences and unique perspectives to the reading event. In responding, readers can make connections, ask questions, and expand on the ideas and information provided by the author or illustrator. They can employ various sign systems to express their responses. Responding to text is not a retelling of a story or a restatement of the facts.

reading transaction. Rosenblatt (1978) developed a theory of reading as a transaction among the reader, the text, and intention of the author. She posited that each reader brings her own feelings, personality, and experiences to the text and that each reader is different each time she revisits a particular text. Meaning does not reside in the text itself but is made by the reader during the transaction with the text.

scaffold. Scaffolds are structures or tools implemented by educators that support students' learning. Scaffolds help the learner reach a level of achievement that he may not be able to reach without the scaffold. A lesson plan format is a procedural scaffold. Outlines and graphic organizers are examples of instructional scaffolds.

schema. The schema theory suggests that knowledge is stored in abstract structures called schemas. People organize and retain information in their memories based on a hierarchy of characteristics. For instance, in my schema for my dog Tessa, I have an overarching concept of animal, then pet, then dog, then poodle, then finally the specific traits of this particular dog. When applied to reading comprehension, schema theory postulates that readers have preconceived concepts that influence their understanding of texts. This background knowledge is applied when texts are being read. Schemas change when new information supplants old or is integrated into prior understandings.

semantic cue. Semantics is the study of meanings, often meanings conveyed by words. Readers learn to recognize semantic cues that authors provide to help fine-tune meaning. These meanings are influenced by the reader's background knowledge and are often culturally specific. Example: "His knees began to knock as the dark figure slinked out of the shadows." The reader can use semantic cues to infer that the character is frightened (knocking knees) and that the dark figure may be a threat (slinked out of the shadows).

sign system. Sign systems are ways to express meaning and understanding. Readers can respond to literature and information using different modalities, including language, art, drama, music, and math.

story element. Characters, setting, plot, conflict, and theme are the basic story elements. Point of view, style (which includes cultural features), and visual elements in illustrated works can also be considered story elements.

text. The text is the totality of the work that weaves together print and illustration, whether in paper or electronic format.

text feature. Text features help organize information. Tables of content, indexes, timelines, glossaries, graphics (including illustrations, photographs, charts, maps, tables, and captions and labels), headings or titles, subheadings or subtitles, font variations, and other print effects are text features often used in informational texts.

text structure. Text structures are frameworks that can be used in both narrative and expository texts. Examples include cause and effect, comparison and contrast, question and answer, problem and solution, and sequencing. In some cases, certain words signal particular structures. For instance, sequencing can be indicated by words such as *first, next, then,* and *finally.*

think-aloud strategy. Think-alouds are used by educators and students when they wish to share their thinking processes orally. In how-to strategy lessons, educators use a think-aloud strategy in modeling. Think-alouds help others understand what is going on inside a person's head when she is learning. Think-alouds are a form of metacognition—thinking about thinking. When students understand their own thinking processes, they learn better.

think-pair-share. In this procedure, a question or problem is posed. Students think about a response or solution and turn to a partner to share their responses, and then the educators ask for volunteers to share with the larger group or whole class.

References

AASL and AECT American Association of School Librarians and Association for Educational Communications and Technology. 1988. *Information power: Guidelines for school library media programs.* Chicago: American Library Association.

———. 1998. *Information power: Building partnerships for learning.* Chicago: American Library Association.

Ackerman, Diane. 1990. *A natural history of the senses.* New York: Random House.

Allen, Janet. 2004. *Tools for teaching content literacy.* Portland, ME: Stenhouse.

Arnold, D. S., and Grover J. Whitehurst. 1994. Accelerating language development through picture book reading: A summary of dialogic reading and its effect. In *Bridges to literacy: Approaches to supporting child and family literacy,* ed. D. K. Dickinson, 103–28. Cambridge, MA: Basil Blackwell.

Barth, Roland S. 2006. Improving relationships within the schoolhouse. *Educational Leadership* 63 (6): 9–13.

Beck, Isabel L., Margaret G. McKeown, Rebecca L. Hamilton, and Linda Kucan. 1997. *Questioning the author: An approach to enhancing student engagement with text.* Newark, DE: International Reading Association.

Bloom, Benjamin S., et al. 1956. *A taxonomy of educational objectives: Handbook I. The cognitive domain.* New York: David McKay.

Champlin, Connie. 1998. *Storytelling with puppets.* Chicago: American Library Association.

Christie, James F., Billy Enz, and Carol Vukelich. 2003. *Teaching language and literacy: Preschool through the elementary grades.* 2nd ed. Boston: Allyn and Bacon.

Cushman, Karen. 1996. Newbery acceptance speech. *Horn Book Magazine* 72 (July/August): 413–19.

DuFour, Rick. 2001. In the right context: The effective leader concentrates on a foundation of programs, procedures, beliefs, expectations, and habits. *Journal of Staff Development* 22 (1): 14–17.

Echevarria, Jana, MaryEllen Vogt, and Deborah J. Short. 2004. *Making content comprehensible for English language learners: The SIOP model.* 2nd ed. Boston: Allyn and Bacon.

Eisenberg, Michael, and Robert Berkowitz. 1990. *Information problem solving: The Big Six approach to library and information skills instruction.* Norwood, NJ: Ablex.

Friend, Marilyn, and Lynne Cook. 1996. *Interactions: Collaboration skills for school professionals.* 2nd ed. White Plains, NY: Longman.

Gardner, Howard. 1993. *Multiple intelligences: The theory in practice.* New York: Basic Books.

Glass, Gene V., and Mary Lee Smith. 1979. Meta-analysis of research on class size and achievement. *Educational Evaluation and Policy Analysis* 1 (1): 2–16.

Hall, Susan. 2002. *Using picture storybooks to teach literary devices,* volume 3. Westport, CT: Oryx Press.

Harada, Violet H., and Joan M. Yoshina. 2005. *Assessing learning: Librarians and teachers as partners.* Westport, CT: Libraries Unlimited.

Hartzell, Gary. 2002. *What's it take? White House conference on school libraries.* http://www.imls.gov/pubs/whitehouse0602/garyhartzell.htm.

Harvey, Stephanie, and Anne Goudvis. 2000. *Strategies that work: Teaching comprehension to enhance understanding.* Portland, ME: Stenhouse.

Haycock, Ken. 2004. Priority-setting: The tough work. *Teacher Librarian* 31 (4): 6.

Jackman, Hilda L. 1997. *Early education curriculum: A child's connection to the world.* Albany, NY: Delmar.

Keene, Ellin Oliver, and Susan Zimmermann. 1997. *Mosaic of thought: Teaching comprehension in a reader's workshop.* Portsmouth, NH: Heinemann.

Koechlin, Carol, and Sandi Zwaan. 2006. *Q tasks: How to empower students to ask questions and care about answers.* Portland, ME: Stenhouse.

Krashen, Stephen D. 2004. *The power of reading: Insights from the research.* Westport, CT: Libraries Unlimited.

Lieberman, Ann. 1995. Restructuring schools: The dynamics of changing practice, structure, and culture. In *The work of restructuring schools: Building from the ground up,* ed. A. Lieberman, 1–17. New York: Teachers College Press.

Loertscher, David V. 1988. *Taxonomies of the school library media program.* Englewood, CO: Libraries Unlimited.

Loertscher, David V., Carol Koechlin, and Sandi Zwann. 2004. *Ban those bird units: 15 models for teaching and learning in information-rich and technology-rich environments.* Salt Lake City: Hi Willow.

Manzo, Anthony V. 1969. The request procedure. *Journal of Reading* 13 (2): 123–26.

Marzano, Robert J. 2003. *What works in schools: Translating research into action.* Alexandria, VA: Association for Supervision and Curriculum Development.

———. 2004. *Building background knowledge for academic achievement: Research on what works in schools.* Alexandria, VA: Association for Supervision and Curriculum Development.

Marzano, Robert J., Debra J. Pickering, and Jane E. Pollock. 2001. *Classroom instruction that works: Research-based strategies for increasing student achievement.* Alexandria, VA: Association for Supervision and Curriculum Development.

McGee, Lea M., and Donald J. Richgels. 1996. *Literacy's beginnings: Supporting young readers and writers.* 2nd ed. Boston: Allyn and Bacon.

McKenzie, Jamie A. 1997. Questioning toolkit. *From Now On: The Educational Technology Journal* 7 (3). http://fno.org/nov97/toolkit.html.

Meek, Margaret. 1988. *How texts teach what readers learn.* Stroud, UK: Thimble Press.

Miller, Nancy A. S. 1998. *Impact! Documenting the LMC Program for Accountability.* Salt Lake City: Hi Willow.

Moreillon, Judi. 2003. *Peace doves and Picasso poems: Literature, art, technology, and poetry.* ReadWriteThink.org. http://www.readwritethink.org/lessons/lesson_view.asp?id=93.

———. 2005. Two heads are better than one: The factors influencing the understanding and practice of classroom-library collaboration: Preliminary report on the pilot study. In *Understanding in the library: Papers of the Treasure Mountain Research Retreat,* no. 12, ed. David V. Loertscher. Spring, TX: LMC Source.

O'Brien-Palmer, Michelle. 1998. *Sense-abilities: Fun ways to explore the senses.* Chicago: Chicago Review Press.

Ouzts, D. T. 1998. Enhancing literacy using the question-answer relationship. *Social Studies and the Young Learner* 10 (4): 26–28.

Partnership for 21st Century Skills. 2006. *Results that matter: 21st century skills and high school reform.* http://www.21stcenturyskills.org.

Reichardt, Robert. 2001. *Reducing class size: Choices and consequences* [policy brief]. Aurora, CO: Mid-continent Research for Education and Learning.

Rose, Laura. 1989. *Picture this: Teaching reading through visualization.* Tucson, AZ: Zephyr Press.

Rosenblatt, Louise M. 1978. *The reader, the text, the poem: The transactional theory of the literary work.* Carbondale, IL: Southern Illinois University Press.

———. 1995. *Literature as exploration.* 5th ed. New York: Modern Language Association of America.

Scholastic Research and Results. 2006. *Research foundation paper: School libraries work!* New York: Scholastic.

Schomberg, Janie. 2003. TAG team: Collaborate to teach, assess and grow. *Teacher-Librarian* 31 (1): 8–11.

Serafini, Frank. 2006. *Around the reading workshop in 180 days: A month-by-month guide to effective instruction.* Portsmouth, NH: Heinemann.

Short, Kathy G., Jerome C. Harste, with Carolyn Burke. 1996. *Creating classrooms for authors and inquirers.* 2nd ed. Portsmouth, NH: Heinemann.

Short, Kathy Gnagey, and Kathryn Mitchell Pierce, eds. 1990. *Talking about books: Creating literate communities.* Portsmouth, NH: Heinemann.

Smith, Frank. 1998. *Joining the literacy club: Further essays into education.* Portsmouth, NH: Heinemann.

Sousa, David A. 2001. *How the brain learns: A classroom teacher's guide.* Thousand Oaks, CA: Corwin Press.

———. 2005. *How the brain learns to read.* Thousand Oaks, CA: Corwin Press.

Stahl, Katherine A. Dougherty. 2005. Improving the asphalt of reading instruction: A tribute to the work of Steven A. Stahl. *Reading Teacher* 59 (2): 184–91.

Tate, Marcia L. 2003. *Worksheets don't grow dendrites: 20 instructional strategies that engage the brain.* Thousand Oaks, CA: Corwin Press.

Todd, Ross. 2001. Evidence based practice: The sustainable future for teacher-librarians. *SCAN* 20 (1): 1–8.

Wells, Gordon. 1986. *The meaning makers: Children learning language and using language to learn.* Portsmouth, NH: Heinemann.

Whitebread, David, ed. 2000. *The psychology of teaching and learning in the primary school.* New York: Routledge.

Wiggins, Grant, and Jay McTighe. 1998. *Understanding by design.* Alexandria, VA: Association for Supervision and Curriculum Development.

Wilhelm, Jeffrey D. 2001. *Improving comprehension with think-aloud strategies: Modeling what good readers do.* New York: Scholastic.

Wolfe, Patricia. 2001. *Brain matters: Translating research into classroom practice.* Alexandria, VA: Association for Supervision and Curriculum Development.

Young, Ed. 1992. *Seven blind mice.* New York: Philomel.

Zimmermann, Susan, and Chryse Hutchins. 2003. *Seven keys to comprehension: How to help your kids read it and get it!* New York: Three Rivers Press.

Index

Note: Page numbers in bold type indicate
glossary definitions

A

B

Judi Moreillon is a literacies and libraries consultant. She also serves as an adjunct assistant professor in the Department of Language, Reading, and Culture (LRC) and in the School of Information Resources and Library Science (SIRLS) at the University of Arizona in Tucson. She teaches courses in children's and young adult literature and school library administration. Dr. Moreillon earned her master's degree in library science from SIRLS and her doctorate in education from LRC. During her twelve-year tenure as a teacher-librarian, she collaborated with classroom teachers, specialists, and principals at the elementary and high school levels to integrate literature and information literacy into the classroom curriculum. Two of the elementary schools were Dewitt Wallace–Reader's Digest Library Power schools. She has also served as a district-level teacher-librarian mentor, a literacy coach, a classroom teacher, and a teacher educator. Dr. Moreillon's current research centers on the factors that influence preservice and first-year classroom teachers' understanding and practice of classroom-library collaboration.